Crippling Epistemologies
and Governance Failures

GOVERNANCE SERIES

Governance is the process of effective coordination whereby an organization or a system guides itself when resources, power, and information are widely distributed. Studying governance means probing the pattern of rights and obligations that underpins organizations and social systems; understanding how they coordinate their parallel activities and maintain their coherence; exploring the sources of dysfunction; and suggesting ways to redesign organizations whose governance is in need of repair.

The series welcomes a range of contributions — from conceptual and theoretical reflections, ethnographic and case studies, and proceedings of conferences and symposia, to works of a very practical nature — that deal with problems or issues on the governance front. The series publishes works both in French and in English.

The Governance Series is part of the publications division of the Centre on Governance and of the Graduate School of Public and International Affairs at the University of Ottawa. This volume is the 22nd volume published in the Series. The Centre on Governance and the Graduate School of Public and International Affairs also publish a quarterly electronic journal www.optimusonline.ca.

The published titles in the series are listed at the end of this book.

Crippling Epistemologies and Governance Failures
A Plea for Experimentalism

Gilles Paquet

University of Ottawa Press
Ottawa

Library and Archives Canada Cataloguing in Publication

Paquet, Gilles, 1936–
Crippling epistemologies and governance failures:
a plea for experimentalism / Gilles Paquet.

(Governance series, 1487-3052)
Includes bibliographical references and index.
ISBN 978-0-7766-0703-0

1. Social epistemology — Canada.
2. Social sciences — Philosophy.
3. Social sciences — Methodology. 4. Policy sciences.
I. Title. II. Series: Governance series (Ottawa, Ont.)

H61.P36 2009   300.1   C2009-900459-3

University of Ottawa Press
542 King Edward Avenue
Ottawa, Ontario K1N 6N5   u Ottawa
www.uopress.uottawa.ca

The University of Ottawa Press acknowledges with gratitude
the support extended to its publishing list by Heritage Canada
through its Book Publishing Industry Development Program, by
the Canada Council for the Arts, by the Canadian Federation
for the Humanities and Social Sciences through its Aid to
Scholarly Publications Program, by the Social Sciences and
Humanities Research Council, and by the University of
Ottawa.

... the economist needs to be a great enjoyer of ideas and a connoisseur of their means of expression, a daring sculptor of argument, an eclectic, and sometimes an heresiarch.
—G. L. S. SHACKLE

Table of contents

PART III   Less than Effective Bricolage

Foreword

*If a path to the better there be,
it begins with a full look at the worst.*
— THOMAS HARDY

This book reports on certain recent episodes in the long voyage of the human sciences from a focus on understanding to a fixation on "methodism" and back. A truly comprehensive treatise would go back to the birth of the human sciences, track down the corrosive effects of the ebbs and flows of positivism, scientism and methodism (but also of many other ideologies), bemoan the "dark ages" of the second half of the 20ᵗʰ century, and celebrate the signs of rejuvenation that one has been able to detect in the last little while. Such a long and arduous task will have to await a younger, more ambitious and more dispassionate travel writer.

My ambitions are much more limited. I wish only to look at the more recent segments of this evolution; to expose some of the slippages that the "methodist" drift in particular, but other drifts too, have generated in the world of the human sciences, in Canada and elsewhere; and to probe in a provisional way the renaissance of refurbished human sciences by underlining some of its most promising offshoots.

This search for more useful practical professional (not professionalized academic disciplinary) social sciences has led me to focus on the nihilistic era, when the effectiveness and relevance of the human sciences have been seriously impaired. This impoverishment of their perspectives through the ascent of crippled and crippling epistemologies of all sorts — skewed theories of knowledge, flawed views of its nature that truncate the scope of what one may justifiably count as knowledge and generate false consciousness — has had an important negative impact on the process of governance (Hardin 2002).

Finally, before we proceed, let me explain the crucial distinction between two aspects of the world of the professions that will be central to our discussion. Professionals are individuals who have not only academic knowledge but also practical knowledge. Professional knowledge is acquired in large part by doing (articling, residency, experience, and so on) out in the field. Such practical knowledge usually complements and enriches academic knowledge, making it more socially useful. I will refer to "professional knowledge" to connote the amalgam of this academic-cum-practical and socially useful knowledge, and to the "professional social sciences" as the enriched sort of intellectual capital and praxis that ensues. "Professionalized academic disciplinary knowledge" connotes the sort of knowledge generated by academic disciplines as ways of seeing according to codes and rules approved by professional disciplinary guilds, and enforced by union-type strictures in universities and colleges over the past fifty years or so. This last label connotes a very stylized, reductive and largely sterile version of professional knowledge.

MUD TIME, MENTAL PRISONS

Exposing such impoverishment and its consequences for governance is necessary if one is to help to engineer a full return to richer and less crippling epistemologies, and, consequently, to a fuller contribution by the professional human sciences to the design of more effective governance of human organizations and societies.

This fundamental slippage of the human sciences as a result of scientism was forcefully denounced by Friedrich Hayek in his *Scientism and the Study of Society* (1952). Without denying that the methods of natural science might be useful in some segments of the study of man and society, Hayek rejected the idea of reducing the human sciences, which are fundamentally moral sciences, to a natural science of man (Paquet 1985; 1987).

Hayek's warning came at the very moment of John Dewey's death, when the social sciences had begun to shift their focus in a fundamental way from Dewey's imperative — "in the beginning is the issue" — to a fixation mainly on the exclusive use of a conceptual toolbox supposedly able to offer incomparable help in handling these issues. This new fixation was built on a set of reductive assumptions that promised particularly important insights to those using this apparatus.

This meant a shift away from efforts to deal with important issues in eclectic and experimentalist ways, to a focus on particular angles of vision. Social scientists became less interested in finding ways to cope with the new "wicked problems" facing societies, and more intent on promoting the heuristic power of disciplinary languages of problem definition, which purported to disclose coherent visions of the world.

Such a drift meant that the social sciences experienced a loss of the sense of their original purpose, which was to make sense of the life-world. This slide was greatly accelerated by the professionalization of academic disciplines, which sanctified disciplinary perspectives as the only available avenues for gaining access to meaningful knowledge. This latter development ensured, by carefully designed rules of credentialism, regimentation, and control over tenure and promotion in academe, that such avenues would become the normal channels of

development and dissemination of the corpus of knowledge in the social sciences, to the exclusion of others
(Katouzian 1980). Disciplinary academic snobbery was
sanctified too.

This hijacking operation never succeeded in imposing a complete monopoly of the social sciences by the
professionalized academic disciplines and their ruling
ideologies, but their control of the institutions and organizations producing knowledge in the social sciences was
extremely important in the last thirty years or so of the
20th century. The sanitized notion of knowledge that
ensued relegated much useful knowledge to the margins
and the underground of the main terrain of operations.
This marginalized, devalued, damned and occluded, in
particular, much of the knowledge produced by practitioners—consultants, activists, mavericks in professional
schools, non-academic institutions or think tanks, or
freelancing thinkers and public intellectuals.

Scientism, with its disciplinary reductionism and
its emphasis on method, was the most important and
enduring calamity plaguing the social sciences over the
past fifty years, but it was by no means the only one.
However unsuccessful, on the whole, the attempts to
constrain the wave of scientism were, the resentment this
reductive approach generated promoted a craving for
less sanitized versions of the social sciences. This led to
the emergence of a multitude of other partial but equally
crippling perspectives.

These new approaches, under the broad banners of
Marxism, structuralism, postmodernism, and the like,
permeated major portions of the humanities and the
social sciences. However, more often than not, these
ideological approaches, instead of triggering focused
experimentalism and innovation, developed alternative
canons that proved just as rigid, reductive, constraining
and obscurantist as the scientistic canon. The multiplication of such perspectives was celebrated as a liberation from scientism, but, given the fact that they were

only proposing new dogmatisms, the "liberation" often amounted to nothing more than new forms of mental servitude, hence new mental prisons.

The multiplication of such epistemological blinders and the new legitimacy of ideological lenses have generated a whole array of wannabe hegemonic perspectives, each equally dogmatic in defending its reductive outlook. As a result, social scientists have not been better equipped to deal with the critical issues at hand. Some university disciplinary departments in the social sciences are now segmented into quasi-religious cult-like sects at the periphery of the scientistic canon, a canon which remains, on the whole, hegemonic.

The musings that follow provide evidence of false consciousness, misplaced academic snobbery, obscurantist ideological cults and intellectual ventures gone sour. They reveal not only how inadequate our intellectual toolbox has been, but also how institutional and organizational design have gone awry as a result of these truncated perspectives, and how efforts at repairs have failed.

Fundamentally indicted are, first, the limits of the Eleatic mindset that rejects the epistemological validity of sense experiences, and, second, the incapacity of the social sciences in general to provide meaningful and effective responses to the important challenges facing crucial institutions and organizations charged with important collective tasks.

These forays into the world of crippling epistemologies, inadequate intellectual apparatuses and failures of governance are presented with the explicit purpose of identifying some of the most toxic mental prisons, and providing suggestions as to how one might escape from them.

It would be nice to be able to announce that the examination of these pathologies and bad experiences has led to the discovery of the intellectual and moral equivalent of penicillin, providing a cure for crippling epistemologies, a remedy that would annihilate or at least contain the toxic forces that have been at work for the past one hundred years and more. Unfortunately, we are not there yet, but this does not mean that there is no progress to report.

ESCAPE ROUTES AND BLOCKAGES

Out of the failures of the past thirty years and the decline of the valence of the social sciences in public policy, much has been learned. There have been of late renewed efforts to get back to Dewey's central question, and to design modes of inquiry that recognize the value of experimental approaches to problematic situations; that condone more eclecticism and pluralism in the choice of instrumentation; and that legitimize the adoption of heretical positions *vis-à-vis* established doctrines, in order to deal more effectively with the issues at hand. This is the case, at least, in the saner institutions of higher learning.

However, this new wave is only now emerging, and it remains quite fragile and diffracted. It has to undergo a painful confrontation with the dynamic conservatism inspired by fifty years of scientism and other ideologies that are now very deeply and institutionally rooted in the academic world, and that continue to act as toxic viruses. Forensic studies have, however, revealed a clearer image of some of the families of blockages that have generated the highest degree of false consciousness, and significantly diminished the capacity of the social sciences to contribute helpfully to the design of effective governance.

The first family of such blockages has to do with the very notion of knowledge. Contrary to the view in good currency, knowledge is not discovered from the world but is constructed by inquirers, and there is not just one valid methodology to do the job, but a large variety of methodologies that can be developed from different sorts of inquiries. This gives a constructivist and a non-Cartesian twist to the production of knowledge: at the core of it is *ingenium* (Laurent and Paquet 1998; Le Moigne 2007).

This richer approach to the production of knowledge entails that one does not restrict oneself to striving to "represent" what would be an objective reality out there, in the name of metaphysical realism, but would rather seek to match knowledge with reality, construct one's knowledge to fit with the empirical world one observes, and contribute a viable way to pursue the objectives one has chosen in these particular circumstances. This is the pragmatic approach that will permeate this book.

Additional critical work will be required before this new social science becomes hegemonic, and generates the requisite amount of experimentation and innovation necessary to establish its credibility. This would mark the return of practical reason, a refurbishment and modernization of the intellectual toolbox used by the social sciences, and a better understanding of the forces at work that prevent the highest and most effective use of applied social sciences in public policy. Developing some ideas that might speed up the emergence of these new freer, more experimentalist and more open-ended approaches is the main purpose of this book.

The second family of blockages pertains to the notion of evidence. It stems from a tendency of the fundamentalists to summarily reject a whole range of types of knowledge as irrelevant if not meaningless, if that knowledge does not originate from the credentialized tribe and is not the result of work done according to certain prescribed protocols.

This tendency is cartoonishly illustrated by the determination of the quality of research results in many universities according to the ranking of the journals in which they are published, without any first-hand critical examination of their quality and relevance. This leads, by definition, to the routine and senseless disregard for the research results of consulting reports that are prejudged as not of a quality or significance comparable to credentialized knowledge. It becomes grotesque when such a credo is taken to mean, as in the case of an excessively narrow definition of evidence-based medicine, "therapeutic nihilism in the absence of evidence from randomized trials" (Straus and McAlister 2000: 838).

These fundamentalist versions of evidence are pathological and derive from a gross misunderstanding of the notion of evidence. Only poorly informed fundamentalists, lacking any critical judgement, would presume to infer that the best sources for answering questions about diagnosis, prognosis or harm are select refereed journals or randomized clinical trials. This does not mean that any babbling by anyone more or less informed should be regarded as usable knowledge, but nor does it mean that other sources may not contain something of interest. This is a matter to be ascertained, not presumed.

The third family of blockages pertains to the very weaknesses of inquiries in the social sciences, which remain marred by: (1) factitious questions and reductive approaches; (2) leading, in consequence, to truncated analyses and narrow alternatives; and (3) as a further consequence, to failures in designing workable organizations and institutions.

This latter family of blockages is ascribable to a poor understanding of the psychosocial process of inquiry, and, as a result, to poor design of the process that Dewey defines as "intelligence in operation" (Boisvert 1998): the situation being problematic, how much of the context needs to be taken into account; whose perceptions and views should be taken into account; how different points of view and interests should be dealt with; how both the past and the future are factored in; how to escape the positivist fixation on occurrence, and to encompass the psychosocial dimensions of uncertainty and social learning (Power 2007; Pahl-Wostl et al. 2007).

In that sense, effective inquiry must have a deconstructive and reconstructive quality. It requires a deconstruction and reconstruction of the evolution of a dynamic open-ended process that is interfered with by a plurality of actors attempting to modify it in a conversation with the situation, with such actions having as a consequence the inventing of structures that in turn reveal conflicts and dilemmas in the appreciative system. Such adjustments are the results not only of external shocks, but also, and mainly, of internal shocks emerging from the uncovering of one's own intentions, projects and actions, from critiquing them, and from acting upon the lessons learned. This is what is meant by reflexivity: knowledge acquired gets integrated during the process; it influences the design, and thereby modifies the outcome.

This reconstructive work aims at carefully probing the evolutionary process, its evolving design and its imperfect reflexivity. It is akin to the sort of inquiry referred to in Arturo Pérez-Reverte's novel *The Flanders Panel* (1994), in which the action pivots around a painting of a nobleman and a knight playing a game of chess. The painter is said to have painted it two years after the death of the knight, and has inscribed on the painting the cryptic statement "Who has taken the knight?", which might also be taken to mean "Who has killed the knight?". A restorer obtains the help of a skilled chess player to reconstruct the game and to discover who has taken the knight. The expert proceeds to this difficult reconstruction, starting from the end situation on the chessboard and working backward, eliminating the impossible moves and logically arriving at the conclusion that the black queen took the knight.

This is the genius of reconstruction: starting with the structure to reconstruct the process that has resulted in this structure, so as to gain "a properly historical understanding of the given situation" (Ferry 1996, 9ff). But the Deweyan inquiry goes a bit further: it also factors in the future, so that the inquiry takes possibilities into account. Ours is a world of "affairs", as Dewey calls them, that is never frozen, it is a world of actualities open to a variety of possibilities, and knowledge is awareness of, and sensitivity to, these possibilities. Indeed, it is often only the seeming inevitability of some of these possibilities that can trigger action, but without them one cannot even imagine how an action-oriented inquiry could make any progress (Boisvert 1998: Chapter 1; Paquet 2008).

To remove these families of blockages one may propose correctives. They are not in the nature of fixes or recipes, but in the nature of (1) a different philosophy of the social sciences; (2) a different conceptual toolbox based on anti-reductionism, experimentalism and social learning; and (3) a new approach to policy, focusing on design, prototyping and "serious play" (Schrage 2000). Underpinning this alternative approach and the new mindset are a philosophy of process, and a focus on design and the centrality of reflexivity.

THREE FOUNDATIONAL ASSUMPTIONS

PROCESS

The process approach is a general strategy for the description and explanation of reality. It is a generalized approach rather than a unified doctrine. It does not deny that things exist, but it suggests that material bodies, like all stable structures, are rooted in process, and constitute only temporary bundles of powers generated by a process that remains unfinished and open-ended.

The process approach and the object approach are traditions that have their roots in classical Greece, in the opposition between Heraclitus and Parmenides, and the lineage of each tradition is impressive. But the object tradition has been overwhelmingly dominant as a result of the dominant impact of positivism. Émile Durkheim (1895/1988), maybe more than anyone else, has been associated with the doctrine that "social facts are things" and should be approached as such. More or less at the same time as Hayek was denouncing scientism, Jules Monnerot (1946) wrote a denunciation of Durkheim's stance, but it did not have a determinative impact. Most of the mainstream social sciences remain associated with the object approach.

The vision of the world in good currency until quite recently remained some version of social physics, but a pre-quantum physics: still enamoured with reversible-time equilibrium analysis, as exemplified most clearly by economics.

This is not to say that heterodox movements did not emerge. The Austrian school in economics challenged the economic orthodoxy typified by Paul Samuelson. The same may be said of the other social sciences. But the mainstream social sciences remained dominated by the object approach, and human agency played second-fiddle.

The renaissance of the social sciences has been fuelled by a shift to a process approach, emphasizing a dynamic open-ended approach in terms of flows (Rescher 1996; 2000). It has aptly restated the basic tenets of process philosophy, and anti-reductionist social scientists have begun to see the human world as consisting of processes, with "objects" having a derivative status.

DESIGN

An offshoot of the process perspective is that intervening in a process is in the nature of design. The design process has too often been sanitized to make it fall in line with the scientistic regime, by being reduced to problem-solving steps fully programmable under a set of rules (Schön 1990: 112). This assumes that the problem space has, like an actual maze, a structure that is already given. Design is reduced to problem-solving in a world where the problem is given.

The design process does not really start with such givens. Schön has defined it in a Deweyan way as intelligent exploration of a terrain (Schön 1990: 125), as an inquiry guided by an appreciative system, carried over from past experience, that produces "a selective representation of an unfamiliar situation that sets values for

the system's transformation. It frames the problem of
the problematic situation and thereby sets directions in
which solutions lie and provides a schema for exploring them" (Schön 1990: 131–132). In fact, designing is
a frame experiment: a conversation with the situation
that leads to inventing structures that in turn reveal
conflicts and dilemmas in the appreciative system. Since
participants talk across discrepant frames, designing,
according to Schön

> is a process in which communication, political struggle,
> and substantive inquiry are combined ... [That] may
> be judged appropriate ... if it leads to the creation of a
> design structure that directs inquiry toward progressively
> greater inclusion of features of the problematic situation
> and values for its transformation (1990: 138–139).

Such exploration or inquiry leads designers to learn
by doing, but more importantly to escape from straight
deductive thinking (proving that something must be)
and indulging in abductive reasoning (suggesting that
something may be and reaching out to explore it)
(Martin 2004). This is fundamental in the world of
design, which "involves inquiry into systems that do not
yet exist" (Romme 2003: 558).

This new way of thinking underlies the whole new
generative governance of social systems, building on
experimentation and "serious play," and making the
highest and best use of grappling, grasping, discerning
and sense-making as parts of reflective learning (Chait
et al. 2005: Chapter 6).

REFLEXIVITY

A final assumption of the new approach is that reflexivity is taken into account as a fundamental condition for
social learning on which effective governance is based.
Reflexivity is defined by Bob Jessop (2003: 7) as "the
ability and commitment to uncover and make explicit

to oneself the nature of one's intentions, projects and actions and their conditions of possibility; and, in this context, to learn about them, critique them, and act upon any lessons that have been learned." Reflexivity means that knowledge acquired gets integrated during the process and unfolds in order to modify the outcome.

As Douglass North (2005) states clearly, the traditional social sciences have done a very poor job of factoring in human intentionality and the human capacity for representational redescription. The belief systems underpinning these representations have an immense impact on the institutions themselves.

The new mindset recognizes that the complexity and turbulence of the context is such that agents cannot fully understand and grasp it. This entails a process of inquiry with a built-in and ongoing critical ability to think about the implications of particular choices, and an ongoing capacity to modify means and ends as learning evolves. It entails learning how to learn reflexively, in a double-looped manner (Argyris and Schön 1978).

These three assumptions of the new mindset are ways to respond to three weaknesses of the old mindset. The old mindset is plagued by its assumptions about an object-world; its view of intervention as problem-solving within a maze-like world where the problem is already set; and its neglect of human intentionality and its key role in a process of governance that must be reflexive. This explains the static and timeless dimensions of the traditional approaches.

CROSSROADS

Exploration in search of renewed social sciences faces a major strategic choice. Should it proceed by adopting a step-by-step research strategy that would attempt to take some distance from scientistic approaches by progressively relaxing some of its most taxing assumptions? Or should it follow the more draconian lead of Hayek, and explicitly build on the assumption that the natural sciences are as different from the social sciences as chalk from cheese, and that, even though there may be certain areas of overlap, they have to be constructed on entirely different grounds?

It is our view that the step-by-step strategy will not work. Herbert Simon (1981) is the most eminent proponent of the strategy. He has done as much as anyone could to build the foundations of the new social sciences in this manner, in a very timid way and in a spirit of compromise. His impact has been minimal, if not negligible, because of this very timidity. The positivistic and scientistic approach that permeated the old social sciences in the 20th century remained too powerful a dominant logic, so his alternative approach did not take hold. His bounded-rationality-cum-satisficing approach triggered only minor challenges to the conventional wisdom. It led to a range of other modifications of the canon without mounting any real challenge to the dominance of scientism as the paradigm of the dominant way of seeing.

A more promising trail suggests that one should start with a clean break between the natural sciences and the social sciences. A version of this alternative strategy has been sketched by Bent Flyvberg (2001) under the general rubric of "phronetic social science". It has a Deweyan flavour, and builds on the work of the "fifth column" of practitioners that has continued to defend practical reason and social learning throughout the years.

Flyvberg (1) frontally challenges the pretensions of scientism; (2) develops an alternative composite approach to the social sciences that is pluralist, and gives much more valence to *phronesis* than to *episteme* or *techne* in attempts to comprehend the social life-world; and (3) questions the dominant importance of technical rationality in the sort of expertise required by social scientists.

Flyvberg's approach may be regarded as an extension of Dewey's imperative — in the beginning is the issue — and is underpinned by four questions: where are we going? is this desirable? what should be done? who gains and who loses? (Flyvberg 2001: 60). From the answers to these questions action follows. It underlines the extent to which the social sciences, as opposed to the natural sciences, are context-dependent; it insists that *phronesis* (prudence, a sense of what is ethically practical) dominates the practice of social scientists, and that *episteme* (science) and *techne* (art and technology) play only subsidiary roles; and it emphasizes that, in the development of expertise and virtuosity, social scientists have to evolve beyond the world of rules into a world that gives significant importance to context, experience and intuition in its practice.

A WORD OF CAUTION AND A PLEA

This book complains about the tendency for so many social scientists to presume that there is a fairly specific, determinate and identifiable social reality waiting to be discovered out there through the use of certain conventional methods that are purported to ensure reliable knowledge.

This conventional view is flawed in two ways. First, as John Law has put it, "much of the world is vague, diffuse or unspecific, slippery, emotional, ephemeral, elusive or indistinct, changes like a kaleidoscope, and doesn't really have much of a pattern at all" (2004: 2). Second, there is no reason to believe that these realities can be approximated only through the limited repertoire of tools usually covered in the traditional courses on research methods. This does not mean that there is no room for common-sense assumptions about the world or for such conventional research methods. Rather, it means that these represent very reductive and truncated views of social science inquiry. There are many realities out there that one may construct and reconstruct, not a single one, and there are many methods that may be used while doing so.

From our efforts to expose the weaknesses of certain dogmas and ideologies, such as scientism, Marxism, feminism and the like, on these matters, it should not be concluded that these approaches are not yielding any new insights. Rather, it should be understood that what is under attack is the pretension to have found a universal lens through which social realities can and should be analyzed. Meaningful knowledge about these realities can be gained in various ways, and often only cumulatively, by trial and error, and making use of eclectic instruments.

This is where the centrality of experimentalism lies. Nothing but an assemblage of methods acting as "a combination of reality detector and reality amplifier" in the overwhelming fluxes of the real will do (Law 2004: 14). This is in turn the role of experimentalism: to trigger the assembling and applying of methods, processes of experimentation as ways to learn about which kind of institution can best coordinate ongoing interactions across various social domains. Reflexivity is at the core of experimentalism: it allows members to collectively revisit decisions and revise collective interactions, and fosters the emergence of new ideas, perspectives, interests, constituencies, oppositions. It structures disagreement. A commitment to experimentalism is a commitment to ways of coordinating our various forms of disagreement.

Our plea for experimentalism entails, therefore, (1) freeing ourselves from the shackles of partial views of realities, and (2) committing ourselves to the development of an assemblage of methods promoting maximal reflexivity.

INTRODUCTION

The difficult emergence of a new mindset

It may be a superior survival trait to have any explanation rather than no explanation for the problems we confront.
— DOUGLASS C. NORTH (2005)

The experience of the aftermath of World War II gave the scientistic social sciences a quite artificial boost. In particular, Keynesian economics promised a new capacity to govern the economy as a result of the lessons learned during the difficult period of the Great Depression and the war. "Big G government" boasted that it would now be in charge, and that it would ensure prosperity, stability and fairness.

A great deal changed from the late 1960s onward. Inflation raged and later stagflation hit hard. Advanced economies were plagued with more complex challenges and became more pluralistic, and, as a result, less easily governable. These polities displayed considerable disarray, and confusion became the dominant tone on the national scene. There was chaos on all fronts, economic, political and social, both in Canada and elsewhere. Citizens lived in Yeatsian times: it appeared that the centre could no longer hold. Yet there seemed to be no alternative to the view that "big G government" had to be in charge, despite the fact that it seemed to be failing miserably at its governing tasks.

In the rest of the western world experiments were carried out that indicated that one might govern in a less state-centric and centralized way, but there was considerable reluctance to abandon the centralized and state-centric perspective that appeared to have served advanced economies so well after 1945.

It would take some time before an alternative cosmology would be permitted to emerge. Newer problems seemed to call for much less "big G government", and much more mass collaboration, provided by market mechanisms; more public consultation; and, for groups and parties whose fates had previously been perceived as negatively correlated, more imaginative ways to coordinate their actions. These initiatives were discussed to some extent, but the citizenry seemed intellectually, emotionally and politically unprepared to deal with this new reality where, in the phrase of Harlan Cleveland (2002), there is "nobody in charge."

OLD VISTAS, NEW VISTAS

The core message of old-vista scientism is that the social sciences, like the natural sciences, deal with an object-world. Their theoretical studies of social facts are designed to meet clear scientific standards: they are explicit, universal, abstract, context-independent, systematic and predictive. They search for context-independent rules.

New-vista social scientists, in contrast, suggest that the social sciences deal with context-dependent, open-ended relations among contexts, actions and interpretations. They draw attention to the fact that a grammar is not a language and rules are not the game (Flyvberg 2001: 49). Consequently, the standards defined by the natural sciences for theories are irrelevant.

This does not mean that the social sciences have no standards. The standards are simply different. The relevant model for phronetic social sciences is the design professions. As a result, context is crucial, for each situation is unique, and the key values are participation, discourse and experimentation. The focus is on getting close to reality, looking at practice, studying cases and contexts, and conducting dialogue with a multiplicity of voices.

However, these new vistas are not yet in good currency. Simplistic schemes of so-called rational decision-making, based on imaginary objective functions and equally contrived constraints, remain hegemonic. Indeed, in recent years the chasm between the social sciences templates and the critical issues of the day has grown considerably wider. More and more, social science paradigms have triggered esoteric and formalized research programmes that have become less and less capable of grasping the complexities of the evolving environment or responding effectively to the various crises that have emerged.

Disciplinary academic social sciences have become so disconnected from the issues of the day that their contribution to policy responses has diminished considerably. The stylized models suggested by disciplinary academic research have become more and more solipsistic, and "muddling through", in the shape of practical social-science-inspired policy research, has proceeded almost in parallel with the work done in academic circles. One would find it difficult to demonstrate how academe has contributed in any significant way to the design of an effective policy response to recent problems (Slater 1967; Paquet 1971).

The phronetic way of approaching policy research was developed to a certain extent during the 1970s, albeit without this particular label, through the work of John Friedmann and George Abonyi (1976; Friedmann 1978; 1979). They proposed an interactive or transactive style of planning, based on reflection in action, dialogue, and mutual learning by professional experts and clients. Their

work was based on four sub-processes (see Figure 1):
(1) the construction of appropriate theories of reality;
(2) taking the formation of social values into account;
(3) gaming, leading to the design of political strategies;
and (4) the ways in which collective action is carried out.
These sub-processes were meant to come to life in concrete situations and might be stylized starkly as defining
an approach that tried to generate a meaningful response
to four simple questions: is the policy being proposed
technically feasible? is it socially acceptable? is it too
politically destabilizing? can it be implemented?

EXPERIMENTS IN THE
1980s AND 1990s

Some terrains were explored with this new type of
instrumentation in the 1980s and 1990s (Paquet 1999a),
and revealed the power of this approach. However,
these experiments were few in number and they also
revealed the great difficulty in meeting the standards
required to ensure the integrity of this four-dimensional
framework.

Very often the four families of maps of the world
that were of interest to policy analysts could not be

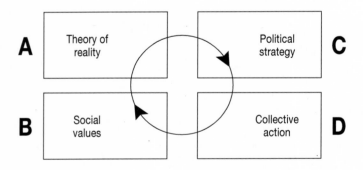

FIGURE 1 A social learning model of policy research
Source: Friedmann and Abonyi (1976: 88)

kept in balance. Allocative efficiency, social values, political stratagems or collective action were often out of kilter. For instance, in relation to energy policy it was found that considerations of allocative efficiency came to overtake the whole process and thwart the policy research in some particular direction or other. I have shown elsewhere, in a critical evaluation of the Energy Options Process, that the efficiency framework trumped the other three, and led to policy research and policy initiatives that were quite unsatisfactory (Energy, Mines and Resources 1988; Paquet 1989a).

The same fragility of this balance among the four components was revealed in other areas. In fact, my *Governance through Social Learning* (1999) might be regarded as a catalogue of errors, showing how good governance through social learning failed in many areas, from education to multiculturalism to funding agencies, because of the incapacity to conduct policy research in a manner that would keep the four dimensions of the framework in balance. More often than not, one particular quadrant or block — mainly the analytical quadrant, focusing on the question of whether a policy is technically feasible — hijacked a policy research process that often proved to be insufficiently robust to rebut such attacks.

SLOW PROGRESS

Yet, across these different terrains, some progress was made. It became obvious that the key reasons why the governance process often failed were the presence of certain epistemological blockages and a lack of appropriate tools to operationalize whatever work appeared to be necessary to design effective responses.

One of the main epistemological blockages came from a fixation of policy research on goal-setting and control mechanisms to ensure the pursuit of these goals. This simplistic perspective proved of little use in a world where (1) goals could not be unambiguously defined;

(2) means–ends relationships proved unreliable; and (3) "big G government" was no longer in a position to rule the roost anyway. Yet it proved extraordinarily difficult to discredit this narrow stylization of the policy research paradigm and to come to terms with the new reality where there is "nobody in charge".

As early as the 1970s there had been suggestions that in our complex, turbulent and evolving environment, "the problem formulation itself is open, the evaluative function involves designing an information system to provide the medium for effective feedback between analysis and problem formulation". In this new context, "the interplay between norm-setting, goal-setting, course-holding, control on functioning, and organizational/institutional innovations becomes fundamentally dependent on organizational intelligence" (Paquet 1971: 54). This social learning view gained some notoriety with the work of Chris Argyris and Donald Schön (1978), but did not come to be in good currency because it appeared to be too intellectually messy and complex. Moreover, the policy researchers who might have been tempted to adopt this experimentalist approach did not have templates or instrumentation that could easily be used to guide such probing. It was only with the development of new tools such as search conferences and other forms of instrumentation based on significant consultation, deliberation and negotiation, that this alternative approach gained some legitimacy, if not credibility. Indeed, the credibility-building phase is still in progress (Williams 1979; Rosell 1992; Schön and Rein 1994; Emery and Purser 1996; Taylor 1997; Thacher and Rein 2004).

A FEW KEY CHARACTERISTICS
OF THIS EMERGING MINDSET

It is possible to identify a few key characteristics of the new mindset. First, in the beginning is the issue, as John Dewey (1927) put it. This calls for a pluralist approach to dealing with the practical problem at hand, in a

manner that is the result of some triangulation among
(1) a fair description of the context; (2) a fair appreciation of the latitude the organization will allow in the
search for a practical answer; and (3) a fair awareness
of what might be regarded as the values and focal points
that might serve as relevant references and constraining
guideposts. This triangulation defines the corridor of
acceptable and therefore viable directions for repairs.

Second, front and centre in this work is the need for
an enriched, evidence-based exploration of the issues.
As a result, it shies away from ideological and partisan
approaches, which are to be regarded as fundamentally
crippled epistemologies (Hardin 2002). However, since
no one can claim to be free of all bias, it becomes important to work actively at putting on the table, as much
as one can, as many as possible of the assumptions with
which one is operating, and to put a premium on exposing the assumptions one is usually not aware of.

The new mindset grapples with "evidence" wherever it
is, and whatever form it might take. Consequently, it does
not restrict itself to hard material or "quantophrenic"
evidence. It also takes account of intentionality, frames
of reference, belief systems and culture, to the full extent
that these realities have an impact on the issue at hand.

Third, the new mindset puts a premium on the highest
and best use of imagination, experimentation and "serious play" (Schrage 2000) in the exploration of promising
avenues, and in the design of viable responses to difficult
situations. In that sense, it puts at the core of its inquiries
an explicit social learning machine.

The issue must not only be properly contextualized,
but also subjected to a probing that attempts to make
explicit the partiality of the frames used by the different
stakeholders in order to generate the requisite blending
and blurring of frames that allows fruitful multilogues.
There is, therefore, a certain process of reconstruction
that accompanies this work: not only searching for
responses to the original questions, but wondering

whether the original questions were the most useful ones, and exploring ways in which such questions might be modified, transformed or reframed.

This is where the process of experimentation, proto-typing and "serious play" becomes centrally important. It is not sufficient to ensure open access to tinkering for as many stakeholders as possible. One must also ensure that the appropriate motivations are nurtured so that all citizens are willing and able to engage in "serious play" and thus truly become producers of governance through tinkering with the governance apparatus. Governance not only relies on a much more flexible toolbox, but requires that any formal or binding arrangement be revisited, played with and adjusted in order to take account of the evolving diversity of circumstances.

Prototyping means (1) identifying some top require-ments as quickly as possible; (2) putting in place a quick and dirty provisional medium of co-development; (3) allowing as many interested parties as possible to get involved as partners in designing a better arrangement; (4) encouraging iterative prototyping; and (5) thereby encouraging all, through playing with prototypes, to get a better understanding of the problems, of their priorities and of themselves (Schrage 2000: 199ff).

The purpose of this exercise is to create a dialogue (creative interaction) between people and prototypes. This may be even more important than creating a dia-logue between people. It is predicated on a culture of active participation. The sort of democratization of design that ensues, and the sorts of playfulness and adventure that are required for "serious play" with pro-totypes, may not yet be parts of Canadian culture, but there are signs that they are emerging.

Finally, this new mindset is meant to be transforma-tive. It proposes, not an exercise in hypothesis-testing, but a commitment to entering a process of inquiry with a view to transforming the context that has led to the emergence of the thorny issue.

The traditional approaches, focused on attempts to falsify hypotheses about some objective reality, have generated too narrow a focus. For the social practitioner what is central is an effort "to create a wholly new, unprecedented situation that, in its possibility for generating new knowledge, goes substantially beyond the initial hypothesis" (Friedmann and Abonyi 1976: 938). This in turn calls for different notions of "success" or "failure" that go far beyond those in use in the usual physical-science-based process.

This means that, instead of taking the "problem definition" as a "given", as if one were in a static, stable or stale environment, what is sought is a process of problem definition based on the simple notion that there is "nobody in charge" and that what is sought is a way to design modes of effective coordination in a world where power, resources and information are widely distributed.

STRUCTURE OF THE BOOK

Part I exposes some of the elements of the crippling epistemology that have prevented this new approach from being developed as fully and successfully as it might have been. It has to do with (1) the drift of the social sciences and the humanities into "methodism"; (2) their failure to develop the sort of practical knowledge required and the education processes underpinning the production of such knowledge; and (3) the risk-averse culture that has plagued the social sciences enterprise and prevented it from being as innovative as it might have been.

Part II, under the general rubric of inadequate scaffolding, explores three major weaknesses that have plagued social science learning: grievously deficient public informational infrastructure, unintelligent accountability, and neglect of organizational design.

Part III defines how the new approach might be used by reviewing some interesting cases of failure of governance. In all these cases the failures are ascribable to a great extent to a lethargic, risk-averse and rear-view-mirror-plagued bureaucracy, shackled to a centralized mindset, and unable and unwilling to experiment and to learn.

This paradoxical approach to some specific policy areas suggests (1) how some *bricolage* might help in developing both a greater capacity to acquire this new way of seeing, and a greater ability in using new tools, and (2) how different forces of dynamic conservatism have been and are preventing such action from succeeding.

It is beyond the scope of this book to flesh out the new way of seeing, or to provide a manual for the use of the new tools. I have attempted to deal much more adequately with both tasks in two separate books to be published concurrently with this one: *Scheming Virtuously* (Invenire Books) and *Gouvernance : mode d'emploi* (Liber).

In conclusion, I want to reflect on the difficulty of unlearning the old ways, on the variety of very constraining mental prisons still in existence, on the promises and difficulties of open-source and reflexive governance, on the emergence of a strong anti-reductionist current, on the demonstrable viability and effectiveness of mass collaboration and also on the paranoia that still surrounds the world of governance.

The book closes with a call to irony, since it is unlikely that, in Canada, a revolution in the mind can be forthcoming in any other way.

PART I

Crippling Epistemologies

Introduction

Part I may appear to some to be tedious reflective whining about the defective philosophy of the social sciences and their ambient culture, an overlong detour on the way to the sort of practical policy research announced above. This is not the case.

The critique of crippling epistemologies constitutes a necessary first step in the development of good governance. Without some critique of the existing mindset, one will not be able to identify the epistemological blockages and their sources, or to initiate the difficult process of development of an alternative arsenal to the "methodist" model of policy research in good currency, and to the development of better governance. Without such a discussion, neither the critical evaluation of the tools in use nor the case studies would be as illuminating as they might be. Neither is this critique the result of whims and "ad-hocery" only. Failures of governance are most often the direct result of crippling epistemologies.

But there is more. If one is to develop an alternative to the traditional model of policy research, one has to establish the identity papers and credentials of the new approach it suggests, the mindset it is built on, and the different components and stages of its inquiry process. Much of this can be done only by ensuring that it is shown to be standing in sharp contrast with the features of current models.

The chapters in Part I provide the minimal amount of material necessary to make sense of the traditional approach, and to understand its characteristics and its flaws. At the core of this critical work is the central notion of "inquiry" in John Dewey's (1927) sense.

Charles Lindblom (1990: 3) defines inquiry as: "the production of social knowledge as a vast social process in which even relatively uninformed, ordinary people play significant parts along with political and opinion leaders." This process of probing is much larger and more heterogeneous than the process of problem-solving: it "emphasizes persistence and depth of investigation, uncertainty of result, and possible surprise"; it connotes "a continuing varied, diffuse, and interactive process."

Lindblom's (1990) choice of this prudent approach to social problems stems from his conviction that one cannot expect anything meaningful from "scientific problem-solving" or "ideology". Neither the simplistic technical rationality of means and ends, nor the anamorphosis of the present situation via a single Great Idea, can generate much usable knowledge. In both cases, nothing can be expected except a caricature of the situation based on a systematic effort to distort the situation in order to make it fit the dominant perspective.

Probing is clearly not the preserve of professionals. Lay persons probe as much as professionals do, and both groups depend on each other. In fact, some of the worst outcomes might be ascribed to a lack of coordination between the two sorts of probing.

Chapter 1 examines the crisis of confidence that has plagued the human sciences as the result of the gradual displacement of content by "methodism" and the professionalization of the academy, without the parallel growth of a sense of professionalism, that has led the human sciences to desert their founding questions, and to focus on generating unhelpful maps. It is argued that the only way out is to redirect the human sciences toward their original questions.

Chapter 2 indicts the post-secondary education system not only as a significant victim, but also as a continuing source of this perversion, this professionalization without professionalism, and suggests a refoundation of the post-secondary education system in a manner that would preserve the core importance of *savoir-faire* and *savoir-être* within a transformed educational paradigm that would give access to a broader varieties of knowledges, and might provide some of the winning conditions for the renaissance of a less crippling and more inclusive process of acquisition of knowledge.

Chapter 3 deals with a complementary source of crippling epistemologies: the surrounding national and corporate cultures. Culture is used as a focus for examining many of the hidden forces that shape our acquisition of knowledge, and our decisions outside the realm of education and research. It is suggested that various neuroses act at the cognitive and ethical levels to shape learning, and thereby to influence the capacities to experiment and innovate.

These diverse sets of constraints and sources of crippling epistemologies, intellectual, institutional, educational and cultural, have been mental prisons preventing the human and social sciences from evolving the breadth and depth necessary to deal effectively with the challenges of governance in a complex and turbulent world.

Identifying these prisons is a not insignificant accomplishment, as it helps to focus social scientists' attention on the main sources of distortion. Such distortions are to a significant extent responsible for flawed informational infrastructure, inadequate instrumentation and governance pathologies, but these are reparable once their sources and causes have been properly diagnosed.

CHAPTER 1

Two tramps in mud time

Only where love and need are one,
And the work is play for mortal stakes,
Is the deed ever really done.
— ROBERT FROST

There may be no better description of the humanities
and the social sciences, and no better characterization
for the time, than the title of Robert Frost's poem quoted
above, "Two Tramps in Mud Time". My argument raises
questions about two basic assumptions on which, at present, most demands made on governments by humanists
and social scientists rest: first, that the humanities and
the social sciences play an important and useful role in
modern society; and, second, that governments should
therefore provide important additional resources for their
support. Unless human scientists change their ways, it
may be argued, the case for their social usefulness and
their deserving of funding is not very strong.

Here is a road map of my argument. First, the humanities and the social sciences are quarrelsome twins that
may not be identical, but are also not fundamentally
different. They are sets of languages of illumination,
exploration and interpretation of the physical and human
worlds.

Second, a crisis of confidence in the humanities and social sciences has developed recently, but analysis of this crisis has generally evaporated into a boring enumeration of troublesome symptoms. The real source of the crisis, I will argue, is in a loss of origin, in the fading away of the founding questions from which the social sciences and the humanities originated. This has led to a gradual displacement of content by method in the practice of both the humanities and the social sciences.

Third, such a displacement is particularly unfortunate when the substantive form of our social and economic order is mutating. The fixation on procedures has induced a great deal of irrelevance in their discourses, just when the humanities and social sciences appear to have the most to contribute.

Fourth, the professionalization of the academy, without a parallel growth of professionalism as part of its duties, appears to be at the roots of this loss of origin. Since World War II, academics have professionalized the practice of both the social sciences and the humanities, and self-regulating corporations have transformed and perverted the use of their languages. The much-needed shift back from method to content is unlikely to occur as a matter of course, and additional public funds will not suffice either. Despite specious arguments to the contrary, governments have legitimate concerns about affairs of the mind, and have to accept responsibility for stewarding the humanities and the social sciences back toward substantive questions.

Fifth, what is required is nothing less than a strategy of culture, to serve as a sextant for such government action.

The intent of this chapter is not to deny that much work of great value has been done, and is being done, in the human sciences. Rather, the point of my argument is that despite their technical and sometimes substantive contributions, the human sciences have not lived up to what could reasonably be expected from them and that,

if anything, the situation is likely to continue to deterio-
rate (although there are signs that a true renaissance may
be in progress). Thus, it seems important to ask why this
is so, and how one might correct such a situation.

THE QUARRELSOME TWINS MAY
NOT BE IDENTICAL, BUT ...

Scientists, social scientists, humanists and artists illuminate reality, explore the unknown, and interpret the
physical and human worlds. It is their common fundamental task, and it is instructive that "theory" and
"theatre" have the same ancient Greek roots (Nisbet
1976: 10–12). Robert Nisbet has argued that art and
science are simply different paths, different logics of discovery of synthetic, self-consistent worlds. In this array
of perspectives, the humanities and the social sciences
are close neighbours.

Even though reality is the quest of the artist as much
as of the scientist, a sort of division of labour has
occurred and each group appears to be attempting to
illuminate, explore and interpret alternate realities.
Lawrence LeShan and Henry Margenau (1982) have tried
to illustrate the multiplicity of those alternate realities
through an account of a businessman's day, as, succes-
sively, a tycoon closing a profitable deal at lunch; a hus-
band almost telepathically communicating with his wife
on the dance floor in the early evening; a worried father
praying for the recovery of his sick child later in the
evening; and, at night, a dreamer of kangaroos and mer-
maids. LeShan and Margenau (165–166) propose four
different classes of ways to organize reality: the sensory
reality of everyday common sense; clairvoyant reality
(as on the dance floor); transpsychic reality (as with
the father praying); and mythic reality (as in the man's
dreams). Which of these is reality? The answer is that
none of them are: there are many realities. Science, the
social sciences, humanities and art illuminate, explore
and interpret alternate realities, alternate domains of

experience, alternate realms, whether observable or not.

The logics used to explore these alternate realities are not, however, contradictory. They *are* different, but they are also compatible and complementary. Methods of study appropriate to each obviously differ, and different kinds of languages must be found to describe and interpret different experiences, but there are often more differences between such languages within the humanities or within the social sciences than one category or the other.

A CRISIS OF CONFIDENCE

A crisis of confidence has developed among humanists and social scientists in North America over the last thirty years or so of the 20th century and the early years of the new century (Andreski 1974; Kaufmann 1977; Woods and Coward 1979). This crisis is akin to the one that has developed in relation to professional knowledge (Schön 1983). Practitioners in the humanities and the social sciences experienced this crisis first in their practice, but the concerns of their clients have been echoed widely and rapidly in the broader social context. Consequently, patrons, including governments, have become less willing to fund the activities of both humanists and social scientists.

Any community suffering such a fall from grace and a loss of legitimacy, might react to the new situation by reflecting on its goals and rejuvenating itself through re-education, entrepreneurship and creativity. Alternatively, it might take refuge in clichés "about knowledge being its own reward and about following the truth wherever it may lead" (Kaufmann 1977: xvi), and refuse to take notice.

On the whole, humanists and social scientists have refused to reflect on their goals and essentially have indulged in a process of rationalization or defence of what they have been doing. However, the two groups

have developed divergent rationalization strategies. On
the whole, social scientists have explicitly sought a new
legitimacy for their work through rapprochement with
the "hard" sciences on matters of method. Humanists
have done so more hesitantly, while articulating a stub-
born defence of their existing practices as the only road
to knowledge. While this general statement probably
holds for most humanists, it does not mean that there has
been no change in the practice of humanists over time.
Indeed, for many humanists the temptation to emulate
the strategy of social scientists has been compelling.
Structuralism, post-structuralism, semiotics, semiology,
grammatology and deconstructionism, with their different fixations on method and on the syntactic dimensions
of their realities, have obscured or even discarded their
quintessential semantic dimensions (Sturrock 1979;
Searle 1985). However, on closer scrutiny it becomes
clear that the differences are a matter of degree. Both
groups, despite their rhetoric, have drifted in the same
direction.

THE REACTION OF THE SOCIAL SCIENCES

The social sciences have become beset by what Lewis
Thomas has aptly called "physics envy": they have
promoted wholesale borrowing of epistemology and
methodology from the physical sciences. This borrowing has tended to reinforce a pervasive undercurrent in
the social sciences that goes back at least to the beginning of the 20th century. A machine model of reality
became the norm, the epistemology and methodology
of physical scientists were lionized, and the existence
of alternate realities was denied (LeShan and Margenau
1982: Chapter 12). This process has almost succeeded
in emasculating the human dimension of the human
sciences. The heritage of Bacon and Descartes was
rediscovered and became hegemonic. Concentrate on
method and the discovery of knowledge would follow:
such was the new dogma. Little did social scientists care

that Bacon and Descartes disagreed on what the method was to be (the inductive method or the deductive method, respectively). Emphasis on method *per se* became central (Nisbet 1976: 13–14).

This development brought together two strands of arguments from different epistemological traditions, which jointly have done considerable damage to the social sciences. From Bacon came a narrower definition of reality: as Jürgen Habermas (1971: 78) has put it, "exclusive reality is now claimed for phenomena which have previously been considered trivial." This narrower reality has been imposed and other realities have been obliterated. From Descartes came the sanctification of the priority of method over substance. Epistemology is reduced to methodological procedures, it being understood that the only acceptable methodological procedures are those borrowed from the physical sciences (Paquet 1985).

THE REACTION OF THE HUMANITIES
The general reaction of humanists appears to have been almost the obverse: all realities and all methodologies are declared admissible. Indeed, humanists often "take the high ground" and declare the existing practices, by definition, best practices. While this sort of "anything goes" approach to both substance and method may not be reprehensible in itself, it often rationalizes pointlessness and characterizes as uncouth any discussion by humanists about the point of their studies.

To confront the accusation (by humanists themselves) that research in the humanities has tended to produce "irrelevant museum culture" (Grant 1979: 47–50), the standard defence has been for pure humanists to point an accusatory finger at the institutional entrapments produced by the "external environment". Practitioners have been led astray, so the argument goes, by the worship of false idols brought in from outside the academy, to the detriment of the progress of knowledge. If only those false idols and their institutional entrapments could be removed, the workings of the "invisible hand" would generate optimum knowledge through a union of substance and method.

This was the technique used by Francis Bacon (1620) with his four idols: the idol of the tribe, the idol of the cave, the idol of the marketplace, and the idol of the theatre. Guy Rocher (1985) has used the same strata-gem to analyze the obstacles facing social scientists in Canada. These "idols" refer to the mental weaknesses typical of the human species (the tribe); to distinguishing peculiarities, such as the colonial status of our scientific enterprise (the cave); to the influence of language, as words are "confused, badly defined and hastily and irregularly abstracted from things" (the marketplace); and to erroneous systems of philosophy (the theatre) (Quinton 1980: Chapter 5).

E. H. Gombrich (1979: 112–122) uses a similar strata-gem to explain why the humanities have been diverted from their optimal path. He identifies four classes of idols to be blamed for their fall from grace: *idola quanti-tatis, idola novitatis, idola temporis* and *idola academica.* He complains that research in the humanities has been distorted and somewhat perverted by the influence of the physical sciences, with their emphasis on quantification, novelty, the use of the newest intellectual or mechanical tools, and the academy's division into departments and disciplines, subjecting this corpus of knowledge to noth-ing less than sacrilegious dissection. Gombrich claims that, even if unwittingly, the humanities have been cor-rupted by the same set of influences that has afflicted the social sciences, emanating from the model imported from the physical sciences and imposed on them by the academic environment. In this case, as in that of the social sciences, there has been a gradual displacement of content by method.

Such reactions have not solved the crisis of confi-dence and the causes of the failure of the human sciences have not been exorcized. The symptoms are clear. Overspecialization, quantophrenia, methodological naïveté and pretension, and formalism as camouflage have over the past fifty years weakened the credibility of the human sciences. This loss of credibility has come about when public expectations, oversold by earlier human scientists on the usefulness of their knowledge and their ability to solve social problems, were growing exponentially.

The changes that have occurred in the economy, as it grew less dependent on physical and technical production, and more dependent on knowledge and information, have enhanced the possibility of indulging in social architecture and social engineering. However, as symbols, design, research and communication have become larger parts of economic life, the complexity of the issues has grown exponentially. It has been argued that the new demands made on the human sciences have had a crippling effect on them. However, the real source of the crisis is on the supply side, generated by what is called a "loss of origin" (as the contributions by Richard Van Loon, Vincent Lemieux and Lorna Marsden in Souque and Trent [1985] show).

CRISIS AS LOSS OF ORIGIN

The crisis of the human sciences, under which label I include both the social sciences and the humanities, exposed by the crisis of confidence mentioned above, turn out to be more than a simple episode of frustrated expectations. In Calvin Schrag's words, the fixation on methodology has simply echoed the fact that the human sciences have lost track of the substantive questions that were at their very origin (Schrag 1980). Schrag sees the prominence of certain methodological principles and procedures as originating in a "crisis of self-understanding because the primordial motivation of the questioning has been forgotten" (1980: 9).

Originally, according to Schrag (1980), the questions had to do with the "knowledge necessary to human existence". Their point of anchorage was the real world, with its shared meanings and experience. What is needed, in Schrag's view, is to return to what William James called the "world of pure experience" or what Gaston Bachelard called *"l'homme des 24 heures de la journée"* (the man of the 24 hours of the day) (Bachelard 1972: 47ff).

This crisis was long ago diagnosed slightly differently by Edmund Husserl, who argued that its roots were in a "misguided rationalism". Instead of accepting the job of constituting special worlds (in the sense that people commonly speak of the "world of the child", the "business world", the "academic world" or the "world of sports") out of an original experience that serves as a sheet anchor against the tendency to declare a particular methodology absolute and paradigmatic, the human sciences seem to be running away from their basic data because they regard such data as inadmissible. Values, purpose, inner experience, creativity, love, courage, dignity and the rest are obliterated. This loss of origin explains the drift of the human sciences and their consequent growing irrelevance.

Both George Grant (for the humanities) and Stanislav Andreski (1974) (for the social sciences) have delivered verdicts on the consequences of this loss of origin for the human sciences. According to Grant (1979: 49), "the more the humanities have gained wealth and prestige in the last decades by taking on the language and methods of the progressive sciences, the less significance they have in the society they inhabit." In a letter to the editor in *Science* (July 9, 1982) Wassily Leontief, a Nobel laureate in economics, chastised his colleagues and wrote of the death of economics as an empirical science dealing with phenomena of common experience. He also commented on the latter-day "feudal system of the intellect" (Norbert Wiener's phrase) used to enforce this idolatry of method: "The methods used to maintain intellectual discipline in this country's most influential economics departments can occasionally remind one of those employed by the Marines to maintain discipline on Parris Island (p. 107)."

To correct the "fallacy of misplaced concreteness" that, according to A. N. Whitehead, results when a methodological abstraction becomes reified and considered in lieu of reality, one needs not only philosophy, which, according to Maurice Merleau-Ponty, is "the vigilance which does not let us forget the source of all knowledge" (Merleau-Ponty 1964: 110), but also alternative foundations for the human sciences. These, in turn, must be rooted in a critique of modern reason and in a replacement of formal reason by substantive reason (value rationality) as the foundation on which one might construct the human sciences (Schrag 1980; Ramos 1981).

Modern reason was defined by Thomas Hobbes strictly in terms of the reckoning of consequences. It has been claimed that this insight has contributed significantly to the derailment of the human sciences into different forms of qualified functionalism. Max Weber has been credited with doing a great deal for such a devaluation of reason, "leading to the conversion of the concrete into the abstract, of the good into the functional, and even of the ethical into the a-ethical" (Ramos 1981: 5), in showing the centrality of formal reason in modern capitalistic society.

However, Weber was not a fundamentalist about these issues. He maintained a clear distinction between two types of rationalities, *Zweckrationalität* and *Wertrationalität* (Weber 1978, Vol. 1: 24ff). The former corresponds to formal and instrumental rationality, the latter to substantive rationality. Weber developed his functional analysis on the basis of the former concept, but he had an acute sense of its limitations. He may not have fully anticipated to what perversions it would eventually lead. Otherwise, he might have explored the alternative foundation more fully.

A. G. Ramos develops the points made above extremely well (1981: 6–7 and 24–27). Either of the two rationalities may serve as a foundation for different theories. Substantive rationality offers insights into reality, while formal rationality merely supports the development of "language tools descriptive of operational procedures".

Though this is not the place to develop in full the consequences of such a change for the practice of the human sciences, it is clear that challenging the idolatry of method and instrumental rationality would bring the human sciences closer to a cultural hermeneutic. Technical reason, objectivity and method would not be suppressed. Rather, their roles would be changed. The task of the human sciences is paradoxical: to make use of technical reason without accepting the reductionism that it might appear to dictate. However, as Schrag (1980) aptly states, a paradoxical task is not necessarily an impossible one.

MINDS, LANGUAGES AND MAPS

In a knowledge-based economy the rich texture of human associative life evolves rapidly: it is a mix of totally and irreducibly intermingled facts and values. This complex, substantive whole is what the human sciences must illuminate, explore and interpret through the development of different languages, resulting in different philosophical maps.

FOUR KINDS OF MINDS

Walter Kaufmann (1977: Chapter 1) has proposed a typology of four ideal types of minds, which may prove helpful for our purposes: the visionary, the scholastic or technician, the Socratic or critic, and the journalist.

> Visionaries are loners. Alienated from the common sense of their time, they see the world differently and make sustained attempts to spell out their vision.
> Scholastics travel in schools, take pride in their rigour and professionalism, and rely heavily on their consensus or their common "know-how." They are usually hostile toward contemporary visionaries, especially in their own field, but swear by some visionaries of the past.

Socratics or critics make a point of not developing a vision and of being anti-scholastic. Socrates was a critic: he examined

> the faith and morals of his time, ridiculed claims to knowledge that were based on an uncritical reliance on consensus, and exerted himself to show how ignorant, confused and credulous most people are—including the most famous teachers, politicians and popular oracles.

The journalist, finally,

> writes for the day, for instant consumption, knowing that his wares have to be sold now or never because they will be stale tomorrow. He has no time for extensive research and no taste for scholastics' rigour.

Every researcher in the human sciences may be regarded as a blend of two or more of these types and, as a result of this blend, is likely to develop a different configuration of special worlds from the world of experience. There are few visionaries, and in any case "anyone as innovative, eccentric and provocative as Kierkegaard—for instance—could hardly hope to make it in the academic world." There are a small number of journalists concerned with exciting, up-to-date material, but not feeding their students much worth remembering, and an even smaller number of Socratic teachers stressing the need for a critical examination of alternatives and self-evaluation. On the other hand, there are legions of scholastics and technicians, whose work may be trivial, but is funded by foundations and agencies because they rely on the advice of other scholastics.

A BABEL OF LANGUAGES
Scholastic languages have been developed by human scientists to illuminate, explore and interpret the world, but much of the analysis based on these dominant

languages has been perverted by the fixation on method and by emphasis on "the disciplinary way" as the only appropriate route to knowledge. The result has been an increase in the volume of publications read by an ever-diminishing number of people, both because of a general lack of interest in the issues discussed, and because of the technical and opaque verbiage in which it is couched.

Normal science is defined by Thomas S. Kuhn as a series of puzzles and rules about what language of problem-solution has to be used to tackle them. Normal science bears little relationship to modern society, which has not been organized, as universities have, into departments or disciplines. Consequently, there is often no clear congruence between the issues raised in the languages of the disciplines and important social issues. Indeed, situations are trimmed, sanitized and redefined to fit the categories of the languages of problem–solution. This cleavage between the possibilities of the languages of the disciplines and the social issues has led the disciplines, as expressed in their journals, to concentrate less and less on empirical policy-oriented or problem-solving studies, and more on modelling and analysis without data.

The chasm between the disciplinary organization of the production of knowledge and the fact that many, if not most, of the problems most important for humanity demand an interdisciplinary approach, has meant that a great deal of scholastic work has been trivial, and that some of the most useful work has been done by amateurs (in the best sense of the word), or people who have transcended or at least shaken off the shackles of the disciplines.

UNHELPFUL MAPS
It is hardly surprising that the dominant scholastics, like the cartographers of earlier times, have produced maps that may be elegant, but certainly are not helpful to navigation. E. F. Schumacher (1977) has compared the philosophical maps produced using the so-called

"scientific method" to maps that ignore the things that we care most about and that are most important in the conduct of life. Instead of designing maps that eliminate most useful information because of the canons of a pre-vailing philosophy of cartography that dictates, "if in doubt, leave it out", Schumacher gambles on the oppo-site approach: if in doubt, show it prominently.

Our turbulent environment, which is alive with value shifts, technological changes and ever-changing oppor-tunities, calls for this sort of daring map-making. Our survival depends on a better understanding of society, and on the development of new maps and new languages to depict and express that understanding. Yet such maps are not being produced, and are unlikely to be produced unless much of our mental output is refurbished and many institutional entrapments are removed.

Those who have critically surveyed the human sci-ences have found that scholars' research does not seem to make a useful contribution to the management of turbulence: elegant answers to meaningless questions are preferred over inelegant answers to good questions. As a result, competence in communication has declined to the extent that it has been systematically distorted by languages that are the province of experts only. This excessive provincialization of knowledge and its detach-ment from society, has meant that the human sciences have not served Canadians well.

Fragmentation of knowledge has also been an obstacle to its full utilization (whenever it could be of use) because it has impeded the cross-fertilization of ideas, but also, and more importantly, because it has generated closed systems and closed scientific societies. According to the second law of thermodynamics, all closed systems are subject to increasing entropy.

AT THE ROOTS OF OUR FAILURES

The epistemological and institutional entrapments identi-fied above did not materialize overnight, but neither do they appear to have been crippling the practice of the human sciences consistently. While there may be competing hypotheses to explain the current malaise, it can be argued persuasively that the professionalization of the academy may be an important source of the problem.

A BIT OF HISTORY

Since the Middle Ages intellectuals as human scientists have had an eventful life as a social group. In the 12th century they were vagabonds and social critics, poor urban nomads, like the group called the *goliards*, who represented a sort of urban intelligentsia that had chosen study instead of war while their brothers were away on the Crusades. They were specialist artisans who evolved from the growth of cities. Like other artisans, they sold their products (lessons) to customers (students), which had the immense benefit of making them entirely independent *vis-à-vis* all civil and religious powers, and allowed them to be somewhat critical of institutions (Le Goff 1957).

The intellectual-artisan class was emasculated in 1179 by the First Lateran Council, at which Pope Alexander III decreed that education should be free. The argument was that poor students should receive an education and that education was a religious responsibility. As a result, intellectuals were deprived of their traditional source of income and condemned to obtain their livelihood from the Church. A tradition of critical thinking ended, and intellectuals came to perpetuate and defend dogmas. They became kept persons.

The 13th century was a time of guilds and corporations. We know little about the emergence of the university corporations during this time, but it is clear that, like others, they were based on a certain jurisdictional autonomy, and obtained a monopoly on the granting of diplomas and the *licentia ubique docendi* (licence to teach anywhere). The corporations used papal protection against local religious and civil powers, and thereby lost their independence. Consequently, the universities struggled to maintain their monopoly against intruders such as the mendicant orders, which were closer to the *goliard* tradition and thus more critical. They threatened the universities with their "unfair" competition. While the university corporations gained some distance from local religious and civil powers through strikes, riots and confrontations, and through the protection of, as Jacques Le Goff put it, "the Apostolic See, which favoured them, the better to tame them", the university corporations were also weakened from within by the scholastic method and the spirit that it nurtured, and both of them in turn were plagued by an incapacity to adjust to the needs of the times.

By the end of the Middle Ages university corporations had attached themselves to new sources of wealth, and to lay and religious patrons. Universities became aristocratic, scholasticism decayed, and, as humanists slowly came to displace the scholastic intellectuals, teaching and research were split. The medieval intellectual was an artisan surrounded by students in the midst of the city; the humanist became a solitary person reflecting at his leisure in his quiet residence in the country. This state of affairs lasted until the Renaissance, indeed, some would say, until the Enlightenment, when a new breed of people emerged, satisfied neither with the approved body of knowledge nor with its social context:

> They had to take real political risks which could cost them their freedom or even their lives. They were not professionals ... their intellectual activity was not the primary means of their livelihood; they regarded it not as a profession but as a *vocation* [my emphasis]: they did not consciously try to specialize in narrow fields although (inevitably) by accident or design they learned and wrote about some subjects more than others; they did not distinguish sharply between living and learning (Katouzian 1980: 125).

These men challenged the monopoly on the production of knowledge that traditional universities still claimed, and became themselves the source of the "new science".

Not until the beginning of the 20th century did universities regain the dominant position they had held centuries before. What ensued was predictable: professionalism replaced vocationalism (Katouzian 1980: 132). The modern university, in some respects, is not unlike the medieval institution, with the difference that, instead of dogmas being inflicted on the academy from the outside, they appear to have been created on the inside.

EXCURSUS ON A SOCIOLOGY OF THE ACADEMIC PROFESSION IN THE HUMAN SCIENCES

The historical excursus sketched above is not meant as an aside. It is more in the nature of an exotic parallel, which is of exemplary value for many observers of the present state of research in the human sciences. According to Homa Katouzian (1980), the period since World War II has witnessed an acceleration in the professionalization of the academy, with extraordinary consequences for humanists. He develops his argument in a series of thirteen basic statements, which can be summarized as follows.

The attributes of mature normal science (à la Kuhn) stem from the emergence and growth of professionalization in all scientific and intellectual pursuits. Such professionalization turns the scientist and the scholar into academics (full-time mental workers), and makes it more difficult, if not impossible, to search for knowledge outside universities or similar institutions. A professional academic enters a career in which his/her primary aim is a combination of material advancement and social recognition; "professional" is used in this context in contrast to "vocational":

> [A] typical professional academic is almost a complete layman outside his own discipline and a narrow specialist

within it. The former makes it difficult for him to make a broader intellectual contribution to life in society; the latter reduces his chances of making significant contributions to the advancement of knowledge in his own discipline ... professional academics are members of narrower groups of disciplinarians whose members communicate with one another through their professional journals (Katouzian 1980: 120).

The attitude of the disciplinary profession determines an academic's chances of appointment and promotion, and his/her reputation as an academic: the more integrated the disciplinary profession, the greater the constraints on intellectual activities. The disciplinary profession exercises this constraint through its control over the means of publication and propagation of disciplinary ideas. As a rule, journals are less tolerant of ideas that threaten established views, preferring shorter papers dealing with narrow topics, and academic promotions and reputations are linked to publication in those journals. Therefore, publication for the sake of publication becomes the overriding objective of the professional academic, an imperative that dictates intellectual cautiousness, a high degree of specialization, and brevity for the sake of brevity. The leaders of the academic disciplinary profession constitute Kuhn's "invisible college", an elite that considers only members of itself as peers.

Katouzian concludes (1980: 121–123) that the following pattern develops as a result of the developments listed above: (a) a tendency to concentrate on the solution of "puzzles" instead of attacking substantial problems; (b) a proliferation of printed material that adds comparatively little to knowledge; (c) a research agenda for academic work that is set by fashion, but itself is mainly determined by the whims of the "invisible college"; and (d) the presentation to the unprofessional academic of three principal choices: to give up resistance and join the professionals; to leave the profession altogether; or

to stand by his/her principles, and take the moral and
material consequences. Katouzian concludes that "the
iron rule of a few learned and respectable oligarchs over
the disciplinary profession ... can do nothing but retard
the pace of scientific and intellectual progress."

A little excursion into the world of academe reveals
that this characterization is not entirely unwarranted.
The process of professionalization has changed the
"social organization" of the human sciences, and anyone who has attempted to work outside the prescribed
mainstream has met with the wrath of the disciplinary
community. The power of the academic disciplinary
professions has grown to the point that it is the main
determining force in the allocation of financial support for research by the funding bodies and agencies in
the human sciences. One may also conjecture that this
will continue to be the case for years to come, which
is hardly surprising, since scholastic academics are the
driving force on the panels that define the priorities and
standards of the funding agencies.

The contrast between the public's occasional demands
for reform of the academy and the defensive tactics of
professional academia is telling. The public has communicated its discontent both at the public hearings of different commissions and in other forums. It has implicitly
and explicitly threatened that unless reforms are carried
out it will direct its governments to ration resources
for academic professionals in the human sciences. On
the other hand, professional academics have been slow
to accept that they no longer have a monopoly on the
production of usable knowledge, and they still resist the
pressures of social demands for more effectiveness, more
efficiency and more economy.

Obviously, not all disciplinary professions have equally
succumbed to this process, or been enslaved by it. We
know little about the extent of the damage in different
areas, but that certainly is not a reason to assume that
it is not there.

GUILDS, GOVERNMENT
AND THE MIND

If one accepts the argument developed in the previous section, based on the work of Le Goff (1957) and Katouzian (1980), one is in a better position to understand both the difficulties of traditional universities and the challenges currently facing the human sciences in modern universities. The great danger faced by traditional universities was that scholastic intellectuals became an intellectual technocracy. This development explains why many great thinkers were not keen to join universities: Galileo, Locke, Rousseau, Voltaire, Faraday, John Stuart Mill, Marx and Darwin were not academics. The same danger has been present since the beginning of the 20th century, when universities "regained their former functions as dominant if not exclusive institutions for the advancement of (modern) learning". However, this danger has been felt more acutely since World War II with the rise of the intellectual technocracy (Katouzian 1980: 126–127).

Modern guilds are no less rigid or effective regulatory instruments than traditional ones were. It is therefore unlikely that the rigidities will be removed by sermons, sporadic dissent or moral suasion. Academic professions are hard-core guilds and have triggered the loss of origin noted above. Katouzian (1980) suggests that only a combination of public consciousness and the growing proximity of the abyss may provoke needed change.

There is some public consciousness of the growing irrelevance of much academic work in traditional human sciences departments in universities, but there is certainly no sense that the abyss is near in academic circles themselves. Government agencies and commissions have drawn attention to the problem in a general way and they may even have identified different root causes, but a major impediment stands in the way of governments taking action to ensure that research in the human sciences attends to the necessary agenda. This impediment is the strongly held presumption that governments have no business in affairs of the mind. Governments, it is assumed, may and should provide generous unconditional financial support for academic research, but that is all. Consequently, the only agent that might be able to end this crisis of legitimacy in the human sciences appears to be disqualified from becoming involved.

Joseph Tussman (1977: 19) has presented a very persuasive argument in support of the "necessity and legitimacy of governmental action in the various provinces of the domain of the mind". He argues that such action is a duty akin to the duty of the state to create and sustain a monetary system or a political order:

> [A]wareness is crucial to the way we conduct our lives and it is important to realize that flawed awareness may betray us ... Consciousness, individual or social, is not, simply by virtue of what it is, always what is should be. It may be inadequate to our needs. It may even be diseased.

The question is whether government has a legitimate role to play in shaping and protecting awareness. My own view is that the state must ensure that research in the human sciences addresses the most important issues. Tussman argues against manipulation, but favours "leadership that enlightens, teaches, and forces us to attend to the necessary agenda" (1977: 19).

When faced with a domain balkanized by regulators of knowledge, one may argue that the *prima facie* case for leadership that would force us to attend to the necessary agenda is yet stronger; for, as shown above, the likelihood of research adhering to such an agenda naturally, as it were, is further reduced. The growing dissatisfaction of governments with research in the human sciences may be measured by the efforts they have made to ensure closer control of funding bodies. There may be some concern that covert action by government may corrupt the forum, manipulate public awareness and manage research. This is a legitimate concern. Such subversion must be avoided. In order to do so, governments should define a strategy of culture elaborated through continuing national debate, a strategy that can then be used to guide government interventions in domains of the mind.

As for the methods that governments might use to deregulate the academic professions, the only one with a proven record is competition. Much of what has been instituted, and to which one might object, is due to lack of competition. While the general directions for action should be judged by their contribution to the accomplishment of the prevailing strategy of culture, the different instruments used should be judged by reference to their contribution to workable competition in the production of new knowledge in the human sciences.

A STRATEGY OF CULTURE

Given the diagnosis presented above, one is led to reflect on the basic principles necessary both to underpin and to constrain the state in its efforts to redirect the human sciences toward the original questions, while not violating the basic tenets of a liberal society. Such principles must be deeply rooted in the liberal social contract and in the reality of Canadian culture.

To avoid the many pitfalls threatening any effort to define culture in Canada, one might start with the bland working definition of culture proposed by the Canadian Commission for UNESCO (1977: 6): "a dynamic value system of learned elements, with assumptions, conventions, beliefs and rules permitting members of a group to relate to each other and to the world, to communicate and to develop their creative potential." A human sciences policy must be seen as an integral part of a cultural strategy for Canada, as a set of interventions designed to more effectively tackle the fundamental questions facing Canadians. Too often, cultural strategies are perceived as

cultural regulations, and condemned as such in the name
of the norms of the liberal social contract. Cultural regulations are seen as violations of fundamental individual
liberties. This is a fundamental misunderstanding of the
liberal social contract. S. C. Kolm (1985) has shown that
liberalism is more than individualism: it is also the basis
for infra- and supra-individual rights.

Some cultural strategies have been propounded in
Canada. An interesting one that has had considerable impact on Canadian thinking was put forward by
Harold Innis. He developed it more than fifty years ago
and called it a survival strategy that would emphasize
"persistent action at strategic points against American
imperialism in all its attractive disguises ... by attempting constructive efforts to explore the cultural possibilities of various media of communication and to develop
them along lines free from commercialism" (1952: 20).
Innis was concerned about technology and the American
presence as the basic challenges facing Canadian society,
and suggested some elements of a strategy as a footnote
to the Massey Report. One can see in the fine analysis
of Arthur Kroker (1984: 109–124) the full implications
of this strategy.

Another strategy of culture that has received attention
more recently is the one proposed in the Symons Report
of 1975. It suggested that at the core of government policies in the affairs of the mind, the notion of Canadian
identity and the centrality of self-knowledge were paramount. The report referred to the universities as "one of
the country's greatest national assets" and suggested, in
line with an argument propounded by Principal Corry
of Queen's University, that:

> ... universities everywhere have been at their vital best when
> they were interpreting the felt needs of society in a discern-
> ing way ... they have been at their worst and their most
> sterile when they have neglected their trust and lost touch
> with the urgencies of their society (Symons 1975: 15–16).

It would be unwise, however, to be swayed even by the great Harold Innis (1952) or the Symons Report (1975) on a matter as important as a strategy of culture. Innis or Symons may have diagnosed some key problems, but not necessarily all of them. Their strategies may have inspired many, but they are not necessarily ones that would satisfy Canadians in the early 21st century.

What is needed is a permanent forum to discuss the nature of the goals and objectives to be pursued, and the strategy to be designed to reach them, in light of what are regarded as the main threats and challenges facing Canadian society today. What we need is a Council of Social Values in Canada (Paquet 1968). Such a permanent forum would replace those episodic occasions given to Canadians to reflect on what should be the basic principles to guide the state, especially concerning affairs of the mind. This council would provide legitimacy for an overt strategy of culture, but also place significant limits on the manoeuvrability of the state in effecting it. Such a forum, or any surrogate institution, would echo firmly the concerns articulated above. It would also lead governments to intervene in the human sciences to end the monopoly on knowledge created by the professional academic disciplines, and to redirect the attention of human scientists to society today.

I have already provided a blueprint for action for the social sciences elsewhere (Paquet 1985). In any case, the guiding principles of social architecture in a liberal society are well-known: variety, competition, progressiveness. The social architecture of institutions likely to reflect these principles best is bound to evolve through time in response to changes in external or internal threats, but, once established, it is also likely to evolve without continuing government interference. The commitment of governments to intervene when necessary would also make it more unlikely that research in the human sciences would again stray far from its real responsibilities.

CONCLUSION

In this chapter I have suggested that there is a crisis of both confidence and legitimacy in the human sciences, which can be ascribed to a loss of origin. This loss of origin has been revealed in the growth of scholasticism, the development of a Babel of languages and the manufacture of unhelpful maps. The root cause of this drift away from the original questions has been the professionalization of the human sciences. To correct the problem, the human sciences have to be redirected toward the original questions through subtle nudges by the state. To guide and constrain the state in this task, we need to create a forum to develop a strategy of culture, and to create research institutions likely to generate, through competition, the requisite variety of new knowledge and a better capacity to attend to the problems faced by society.

Our situation is not new. Richard Nathan (1985) reminds us of a passage in *Gulliver's Travels* where Jonathan Swift describes a voyage to the kingdom of Laputa, which is in a state of disrepair and decay. During his sojourn in the capital city, Lagado, Gulliver finds that, although the kingdom is in crisis, the experts at its Grand Academy have been working for years on problems such as extracting sunbeams from cucumbers. In modern universities the fixation on narrow puzzles has taken forms different from those observed at the Grand Academy of Lagado, but in both cases the central issue is the loss of the sense of the original questions.

Some factors that have led to this state of affairs have been identified in this chapter and plausible solutions have been hinted at. It has been argued that before the human sciences can legitimately demand more resources from society, they may have to redirect their attention to what society considers its main concerns.

Can the academy reflect critically on its practice and initiate such reforms? Many clearly have said no to that question, which is why governments, as representatives of the public, have been asked to take action. One can hardly expect unanimous support from the human sciences community for the diagnosis, and most certainly not for the cure. It may even be that specialized academic pressure groups will prevent governments from taking vigorous action any time soon. But that can only be a temporary respite. Meanwhile, impatient human scientists of good will who do not share the view that the Grand Academy of Lagado should be held up as a model should not despair. One need not be hopeful, but one may have hope. As Harold Innis wrote in a pessimistic moment (as quoted by Neill 1972: 96), "a social scientist in Canada [and I think he would readily have included all human scientists] can only survive by virtue of a sense of humour."

CHAPTER 2

Professional "wrighting and wroughting"

> *To prescribe methods automatically*
> *blocks the development of better methods.*
> — JANE JACOBS

Education (*stricto sensu*), training and personal development are capital goods whose "just price" is difficult to gauge at the time of buying. The just price worth paying is the discounted value of the streams of benefits of all sorts that can be derived over one's lifetime from buying or acquiring such capital goods. Since one never knows for sure what one will be confronted with in life, it is difficult to know in advance what one should invest in: skills? basic knowledge? character-building? a mix of them? Should one learn how to speak another language or how to swim, or take another few courses in physics?

Given this framing of the question, the argument has often been made that education, training and personal development should be as general as possible, so as to be of use in the widest possible range of circumstances. On this basis, literacy and numeracy are often presented as fundamental necessities in primary and secondary schools.

On the other hand, since specialized and therefore specific knowledge is greatly valued, because it is purported to yield extremely high benefits if one invests in the right specialized knowledge base, there has been an equally strong tendency to develop a very narrowly focused, in-depth pursuit of certain disciplines, skills or traits. This specialization has begun to erode the secondary school's "liberal education" curriculum, but it has mostly challenged the post-secondary education system (PSES), where choices become agonistic.

This dilemma is made all the more acute by the fact that the right mix of education (*stricto sensu*), training and personal development that goes into the production of successful human development is somewhat ill-defined. In most professions the three components are extremely important: a surgeon, an architect, an orchestra leader, a mechanic, an engineer, a designer, a lawyer or a social worker must draw heavily from all these sources to be successful.

It has been argued that in many other areas the full complement of these components is not essential. This is a view that, personally, I have some difficulty with. It is difficult not to find a confluence of knowledge, skills and character in most successful activities, even though many observers are prone to occlude the importance of diagnostic skills in the work of a good mechanic, manual dexterity in the work of a surgeon, perceptive skills in the work of an internist or empathy in the activity of a social worker.

The PSES has a variety of functions in society: to produce ever more literate and numerate, active and responsible citizens; to develop the human capital necessary for the maintenance and enhancement of a country's competitiveness and living standards; to develop perception, mind and ability, in order to facilitate entry into the labour market; to supply an adequate mix of knowledge, skills and personal development to students; and so on. Educators, trainers and developers, as crucial producers within the PSES, have suggested different strategies and emphasized different approaches to this multiplex task. Educators have traditionally focused on general principles as means of teaching students how to think critically. Trainers have focused on imparting skills and abilities that cannot be transmitted without focusing on schemata that are highly specific to the task at hand. Personal developers have taken the view that knowledge and skills can be developed only on the basis of a capacity to grow as a human being within the community to which one is acculturated.

Few institutions have chosen to focus exclusively on one approach over the others. Most have elected different mixes of activities, while emphasizing one dimension or another. But most have *not* developed as rich a meshing of that one dimension with the other approaches as they should have, nor have they drawn as much from expertise in the external environment as they should have. Even institutions that have privileged co-operative education have often managed the internal–external interfaces rather shabbily. They have not ensured, for example, that what should be acquired through work experience actually is acquired.

To map the PSES one might imagine a triangle with each of these views at one of the apexes, and most PSES

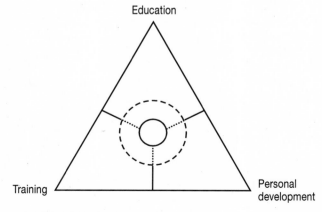

FIGURE 2.1 The PSES triangle

institutions and practices located within this triangle according to the relative importance they give to each of these three pillars (see Figure 2.1).

An inquiry into the future of the PSES is a golden opportunity to get an appreciation of the current state of affairs, to question the assumptions on which the present system is built, to speculate on a desirable degree of mixing for the PSES, and to explore ways of mobilizing all those external and internal partners who have portions of information, resources and power (in the private, public and social sectors), and of coordinating their efforts to make the PSES more efficient and more effective. Good governance is based on effective coordination when power, resources and information are widely distributed, and that is also the case for the PSES.

KNOWLEDGE GAPS, APARTHEIDS AND GOVERNANCE FAILURES

Despite important disagreements about what the best PSES might entail, a fairly standardized version of the system has emerged throughout Canada. Although there may be doubts about the system's effectiveness (doing the right thing) and its efficiency (doing it right), a bizarre quasi-unanimity and uniformity has emerged across the country.

A rationale for not raising too many questions about the optimality of the PSES has evolved through the mutual accolades required by the process of accreditation for new institutions and programmes. The application of this process has ensured some convergence toward a single set of standards and provided some assurance that the PSES would be properly policed. This forced convergence becomes particularly evident when universities seek permission to grant graduate degrees and must, in the process, satisfy the standards and norms imposed by older and more established institutions.

A few professional schools have strived to maintain a curriculum balanced among the three components, but the link to skills and personal development in universities has become more and more tenuous. This tendency has not only unduly sanitized the academic stream of much valuable content, but it has often also disconnected students from other sorts of knowledge, and thereby constrained learning considerably. In community colleges and technical schools the narrow emphasis on technology *per se* has greatly weakened the broader ambitions of technical skills and trades training, and students often graduate without all the knowledge, skills and personal assets that would provide them with an ability to successfully pursue their chosen careers.

More generally, the tight compartmentalization among the different sets of institutions in Canada has prevented the emergence of appropriate mixes of these complementary knowledge bases, even when it has become clear that such mixes are desirable in many issue domains. Thus many students in search of a suitable mix, having completed a degree or diploma at one type of institution, are forced to waste valuable time acquiring another degree or diploma from a different type of institution, when a mixed programme would have been ideally suited for them.

The above diagnosis must be significantly modified when one deals with the PSES in British Columbia. This is the one jurisdiction in Canada where the above indictment applies least. In British Columbia the bifurcation between universities and colleges is certainly significant at the governance and structural levels. Universities and colleges are governed by separate acts of the provincial legislature, and there are no structures that bring the governance bodies or institutional administrators and leaders together. There is also a third sector, the university colleges. Each of these groups — universities, colleges, and university colleges — fund and maintain separate provincial secretariats for the purpose of political advocacy and relations with government.

Notwithstanding the above, there is probably much more integration of courses and programmes in British

Columbia than elsewhere in Canada. All community colleges in British Columbia offer the first two years of university programmes and these first two years are fully transferable to all universities in the province. The universities in turn offer a wide variety of degrees in the third and fourth year, and since 1995 they have each had independent degree-granting authority. In that sense opportunities for learning skills but also for some mixing exist at all universities and community colleges in the province, given that many offer not only technical and trades training, but also substantial academic programming in an integrated and articulated fashion.

Moreover, the British Columbia Council on Admissions and Transfers is a world model in establishing course transfer agreements between institutions. All the public-sector institutions in British Columbia's PSES, as well as a number in the private sector, are included in the *Transfer Guide*, which lists thousands of courses and defines the degree of transferability in specific course numbers among all the institutions in the province. Transferability is brought about and maintained through annual, discipline-by-discipline articulation meetings that bring together representatives from all institutions.

Finally, there is strong government support for private-sector providers within British Columbia's PSES. The provincial government led by Gordon Campbell since 2001 has done a great deal to facilitate the development of these providers through flexible legislation and the appointment of a senior bureaucrat within the Ministry of Advanced Education with this portfolio.

Consequently, while the general points made in the next section of this chapter are still valid, and much more can be done to provide an optimal degree of integration, more progress may have been made in British Columbia than elsewhere in Canada, and the argument in the case of this one province is more about improving a situation that many regard as good than trying to break down barriers among watertight compartments. Still, much remains to be done in a world where some sense of apartheid still prevails in the minds of citizens.

BALKANIZATION

In general, one of the basic assumptions on which the present PSES in Canada is built is the reasonableness of partitioning the system into strands of programmes and institutions purported to cater to entirely different categories of students, and geared to different "types" of intellectual accomplishments, most notably by way of academic and training streams, and secular and religious institutions.

As we mentioned above, this may be much less the case in British Columbia than in the rest of Canada. What British Columbia has accomplished is a significant loosening of the apartheid on the supply side, as the necessary conditions for significant mobility and flexibility have been put in place. But it is not sufficient to ensure full use of these possibilities, the optimal mix of *savoirs*, *savoir-faire* and *savoir-être* in the programmes, and the highest and best use of the extramural knowledge base.

Another assumption is the conviction, underpinning the intelligentsia's celebration of the secular academic stream, that this is the royal road to a superior education, while other colleges are purported to provide inferior if not inconsequential intellectual endeavours, whatever the outcomes might be. Again, while this perception may have been attenuated by some degree of potential mixing in British Columbia, the "university" brand still remains quite important there. I have heard it said by members of the "university elite" that, for example, Thompson Rivers University (TRU) is not a "real" university because it trains mechanics. This is not only a measure of the "snob effect" that still prevails, but also of the lack of curiosity about, and poor appreciation of, types of knowledge other than those privileged by the inner sanctum.

According to the assumptions of the conventional wisdom, there is something fundamentally different about these streams: their educational purposes, the nature of the learning processes, the clienteles for which the programmes are designed, and the basic intellectual abilities of these clienteles. This has led to a quasi-apartheid regime that has kept these sub-systems more or less effectively disconnected from one another, and has produced a fractured and dysfunctional PSES.

This broad consensus stands in contrast to an alternative approach that would aim at creating more mixed institutions, located at the inner core of the PSES triangle, and better connecting with the world or with professionals outside the PSES. As for the disconnect between the world of the PSES and the real world of practising professionals and the rich world of work, it has been bridged in part by co-operative education; however, this provides limited exposure for a minority of students, when it should be an integral part of most students' experience.

Over the last while there has been a higher degree of specialization in the institutions of the PSES — traditional secular universities, religious colleges, community colleges, training schools — and a drift of different institutions toward emphasizing one or the other of these priority approaches. This has not only meant a certain division of labour among institutions (private, public and social), but it has also often meant an impoverishment of the education/training/personal development mix, whatever the quality of the segment any one institution has chosen to emphasize. The result has been some erosion in the capacity of the PSES to produce well-rounded "reflective practitioners" (see Schön 1983).

The professionalization and the unionization of the PSES have somewhat hardened the barriers to cross-fertilization among the different types of institutions, and between "insiders" and "outsiders," across much of Canada. Various actors have either been excluded from the process of production in the PSES, or have excluded themselves as a result of these barriers.

The growing celebration of credentials, the monopoly on the granting of degrees, which is a privilege bestowed by the provincial governments, and the extraordinarily defensive stance of provincial governments in allowing few or no private institutions to enjoy this privilege, have also had a Malthusian effect on the system. While British Columbia stands as immensely less Malthusian than the rest of the country, and Quest University has made the point that one can break into even the inner sanctum, this is clearly the exception rather than the rule. One can only imagine what the Canadian PSES might look like if such barriers to entry did not exist.

Moreover, there has been an ever greater exclusion of practitioners from the teaching function at universities — much less, fortunately, at the community college level, but it is bound to grow with creeping credentialism. This makes it more difficult to provide the right mix. Again, while this is less true in some professional schools, and for British Columbia as a province (at least in principle), it has tilted the PSES toward the pure education apex, and has eliminated from programmes much that could have been provided only by practitioners.

Consequently, there has been a growing chasm between what is happening in schools and what is happening in workplaces. This has had a dual effect: firms themselves have had to do some of the training needed for their employees to be operative, but the employers have also developed a growing lack of interest in truly co-operating with educational institutions, except in crassly self-serving ways. When firms run into serious manpower shortages in certain skill categories, they often realize that the sort of training available in the PSES is so inadequate that they need to get into the training business themselves.

In Canada the contribution of the private sector to the PSES remains a fraction of what it is in the United States and many countries in Europe, but it is to be expected that the inadequacy of the existing PSES is bound to generate much greater interest from that source in the future. This chasm has been identified and taken advantage of by a growing variety of private and civic institutions that have attempted to fill specific gaps in the PSES, such as in languages and informatics. The growth of this parallel PSES has been somewhat chaotic and its unregulated nature has led to many scams, but the demand for a product different from what the official system offers is so great that citizens are willing to take their chances. While these parallel institutions have tended to specialize in very narrow technical training, there are reasons to believe that they will soon become more ambitious. Again, British Columbia stands out as having taken a more liberal approach than most other provinces, and as having done a great deal to facilitate the development of these providers.

There have been some creative and successful efforts to somewhat integrate the academic and trades/technical streams in British Columbia. At the very least, one might say that, structurally, much has been done in British Columbia to facilitate such integration. But how much is effectively being done to overcome the high degree of imperviousness that tends to develop among streams and programmes must be evaluated.

An illustration of the backwardness of current "practices" might be a recent case in Ottawa. The same course, using the same textbook, was given both at a university and at a community college by a university professor who was moonlighting at the community college. Yet a student trying to transfer from the community college to the university could not obtain credit in the university programme for the course taken at the community college.

The multiplicity of blockages among institutions, and between the institutions and professional practitioners, has balkanized the PSES in Canada, and prevented the development of truly integrated programmes, except, again, in certain professional schools, and most certainly at the structural level in British Columbia. This has contributed significantly to the perpetuation of the view that the PSES embodies an either/or option, not a more-or-less choice, and to the persistence of the cultural devaluation of non-academic education.

Much of this cultural devaluation is based on a flawed notion of knowledge acquisition and learning, but it has been exploited by governments to rationalize funding community and technical colleges at a much lower level than universities. This in turn has generated hiring practices at the community and technical colleges that have been stigmatized as "inferior" by the dominant credentialism. It has become a self-fulfilling prophecy that the non-academic stream could indeed be regarded as inferior. Unless one revisits the basics of knowledge acquisition and learning, it may be difficult to challenge these assumptions.

PERCEPTS AND CONCEPTS

The evolution of the PSES appears, then, to have been derailed by some flawed assumptions about knowledge acquisition. Among these are the beliefs that (1) superior intellectual achievement is built on content-free principles and methodologies — what I have called "methodism" — acquired through the ladder of abstraction, and that (2) knowledge flows only one way, from underlying disciplines, to applied science, to actual performance.

Both these propositions are false. Knowledge acquisition and learning do not move solely by climbing the ladder of abstraction, but also emerge from a two-way approach emphasizing knowing in action and reflection in action, where knowledge emerges from groping with situations, and from surprises leading to on-the-spot experiments and knowledge creation.

From this flawed view has emerged, as a corollary, a systematic social devaluation of other forms of knowledge acquired through experience, learning by doing, and the like, and the sense that such "knowledge" could not be as sophisticated as what comes through the ladder of abstraction. From this has arisen a natural repugnance against having a bright child follow that route. Even if these assumptions are ill-founded, they constitute deep-rooted beliefs. They must be effectively attacked and undermined, because otherwise it will be impossible to effect a social revaluation of these other types of knowledge.

Cognitive science has already begun this debunking work. It casts doubt on the idea that there are any general or transferable cognitive skills. It has shown that critical thinking does not evolve from content-free principles and methodologies, but from procedural and substantive schemata that are highly specific to the task at hand. Developing a human being means ensuring that he or she acquires a fair number of these schemata (Hirsch 1987).

The development of this basic currency, which may be capacious and vague, but is fundamental to communicative competence, cannot be ensured by disembodied principles in the manner of the traditional curriculum, or through skill-building in the manner one uses to coach an athlete to success. Facts and skills are inseparable, and background knowledge is of great import in the development of critical reason.

Therefore, it is not enough to see to the accumulation of proven knowledge by memorization of established associations, rules of classification and logical inference, or to teach students to distrust their personal experience as a guide to knowledge. An effective educational system depends on the perception and experience of the individual, and on the training of attention, and higher studies are meant to provide aided modes of apprehension or extraction of information by means of instruments of knowledge, language to make knowing explicit instead of tacit, and pictures to extend perceiving and consolidate the gains of perceiving.

In this Heider/Gibson/Emery "ecological view" of cognition, knowledge is restricted only by our habits of perception, and one may and must educate the student's perceptual systems. This entails recentring education on the process of searching, on learning to explore, because the weight of evidence is that even literate adults find it difficult to use their own perceptions (Gibson 1979; Paquet 1989b).

This approach may be summarized as follows:

- picking up information is a ceaseless activity;
- what are perceived are places, objects, substances, together with events, which are modifications of these things;
- information is the specification of the observers' environment;
- the perceptual system is a mode of overt attention: it can explore, investigate, adjust, optimize, extract;
- the perceptual system registers persistence and change;
- information pick-up can be developed and learned: better extracting, exploring, and so on.

This new theory of active perception has educational implications:

- access to information is limited only by habits of perception;
- perceptual systems can be improved: this is "an education in searching with your own perceptual systems, not an education in how to research in the cumulated pile of so-called social knowledge" (Emery 1981: 29);
- education is "learning to learn" from our own perceptions.

While the usual PSES insists that it must produce "disciplined intelligence ... that is trained in logic and logical analysis", a much broader approach is suggested by a Heider/Gibson/Emery view that covers a variety of types of "thinking": logical, practical, lateral, including "thinking with one's hands" (de Rougemont 1936). This latter view of knowledge acquisition and learning has an immense importance for the question at hand. It underpins a new educational paradigm emphasizing the import of the training/personal development dimensions, both as complementary elements in the education process and as sound bases for an alternative learning experience. Table 2.1. summarizes this new paradigm and compares it to the old one it is replacing.

TABLE 2.1 Two educational paradigms

The Practice	Traditional paradigm	Ecological paradigm
Object of learning	Transmission of existing knowledge; abstraction	Perceptions of invariants; discovery of serial concepts
Control of learning	Asymmetrical Dependence: teacher–students, competition of learners	Symmetrical dependence of co-learners, co-operation of learners
Coordination of learning	School/classroom calendar, class timetable	Community settings synchronized to, and negotiated with, community
Learning materials	Textbooks; standardized lab experiments	Reality-centred projects
Learning activity	Paying attention; memorizing	Discriminate; differentiate; searching; creating
Teaching activity	Lecturing; demonstrating	Creating and re-creating learning settings
System principle (Abrams 1953)	Pedagogy: "the mirror"	Discovery: "the lamp"
Personal development	Conformity; divorce of means and ends	Tolerance of individuality; learning as living

Source: adapted from F.E. Emery (1981: 45)

The motto of Caleb Gattegno used to be that "teaching should be subordinated to learning" (Gattengo 1972). If learning is presumed to be dependent on the ladder of abstraction, and the senses are regarded simply as a medium through which inputs have to be transformed into mental concepts in order to become sources of learning, it is easy to see how much teaching is going to be perverted toward the sort of activities favoured by the traditional paradigm.

It is only when one accepts that percepts are the direct way in which one extracts information from the environment, and learns that the focus will shift to developing the mechanisms of perception and to nurturing the direct processes through which one learns. All the senses then are means of perception that may be mobilized, both in the education of the reflective practitioner and in the world of apprenticeship and practical knowledge.

The difficulty with the rehabilitation of practical knowledge and knowledge based on something other than the ladder of abstraction, is that it goes against the grain of what has been the conventional wisdom ever since the days of John Locke. The emphasis on percepts, and not just concepts, is based on a growing recognition that the perceptual systems have survival value, and that there is no need to force all our knowledge into a mentalistic framework (Noë 2006).

Young children learn how to speak a language through extraction of information from the environment, without any use of the ladder of abstraction. They perceive invariant relations and distinctive features. Gattegno has developed a method of language teaching going back to these principles. What we find in both training and personal development is a much greater emphasis on percepts than on concepts. In that sense, use of IQ as a gauge of intelligence is rather awkward, for it measures, not intelligence, but a capacity to deal with abstract similarities. A high IQ does not indicate an ability to behave intelligently outside the narrow world of academic scholarship.

Percepts are tools of exploration. They are the instruments through which serial-genetic concepts (concepts developed through the serial order generated in nested spatio-temporal events) emerge through becoming aware of invariants. Such learning is central to training and the development of *savoir-faire*. The perceptual system is capable of acquiring a greater capacity to extract information. This is a skill. Percepts are fundamental in developing a different kind of knowledge, which we shall later call "delta knowledge," and such knowledge is central to the dispatch of complex tasks that cannot be easily reduced to routines.

There is no reason to believe that the knowledge acquired via the traditional paradigm is superior to what is made available via the ecological paradigm. Consequently, there is no reason to dismiss the non-academic stream as inferior. On the other hand, this alternative way of learning is not necessarily well-managed or well-governed at present. Indeed, when the technical skills and trades training institutions attempt to emulate academic education, and to get students to master unnatural tasks of abstracting and inferring with symbol systems, rather than making direct use of percepts, the result is often dismal. It would produce a very poor professional.

A reasonable expectation would be that technical skills and trades training should be done in a manner that draws considerably on the new ecological paradigm, but often the Lockean perspective is so deeply ingrained in the norms of the educational establishment that anyone trying to impose these methods based on percepts onto a world permeated by the traditional paradigm risks being ostracized. This is all the more difficult in a conventional academic environment where "experiential" approaches are regarded as primitive and anti-intellectual.

AN ALTERNATIVE PERSPECTIVE: COVERING ALL THE ANGLES

The production of "reflective practitioners" would entail ensuring a more balanced mix of *savoirs*, *savoir-faire* and *savoir-être* in most institutions in the PSES. This might mean (in an ideal-typical way) a programme allowing students to develop their perception systems in a variety of ways, drawing as much on the development of perception skills and on contextual experience as on stylized "re-searching" of stock knowledge.

It is our view that most problems emerge from the fact that there is a fundamental misunderstanding about the essence of post-secondary education. It must be understood that it is a process that calls for a recognition of (1) development of habits of perception as an effective way to approach complexity; (2) the capacity to diagnose what works and what does not work; and (3) the ability to design interventions likely to succeed. These three operations are analogous in all streams, and require the acquisition of a variety of types of knowledge and skills, and this applies equally well in education, training and personal development. It then becomes clear that the present structures and practices in much of the PSES as it stands are less than ideal.

For the time being too much emphasis is being put on the academic stream in general and, within it, often to the exclusion of diagnosis, and almost always to the exclusion of design. Meanwhile, too much emphasis is being put on the design of interventions in the trade stream, often to the exclusion of the requisite work on perceptions and diagnosis. A better appreciation of the range of types of knowledge necessary to perform these different tasks would lead one to the suggestion of a number of fundamental transformations: (1) a decompartmentalization of the system's different streams; (2) a rebalancing of the types of knowledge in all streams to allow a variety of mixes of these three sets of intellectual tools to coalesce in different programmes of research and study; and (3) a restructuring of the PSES into sets of institutions capable of partnering more effectively with different groups of stakeholders.

This will require nothing less than a revolution in the minds of the PSES establishment, as well as in the minds of the citizenry. For generations they have been encapsulated in a world that has valued "disciplined intelligence", and have ignored the contribution of training and personal development to the mental toolbox of the individual. As a result, arts and music education has been devalued, together with "shop", "gym", work experience and the like, as peripheral and therefore non-essential to the main learning programmes, when in fact they were essential.

This quickly led to those students who chose these avenues being regarded as intellectually inferior or socially marginal, and therefore to be seen as either unable or unwilling to tackle the challenges of truly "higher" education. It is only in the recent past, with the explosion of the trades in informatics, computer graphics and the like, that the aura of such trades training has begun to regain some lustre.

Sociologically, this has led over time to a variety of pathological phenomena: (1) a higher high-school drop-out rate, as "academic" subjects came to dominate the curriculum, determining that only certain intellectual capabilities were recognized as valuable; (2) a deterioration of specialized skill and trades education, as it lost much of its social lustre, a consequent decline in the relevance and quality of these skills, as little public investment was made in them, and a greater reliance on "learning by doing on the spot" in the work milieu (outside the PSES), as a result of the unsatisfactory performance of trades schools; and (3) a shortage of skilled personnel.

When, in the recent past, such technical skills and trades training has acquired some notoriety there has been the danger of these institutions being tempted by higher funding and higher prestige to allow their programmes to drift toward a greater "academic" focus, in order to acquire more financial and social gratifications.

Indeed, it has not gone unnoticed that a certain number of community colleges doing extraordinarily valuable work have worked hard at acquiring university status.

This would not be worth noting were it not that in order to obtain such status many (not all) have had to lose their "soul", abandoning their philosophy of education to adopt or mimic that of more narrowly academic institutions. In the best of cases (and again British Columbia has been particularly insightful), this has not been the case, and they have become a sort of laboratory where a new mix of education, skills and personal development has been experimented with.

As for the institutions that have traditionally focused on training and personal development, and have organically adopted the ecological paradigm, the dominant academicism has sometimes perverted their curriculum and programmes. They have not dared to extend their experiential approaches to standard domains of studies in academic institutions. As a result, when it comes to extending training programmes to provide students with a complement of subjects likely to enable graduates to be fully effective in their work environment, and to be able to take on much broader responsibilities as they gain experience, courses grafted onto the basic training programmes are frequently delivered in such an extraordinarily artificial way that the graft does not take, and never becomes an integral part of the intellectual baggage of the reflective practitioner.

Economics and accounting may not be as effectively imparted to persons whose "education" has been acquired in the ecological paradigm as they would be in an academic milieu. My own experience with the teaching of economics to business students has revealed that if the learning methods are not modified, the teaching will be like water off a duck's back.

One may draw a few lessons from these reflections. In the first place, the PSES in general has been unduly reductive in giving access to varieties of knowledge. In the academic stream this has meant a truncation of the educa-tion process that has often left graduates ill-prepared to operate effectively, except in a narrow field. In technical skills and trades training this has frequently meant an unfortunate grafting of artificial branches onto experi-ential programmes to give them academic legitimacy. In the process the hegemony of the traditional paradigm has not been challenged much and the ecological paradigm has had only a partial impact. A mix of learning through both approaches would provide an improved PSES.

However, it is unlikely to emerge organically unless a variety of prerequisites are put in place. It is to be noted once again that British Columbia has been particularly helpful in promoting such mixing. A critical review of the PSES should provide an opportunity to re-examine the balance of the system, and to ensure that the whole range of types of knowledge and modes of acquisition of knowledge is fully exploited. The existing distortions can be ascribed to many causes, including public perceptions, interest groups in place and poor understanding of the knowledge acquisition process. A strategy to refurbish the PSES, and to re-establish a full role for technical skills and trades training in all its former lustre, will require interventions at many levels. There will be great resistance both inside and outside the technical skills and trades training system.

Much learning can be derived from the evolution of professional education. A study of professional educa-tion's successes and failures in both the "nobler" and the less recognized professions in the United States and elsewhere may be quite enlightening. There will be a need for a new vocabulary to deal with these issues.

Since we do not know how to plan such a change, self-organization and effective experimental learning may be the only way to proceed, and permission to do so must be readily granted. A general debate about learning and the different types of knowledge that have survival value will also be necessary.

Given the crucial importance of "learning to learn" in a knowledge-based economy, and the dysfunctions of the PSES, this opportunity to refurbish it is crucial. There is an immense degree of cognitive dissonance and dynamic conservatism in the system. Both the sacred tenet of academic freedom and the credo that putting more money into the PSES is the magic cure will make any quick transformation unlikely. There is a great need for a deeper exploration of the extent to which the PSES is unequally flawed in the different segments of the enterprise. Some additional or refurbished external institutions may be necessary for the improvement of the PSES. One must be willing to explore the fringe of this domain of study, as, for instance, with the contributions of some who are regarded as mavericks when it comes to thinking (de Bono 1979).

Much of this discussion is not without some import for the secondary and primary school systems as well. Reframing will require a massive communication strategy. Restructuring must be done with co-operation at the local level. Retooling must be subtle, because there is still a prevalent view that government has no business in the affairs of the mind, and there is no appreciation of the existing system's main flaw: the fact that it is nothing but an aggregation of private interests.

WINNING CONDITIONS FOR A RENAISSANCE

It would be dishonest not to celebrate the signs, appearing largely in the past thirty years or so, of a renaissance in some sub-segments of the "technical skills and trades training" sub-system, as a result of the information revolution. Indeed, university graduates have recently been observed taking second degrees at community colleges or taking on studies at private institutions to develop their skills in computer graphics and the like, after their university degrees have left them somewhat unemployable. It would also be unfair not to emphasize that British Columbia has been particularly liberal in developing a PSES that has provided a most extensive process of course transfers and transfers of credit among its different families of institutions (colleges, university colleges and universities).

While in British Columbia a silo system remains as far as the governance structure is concerned, from the point of view of the users there is much more integration than elsewhere in Canada. In fact, some colleges and university colleges have become leaders in their trades, and have acquired both pride and recognition. Moreover, there has been an extraordinary burgeoning of private-sector entities that have developed programmes to fill the gaps left by public-sector institutions.

In any case, the information revolution has opened the door to a new appreciation of the most valuable intellectual capabilities being developed in alternative institutions. But it will be a long road to getting this stream fully recognized, funded and nested within the PSES. Three major conditions are necessary for this revolution to occur.

The first is at the epistemological level. It will be necessary to succeed in generating the explicit recognition that all the institutions in the PSES triangle share the same challenges: (1) habits of perception as an effective way to approach complexity; (2) the capacity to diagnose what works and does not work; and (3) the ability to design interventions likely to succeed. This will require nothing less than conveying a new educational paradigm to the population, and nothing less than a new vocabulary that will explain the alternative types of knowledge acquisition. As indicated above, notions of learning and of the ways in which knowledge is acquired will have to be redefined, not only in scholarly circles, but for the general public, if there is to be a challenge to the notion that learning means re-searching the pile of accredited knowledge.

The second is at the structural level: a decompartmentalization of the system's different streams, and a rebalancing of types of knowledge in all streams to allow a variety of mixes of the three sets of intellectual tools to coalesce in different programmes of research and study. This should entail more competition, and therefore more innovation in designing programmes that cover the whole range of the PSES triangle, instead of inhabiting only a small portion of the territory. Such a restructuring can be expected to generate considerable hostile reaction from academic institutions, which have up to now enjoyed an upper hand in the PSES, but may also generate a recombination of the different segments of the "learning enterprise", enabling the private, public and social sectors, the academic, trades, and human development sectors, and the theory and practice sectors to recompose a different ensemble of programmes of learning, better matched to the needs of the different types of reflective practitioners.

The third is at the motivational level: the design of the right system of incentives and rewards to ensure that the most fruitful partnerships emerge, and that the requisite resources flow toward these new alternative institutions. While there may be a need for collibration (putting a thumb on the scales to re-equilibrate things) at the beginning, the intent is that competition among these institutions will keep them at the cutting edge of innovation, and better serve those institutions that are more innovative.

DELTA KNOWLEDGE — A CULTURAL REFRAMING

Knowledge is an elusive notion. Typically, citizens have only the vaguest notion of what it is or of the ways in which it may be acquired. More importantly, when typical citizens are forced to think about knowledge, some clichés dominate their thinking: literacy, numeracy and the like. They have little appreciation of the depth of their own knowledge: they do not realize or know what they know. More important, perhaps, is the fact that they do not realize how much of the knowledge they do have has survival value they have had to acquire on their own, through experience and attention to circumstances.

When it comes to classifying types of knowledge, citizens are typically even more at a loss. Only academics worry about such things. Fritz Machlup (1980–1983) has suggested a three-way classification of what he regards as the most important types of knowledge: humanistic knowledge, scientific knowledge, and social science knowledge. This classification is not only open to criticism, but has been toxic, even though it has become the standard reference in the PSES, because it implicitly suggests that these are the only types of valuable knowledge.

The experience in the Netherlands, which came to my attention by chance a few years ago, has thrown some light on that toxicity. In the Netherlands, according to my colleague the late industrial designer Willem Gilles, these types of knowledge are referred to as alpha, beta and gamma respectively, and are the basis for the different faculties in universities. That has led to certain types of knowledge being unheralded, marginalized, and regarded as mundane, unwholesome, unwanted, illusive, irrelevant and useless. It is a perspective that has been extraordinarily destructive, and has led to many portions of the PSES being excluded from Dutch universities. For instance, in the Netherlands work done in management, architecture, agriculture, medicine and some other "vocational" subjects is routinely conducted outside university compounds.

When Gilles and others tried to understand in what way the types of knowledge generated and transmitted in these excluded sectors were differentiated from those accepted within the universities, it became clear that these sectors all shared a certain dependence on "learning by doing", learning on the spot through reflection in action. Knowledge acquired in this manner is rooted in *savoir-faire*, in some symbiotic relationship between master and apprentice, and it produces a sort of practical knowledge that is quite different from the bookish knowledge imparted by the traditional academic stream. In a generic way, we can refer to "delta knowledge" (Gilles and Paquet 1989) as that which is generated by and for "wrighting and wroughting" (Archer 1978). It depends on learning by doing, a conversation with the situation that focuses on "know-how" more than on "know that", and is produced according to rules that are largely implicit, overlapping, diverse, variously applied, contextually dependent, and subject to exceptions and to critical modifications (Schön 1988).

A lot of technical skills and trades training, as in management, design and many other professions, are based on delta knowledge, yet it is hardly recognized and is most certainly not well-understood. Indeed, this whole dimension of the PSES is not even acknowledged. It is at best considered as a frill to the core curriculum, as an add-on that may be beneficial in some programmes of study, but cannot be regarded as constituting anything but an extra, in the way that case studies, work stages and the like are presented in the publicity materials of most academic institutions. This practical component is considered not as the core, but as the periphery.

However, if one accepts the Heider/Gibson/Emery (1926; 1979; 1981) paradigm, it is clear that, even in the PSES, much depends on the development of perception skills, and therefore diagnostic skills, even though they are mostly occluded. Professional schools used to understand this as being at the core of their mission. Indeed, what they aim at producing is a professional who, when faced with an ailing patient, a distraught child, a disconcerted organization, a stalled truck or a failed state, has the intellectual abilities required to come up with a diagnosis and a coping strategy.

Much depends on a corpus of specialized knowledge, but, more importantly, on a capacity to extract information, understand the difficulties and design a way out.

Professionals are often able to react instinctively, in the blink of an eye, to a pattern of symptoms. Their attention and perception systems have been finely honed, and experience proffers the diagnosis (Gladwell 2005). Yet as long as this tacit knowledge is neither acknowledged nor valued, and as long as only certain types of accredited knowledge are recognized as valuable, no transformation is possible. Why would one work hard to acquire skills and character, or invest in developing better ways to impart such knowledge, when it is not valued? Institutions have a surreal capacity to refuse to accept anything of value outside of their own credentialized metrics. Thus professionals are becoming unwelcome in academic settings. Extraordinary surgeons are led to publish articles on the costs of their surgical operations in order to maintain their publication record and therefore their university accreditation. A retired Supreme Court judge was prevented from directing graduate students at a Canadian law school because her publications dossier was not substantial enough, even though her colleagues were studying her judgments in other courses.

Michael Polanyi (1966) has shown that tacit knowing is equally present in science and in practice, that it guides scientists to problems, promising new discoveries as much as the recognition of mood on a human face. It is also central to the innovation process in industry, which depends on interpretation and "trans-sector conversations" (Lester and Piore 2004). Nevertheless, unless delta knowledge and tacit knowing are recognized, identified and labelled as components at the core of the education process, they will never acquire the status necessary for resources to flow in that direction.

Identifying "delta territory" will not be easy; in the academic world, most professional schools are mesmerized by "scientistic" ideals, and have come more and more to neglect learning by doing and the focus on the perception system. It can be surmised that if any university were to identify a set of fields in its programmes as "delta territory" — as fields where learning by doing and reflection in action formed the core, and where learning would have to be designed accordingly — the "chosen" would rebel and claim their right to be housed with the rest of the herd.

A cultural revolution centred entirely on technical skills and trades training would have little chance of succeeding. What is needed is a mobilization of the nobler professions so that the types of knowledge on which their training is based are more widely recognized. Otherwise, there is little hope that there will be a revaluation of the delta territory recognition of the sort of tacit knowing (*savoir-faire*) that is so central in technical skills and trades training. The bundling of professional schools together into a College of Professional Institutes would not be an innocent move. It would indicate not only that a new covenant is in place, but that a new ethos is in the process of being constructed.

TRIANGLE-WIDE EXPERIMENTS: SOME RESTRUCTURING

It will not suffice, however, to ensure some recognition of the intellectual accomplishments that are anchored in delta knowledge, or of the relative importance of percepts as direct vehicles to knowledge. This may please art teachers, who have been arguing for generations that art education is not about training artists but about nurturing some intellectual and perception developments, but it is unlikely to mobilize a revolution in the PSES unless one is able to explicitly encourage a full exploration of the different modes of production of knowledge, and to put in place supporting structures that will prepare the ground for triangle-wide experiments — experimental designs of teaching and research, and practices attempting to develop different packages of *savoirs*, *savoir-faire* and *savoir-être*.

It is expedient to start by recognizing that there are different types of "research" attached to the different streams. Research has quite an aura, and might prove to be an easier road to credibility than a strict concentration on skill or personal development *stricto sensu*.

In fact, one might usefully begin with some linkages between our triad (*savoirs*, *savoir-faire*, *savoir-être*) and the Aristotelian triad of *episteme*, *techne* and *phronesis*: that is, knowledge that is universal, general, non-contextual; knowledge that is practical, instrumental, product-oriented know-how; and knowledge that is experience-based, prudence, practical wisdom concerning how to exercise ethical and moral judgement in particular and concrete situations. These sorts of Aristotelian credentials can only help. It would be easy to infer that each of these branches lends itself to different sorts of research and such research is most important in generating new knowledge of each sort.

This approach has the double advantage that it not only establishes the principle of different bases for legitimate and credible knowledge, but is also likely to heighten the status of *techne*, because it may be shown that it is at the level of *techne* that the integration of these three strands of knowledge can best be effected (Jentoft 2006). Engineers, architects and other professionals would likely concur.

For such a commitment to *techne* to materialize, a wide range of triangle-wide experiments must be conducted. It might be useful to design research institutions that might provide the different foci and mixes of activities related to these three strands. This would both provide status to *all* institutions (for research is now a mantra), and allow research to be freed from the shackles of academia and its claim to be the only place where meaningful research is conducted.

The Tavistock Institute (1964) has proposed an array of institutions one might see as mapping the research domain in the form of Venn diagrams, with three sets of institutions overlapping (compare Table 2.2). The decision to deliberately locate a large number of "Type A" knowledge creation organizations, focused on client needs, concrete problems, a mix of research and service, and a multidisciplinary approach, in institutions specializing in technical skills and trades training would provide not only a sound basis for developing new knowledge of a special type, such as delta knowledge, but also the necessary platform for the sort of collaborative work that might be done with other organizations ("Type B" or "Type C") that might be located elsewhere.

A VARIETY OF INCENTIVE-REWARDS: SOME RETOOLING

It is not sufficient to modify the frame of mind (theory + culture) and structures. One must also tinker with the social technologies and the incentive–reward systems. Culture evolves slowly and structures take time to establish themselves. Unless there is a bit of collibration, the dynamic conservatism of the forces in place may well block any change.

It is legitimate for governments to interfere in the affairs of the mind (Tussman 1977), and they do so constantly. If a rebalancing in the production processes of the PSES is seen as desirable, the incentive–reward systems

TABLE 2.2 Knowledge creation organizations

	User organizations	University departments	Special institutes
Source of problem	Client needs	Theory/method	General "field" needs
Level of problem	Concrete	Abstract	Generic
Activity mix	Research/service	Research/teaching	Research/ application
Disciplinary	Multiple	Single	Interrelated
	Type A	Type B	Type C

Source: adapted from Tavistock Institute (1964)

have to be tinkered with in such a way as to encourage supply, demand and coordination between them.

On the demand side there is a need for a better system of information about the quality and job-worthiness of technical skills and trades training. This must begin with a relabelling of these activities. This will not be easy because of the "brand name" that universities have carved for themselves, the value of the brand as seen in the United States and the aura that such brand names still carry around the world. Consequently, any change in name is bound not to resonate with those institutions, such as universities, that are trying to shape the future somewhat differently. There are already various categories of universities (undergraduate, comprehensive, research-intensive, and so on), so what might be useful is to identify "new generation universities" (NGUs), a category of institutions built on the whole range of types of knowledge, and explicitly designed to promote creativity and innovation. The Campus 2020 process launched in British Columbia in July 2006 might offer a marvellous opportunity to promote and announce new robust but different standards for these colleges and schools, including a greater sensitivity to the possibility of credits for work experience, and to put in place a robust marketing campaign designed to celebrate this particular strand of the PSES as leading to impressive and lucrative careers. A temporary, special type of scholarships-cum-loans, directed to the students of NGUs, and well-advertised in secondary schools, would probably have some impact on dropout rates and on the nature of secondary school programmes by reintroducing a larger place for non-academic subjects and creativity-focused activities.

On the supply side there will not only be a need to formally recognize the value of different forms of knowledge, but also a need to encourage the production of this new knowledge of different sorts. Instead of slavishly responding only to the demands of the traditional university lobbies, it might be worth exploring a bit further

the real sources of productivity and innovation, and
to fund with some equability the different institutions
according to performance criteria related to their capacity for engendering "innovative conversations" (Lester
and Piore 2004). The development of "Type A" research
centres in NGUs would do much to bestow higher status upon them, to help them to recruit a wider range of
persons with expertise of different sorts, to incite these
institutions to become much bolder in organizing their
modes of production and imparting of knowledge, and
to establish bridges between these institutions and the
other types of institutions in the PSES on the basis of
this comparative advantage.

On the coordination side, British Columbia has
already done a great deal to help the smooth transition
of students from one institution to the other and the new
network of research centres would do much to connect
faculty members.

There might be ways in which the experience of the
Canadian Institute for Advanced Research would be
of use in thinking through ways of generating virtual
networks of researchers from these different types of
institutions, and stimulating joint ventures by institutions
in creating mixed programmes of studies and research. In
this process it would be a mistake to allow local patrio-
tism and protectionism to prevail.

The use of open-source materials provided by the
different segments of the PSES might allow an extraordinarily effective transfer of technology and educational
materials, and help to provide additional "enrichment"
through better integration, to take advantage of the
experience of other institutions. The creation of virtual
research organizations, making the highest and best use
of the personnel in different institutions, might indeed
be the basis of a network of elite "Type ABC" research
organizations that would selectively bring together not
only personnel from different institutions operating
at the same level, but also personnel from different

institutions operating at different levels. The decision to generously fund such coordinated initiatives could produce miracles.

It might even be useful to envisage the creation of new roles for institutions that might be interested in playing an intermediation role in this newly integrated and real-cum-virtual PSES. Such institutions might provide new services. One example might be the evaluation of a wide range of competencies that are for the moment very poorly known, so that they could become properly acknowledged and rigorously assessed (language, particular skills, work experience equivalencies), with the possibility that such recognized competencies, established through rigorous challenge examinations, might be properly recorded electronically on the back strip of a portable "education card" not unlike the health card. The technology exists for such an initiative (proposals to put it in place have been floating about for more than ten years [Authier and Lévy 1992]), and yet no institution has stepped forward to take on the responsibility for such an initiative except (I am informed) in Nunavut. This would allow a much finer appreciation of the pool of knowledges and competencies available, on a level that simply does not exist now, and labour market information would be immensely improved. Still, we appear to be satisfied with much grosser recognition of batches of competencies, such as degrees, when we might get much finer and more easily accessible appreciation of the real competency profiles of individuals and communities if such an intermediation role were to evolve.

Another example might be the development of providers that could offer a whole range of educational packages of accredited courses, either produced locally or acquired from other institutions, that might provide the requisite variety and diversity of programmes one would like to see available. These educational packages, provided *à la carte* by intermediaries, would be possible without the need to replicate every course or programme

in the different institutions, and might produce variety
and diversity at much lower costs.

CONCLUSION

For over fifty years, the PSES has congealed in a certain
form, and institutions have been explicitly encouraged
by financial incentives to focus mainly on only certain
portions of the PSES terrain. Reframing or restructuring of the PSES will obviously generate concern on
the part of those who have thrived under this regime,
for it can only mean raising questions about present
(perhaps) and future (certainly) allocation of resources.
Consequently, the legitimacy and importance of forms
of knowledge other than those that are now dominant
in universities are going to be challenged, or at least
belittled. Such dynamic conservatism has to be actively
countered.

One of the major sources of problems has been the
social architecture of research institutions, which have
been disciplinary and well-interwoven with university
departments ("Type B"). Such an architecture has provided a very limiting context for knowledge creation. A
more reasonable architecture would harbour different
sorts of knowledge creation units.

I have sketched some of the challenges and hinted at
ways in which they could be met, but that might not be
sufficient. More importantly, it might allow less favour-
ably disposed groups to deliberately ignore what has not
been put forward squarely and forcefully. Consequently,
I would like to mention in closing a number of modest
general propositions to complement the various pointed
suggestions made in the body of this chapter.

(1) A mandate to create, teach and disseminate delta
knowledge should be formally integrated into the mission
of all institutions in the PSES.

(2) There should be an effort to trigger a cultural
change that would eliminate the old stereotypes plaguing
the technical skills and trades training sector, and better

inform citizens and business about the sophistication of such training.

(3) Experimentation in the PSES should be robustly encouraged, with an equally robust evaluation process that would ensure that successful experiments are celebrated and disseminated quickly, but unsuccessful ones are quickly brought to a halt.

(4) Certain institutions whose absence currently prevents effective governance of the PSES should be created. (One might, however, persuade existing institutions to shoulder these new roles.) Such institutions might include an electronic system of competency profiles built around an "education card" that might summarize more comprehensively the full range of competencies of an individual as properly and rigorously assessed; and a network of brokers capable of making the highest and best use of the range of courses available in the PSES.

(5) There should be a review of the financing of the different layers of the PSES on the basis of a new and more realistic appreciation of the real costs and benefits of different activities, instead of relying on fanciful historically based formulas that bear no relation to real costs and benefits.

CHAPTER 3

Corporate culture and governance

*We require a framework
for dealing with the unforeseen.*
—DAVID M. KREPS (1990: 90)

Crippling epistemologies may be endogenously generated by the evolving traditions in the human sciences,
or fuelled by a post-secondary education enterprise
that focuses exclusively on *episteme* to the detriment
of *techne* and *phronesis*, but they may also be ascribable to a broader cultural environment that discourages
risk-taking and innovation. Such an environment tends
to reward conformism and does not foster deviance or
entrepreneurship.

In the case of the social sciences, it is not clear how
important the cultural milieu has been in the consolida-
tion of a culture that puts an emphasis on method and
has failed to develop social sciences capable of dealing
with the major social issues of interest to the citizen. My
hypothesis is that the cultural milieu has played a significant role in supporting the dynamic conservatism that
has helped to consolidate the traditional mindset, and
that it explains the extent to which the key institutions
and organization producing and funding research in the
social sciences have played a rearguard role.

CULTURE AS SOUL

The notion of culture is opaque and elusive. It refers to what one might regard as the "soul" of an organization, the nexus of broad and faceless forces that shape the way in which an organization or a society perceives the world, reacts to changes in the environment or challenges from competitors or partners, and governs itself. The concept of culture connotes the ideas, customs and skills of a people or a group that are transferred, communicated or passed along from one generation to the next, and their shared beliefs, behaviours and systems of meanings. In general, a culture is an appreciative system that is both enabling and limiting. It encompasses both a set of readinesses and capacities, and a set of constraints under which the organization labours when faced with unforeseen challenges (Vickers 1965). Culture is "collective programming of the mind" (Hofstede 1991).

In addition, the corporate culture of organizations such as universities is permeated by their national culture. Business organizations also cannot escape the burden of a national culture. In a country that systematically celebrates individualism, it would be surprising to see a collectivist corporate culture. This does not mean that corporate culture is in all respects a mirror image of the national culture, but they share a large segment of common entrenched beliefs.

The corporate cultures in the Americas are quite varied, and are rooted in very different histories and experiences. Even Canada and the United States have corporate cultures that have somewhat different contours, despite their great similarities. Canada's corporate culture appears to stand somewhere on a continuum that spans the whole range from the more individualistic US corporate culture to the more communitarian corporate cultures of continental Europe and East Asia (Courchene 1995). The differences are particularly evident when gauged by the level of tolerance for uncertainty: Canada, like the countries of Latin America, is much more risk-averse than the USA and less likely to accept change.

The next section defines key dimensions of corporate cultures and suggests that these dimensions often aggregate into syndromes revealing different forms of neurosis. Subsequent sections show how corporate culture operates as a cognitive and ethical prime mover in society and the economy, and how it underpins productivity, innovation and resilience. It is then conjectured that the corporate cultures in the Americas are beginning to converge, albeit somewhat uneasily, and little by little. The concluding section of this chapter comments briefly on the reasons why corporate cultures as mindsets and sextants cannot be easily modified, and why converging dissensus may have to suffice.

THE PALIMPSEST OF
CORPORATE CULTURE

Corporate culture, like national culture, is a work in progress. It develops as the context changes, but it maintains a certain hard core of common views that ensures the coherence and permanence of certain key directions of the organization. This hard core mobilizes resources in a meaningful way in times of crisis, and provides a sort of extra-rational capacity to react instinctively to unforeseen challenges. But it also, at times, prevents the organization from shedding ineffective practices deeply anchored in the core. Around this hard core of basic assumptions, deeply rooted in the collective mind, is a large surrounding network of values, beliefs and artefacts (Schein 2001) that are less firmly anchored, and therefore lend themselves to reinterpretation. They are candidates for being tinkered with when they show signs of being dysfunctional. So the cultural process as filter is a double-looped learning engine: the challenges of context generate, in the short run, adjustments in the protective belt of surrounding values and modification of the instrumentalities built on them, but they also provoke, over the longer haul, and much more slowly and painfully, an erosion and modification of the core assumptions.

This evolutionary rewriting of the cultural script means that probing culture at any one moment is like reading a palimpsest (a parchment that has been reused many times). The previous writings are not fully erased or scraped off, making the more recent scribbling decipherable but often difficult to decode. This multi-layered parchment has the particular merit, however, of allowing one to detect a cultural drift from the fading scribbling of the past to the more visible recent one.

For instance, the present differences between the more confrontational corporate culture of Argentina and its more passive counterpart in Brazil cannot be easily understood unless one is aware of the history of these countries. Particularly oppressive colonization and the crucial import of slavery explain to a large extent why Brazil is still a society where a very unequal distribution of power is readily accepted (Risner 2001: 24). Brazilian culture has been identified as hierarchical (tendency to centralize power, passivity, acceptance of authority); personalistic (society based on personal relations, paternalism); permeated by cunning (flexibility and adaptability as ways to manoeuvre); and inspired by a need for adventure (more dreamer than disciplinarian) (Borges de Freitas 1997, cited in Risner 2001: 27).

This is not the place for a detailed analysis of the nature of each national and corporate culture in the different portions of the Americas, but the example of Brazil illustrates how key dimensions of such cultures can have an impact on the conformation of the particular habitus (the propensity to tackle issues and challenges in certain characteristic ways) in each of these countries.

However, the reductive fascination with "national character" and uniformity must be resisted. Countries are convenient as boxes simplifying the global mapping of cultures, but one should not fall prey to the logical fallacy of *ignoratio elenchi*: ascribing causal force to a principle of classification used for convenience. Measuring unemployment by regions, for example, does not allow one to ascribe the differences in observed rates of unemployment to a "regional factor". Such a tautological argument invents a fictional "national character" as warranted when, most of the time, it is not. The cultures of Quebec and Alberta are no more identical than those of the northern and southern parts of Brazil, or those of California and New England (Saxenian 1994).

KEY DIMENSIONS OF CORPORATE CULTURE

Many schemes have been proposed to X-ray corporate culture. A most interesting scheme for comparative purposes has been proposed and continually updated by Geert Hofstede (1967–2003). It focuses on indices of power inequality, individualism, risk aversion and long-term orientation, among other things. A more extensive scheme, proposed by Charles Hampden-Turner and Alfons Trompenaars (1993), is based on seven dilemmas or tensions between pairs of values, in which each of the fourteen values is crucial to success. It is, therefore, a matter of determining where different organizations and countries might appear to stand on the continuum from total emphasis on one value to total emphasis on the other in each pair:

- priority to rules—priority to the particulars of a case;
- analyzing phenomena in parts—relying on detecting patterns of relationships;
- individual priorities—community values;
- inner-directed commitments—signals from the outside world;
- doing things fast—synchronizing efforts so that completion is well-coordinated;
- achieved status of stakeholders—ascribed status of stakeholders;
- priority to equality—priority to hierarchy.

The location of a national or corporate culture on the continuum of these values can be established by interviews that allow managers to reveal their modus operandi by being confronted with case studies and pointed dilemmas. This approach suggests that Canada's culture is "soft universalist", analytical, individualist, inner-directed, oriented to the short term, achievement-focused and biased toward equality (Hampden-Turner and Trompenaars 1993). While this diagnosis requires some adjustment of flats and sharps as one refers to one region or another, it corresponds to a broad characterization that resonates with most observers.

In the rest of the Americas the differences among corporate cultures are sharply contrasted. In Latin America (Central America and most of South America) there is a confluence of factors that have made many features — particularism, integration, communitarianism, outer-direction, status by ascription, hierarchy and a synchronized view of time — play much larger roles than they generally do in Canada. Again, one must be careful not to generalize unduly. The northern and southern parts of Brazil do not have the same corporate cultures, for example. In the north corporate culture has been greatly influenced by colonization and slavery, while in the south it has been shaped much more by European elements, due to the immigration policies of the late 19th century.

HABITUS AND NEUROSIS

Patterns of governance are importantly influenced by "national" and corporate cultures, though these features are never easy to characterize sharply and precisely. Indeed, such cultural factors shape decision-making. Saxenian (1994) has shown that in the high-tech world the same shocks hitting the east coast of the United States, with its more formal and hierarchical corporate culture, and the west coast, with its more informal and more horizontal corporate culture, have led to quite different responses and contrasted performances. The same may be said about a variety of other decisions in different areas where culture makes its impact in a differential way.

In more routine decision-making processes, cultural forces may be repressed, if not totally suppressed, by the standards prevailing in the professional milieus in question. Marketing and accounting have their own internal cultures, with their own rules, and organizations ignore them at their peril. Corporate culture, therefore, often encompasses a variety of sub-cultures that appear quite different, yet share many of the same mores.

The contrasts among corporate cultures become more visible when an organization faces an unforeseen crisis for which there is no routine response and for which it is ill-prepared. As a result the "soul" and "instinctive dimensions" of the organization take over, take charge of defining the problem and shape the response. These responses reveal the dominant features of the underlying culture. Characterizing these features is a daunting and perilous task, for one is forced to "psychoanalyze" the organization, so to speak, and to reveal its neurosis. Often, the best one can do is identify how the organization's habitus (its propensity to act in certain ways) tends to reveal a mix of characteristics that add up to a syndrome or an ensemble of traits that carries with it some general tendencies.

Kets de Vries and Miller (1984) have boldly suggested that this might reveal some forms of "organizational neurosis", and, with it, some fantasies and dangers. Organizational neurosis is a dysfunction that generates affective and emotional problems without disrupting the functioning of the organization. There are different styles of neurosis: paranoid (suspicious), compulsive, dramatic, depressive, schizoid (detached). Each has its own characteristics, dominant motivating fantasy and associated dangers (see Table 3.1). They may as easily be applied to private, public or social

TABLE 3.1 Summary of neurotic styles

	Paranoid	Compulsive	Dramatic	Depressive	Schizoid
Characteristics	Mistrust	Perfectionism	Self-dramatization	Sense of guilt	Non-involvement
	Hypersensitivity	Focus on trivia	Narcissism	Helplessness	Estrangement
	Perceived threats	Dogmatism	Exploitativeness		
Fantasy	I cannot really trust anybody; I had better be on my guard	I don't want be at the mercy of events; I must control everything	I want to get attention from people and impress them	I am helpless to change the course of events; I am not good enough	The world of reality does not offer any satisfaction, so it is safer to remain distant
Dangers	Distortion of reality	Fear of making mistakes	Overreaction to minor events	Inhibition of action	Bewilderment and aggressiveness
	Defensive attitude	Excessive reliance on rules	Action based on appearances	Indecisiveness; excessive pessimism	Emotional isolation

Source: adapted from Kets de Vries and Miller (1984: 24-25)

organizations, and even, with immense care, to regions/
nations.

These sorts of neuroses give rise to a number of common problems: improper allocation of authority, an
out-of-line attitude to risk, inadequate organizational
structures, poor distribution of information, deficient
calibre of executive talent and so on. Such problems are
signs of failures of governance and call for a modification
of the organization's governance to correct them.

Not all corporate cultures are equally neurotic, nor
do the five "neurotic styles" identified by Kets de Vries
and Miller (1984) exhaust the range of flaws in corporate cultures. They are provided as illustrations of the
sorts of syndromes that corporate cultures can embody.
Nevertheless, all organizations suffer to a greater or
lesser degree from such neuroses. Some organizations
are better able than others to overcome these debilitat-
ing traits and to provide a framework that is better at
"guessing" the unforeseen.

Taking a reliable X-ray of Canadian corporate culture,
using this grid of neurotic styles, would require a very
elaborate study. Such a study has not been conducted yet,
and in any case it would have to be constantly updated to
take into account the evolution of the corporate culture.
However, I was privileged to attend a meeting of some
forty representatives of ethical advisers of mainly large
private companies (but some public-sector organizations as well) in Ottawa in May 2006. These relatively
senior officials agreed to fill out a questionnaire that
was prepared by Kets de Vries (2001: 169–173) to help
organizations in determining what neurotic styles appear
to best fit their operations. While the sample is small
and not necessarily fully representative of the Canadian
scene, it provided the opportunity to gain some insight
into what appear to be the dominant styles prevalent
in Canada. The results were surprising. Almost half
the respondents using the Kets de Vries grid came to
the conclusion that their organization was most closely

associated with the dramatic style, while almost twenty percent found that the compulsive style was the best match. As for the type of organization preferred by these officials, the questionnaire showed that a strong plurality of the respondents leaned toward the detached organization as the one in which they would prefer to work.

One cannot and should not draw any but the most careful conjectures from such a small base of empirical data, but one may infer that the dominant organizational type appears to be dramatic/compulsive, entailing a strong degree of hyperactivity, obsession and self-dramatization, while officials appear to be tempted by a milieu that would provide more distance and non-involvement. This "general" misalignment does not seem to be a recipe for success.

THE VARIOUS WAYS IN WHICH CORPORATE CULTURE CATALYZES THE ORGANIZATION

It is not sufficient to identify the traits that define corporate culture. One must also understand the way in which this diffuse reality affects social learning by organizations, and the main channels through which corporate culture affects the functioning of organizations and enhances or impairs their performance. Without a sense of this dynamic, it is not clear that one would be able to determine the repairs that might be required by both the corporate culture and the apparatus of governance.

In the face of accelerated technical change, globalization, and the need to adapt with great speed and to learn quickly, centralized, hierarchical and confrontational structures of governance are usually inadequate. Innovative flexibility and collective learning call for the development of a mix of coordination and collaboration from all stakeholders, establishing co-learning and co-governance in an ecosystem that evolves by finding better ways to "charter" cross-functional teams, from which no important power players are left out, and in which "all major players have some stake in the success of the strategy" (Moore 1998).

Such a "perfect" system of governance does not necessarily materialize organically. Real systems show signs of disconcertation, disconnectedness, misalignment between the governance regime and its circumstances (Baumard 1996). As a result the degree of social learning and collective intelligence is less than it might be, and the performance of the system is less than optimal.

Corporate culture, through its capacity to facilitate interaction among groups that have different objectives and values, can play a most important role at the cognitive and ethical levels.

AT THE COGNITIVE LEVEL

To accelerate social learning in complex organizations one must first gain some appreciation of the ways in which collective intelligence works. An approach by Max Boisot (Boisot 1995; Paquet 2004a; 2005b) suggests a mapping of the social learning cycle in a three-dimensional space, the "information space", which identifies an organizational system in terms of the degrees of abstraction, codification and diffusion of the information flows within it. This information space (see Figure 3.1) defines three continua: the farther away from the origin on the vertical axis, the more the information is codified (the more its form is clarified, stylized and simplified); the farther away from the origin to the right, the more widely the information is diffused and shared; and the farther away from the origin to the left, the more abstract the information is (the more general the categories in use).

The social learning cycle is presented in two phases with three steps in each phase. Phase I emphasizes the cognitive dimensions of the cycle, while Phase II deals with the diffusion of the new information.

In Phase I, learning begins with some scanning of the environment as well as the concrete information widely diffused and known, in order to detect anomalies and paradoxes. Following this first step (*s*), one is led in the second step to stylize the problem (*p*) posed by the anomalies and paradoxes in a language of problem solution; the third step of Phase I purports to generalize the solution found to the more specific issue to a broader family of problems through a process of abstraction (*at*). In Phase II the new knowledge is diffused (*d*) to a larger community of persons or groups in a fourth step. There is then, in a fifth step, a process of absorption (*ar*) of this new knowledge by the population and its assimilation so that it becomes part of the tacit stock of knowledge. In a sixth step the new knowledge is not only absorbed, but has an impact (*i*) on the concrete practices and artefacts of the group or community.

It is possible to identify the different blockages through the learning cycle. In Phase I, cognitive dissonance in *s* may prevent anomalies from being noted;

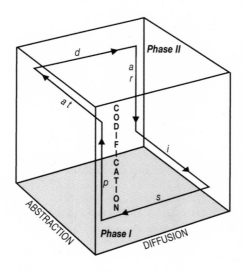

FIGURE 3.1 Learning cycle and potential blockages

epistemic inhibitions of all sorts in p may stop the process of translation into a language of problem solution; and blockages preventing the generalization of the new knowledge because of the problem definition being encapsulated within the here and now (at), may keep the new knowledge from acquiring the most effective degree of generality. In Phase II the new knowledge may not get the appropriate diffusion because of property rights gridlock (d) (Heller 2008), or because of certain values or very strong dynamic conservatism, which may cause those most likely to profit from the new knowledge (ar) to refuse to listen, or because of difficulties in finding ways to incorporate the new knowledge (i).

Interventions to remove or attenuate the negative effects of such blockages always entail some degree of interference with the mechanisms of collective intelligence. In some cases, such as the modification of property rights, the changes in the rules appear relatively innocuous, but in some cases government must interfere significantly in the affairs of the mind. Correcting social learning blockages modifies relational transactions and therefore the psychosocial fabric of the organization.

The lack of the requisite structures to facilitate dialogue and deliberation has contributed to considerably weakening capacities to identify important anomalies, to understand the sources of the difficulties revealed and to generalize the response to a whole range of pressure points that are attributable to the same causes. This, in turn, has hampered the effectiveness of governance. More generally, the lack of adequate information and transparency allows "false consciousness" to thrive unchallenged, and allows dysfunctional arrangements to survive, solely through the force of apathy, inertia and raw defence of narrow vested interests.

Corporate culture serves here as a substitute for these failing structures and as a facilitator in the emergence of workable arrangements, both at the cognitive level and at the level of diffusion. The existence of the different values systems held by different stakeholders can make the diffusion of particularly helpful responses to generic problems more difficult, and lead to counterproductive adversarialism. Corporate culture facilitates alignment among these different value systems.

Still, the collaboration and partnering that are needed entail power-sharing and are often regarded as "unacceptable in principle" by the very groups claiming to want to become partners (Paquet 2001). At a time when the amount and kind of collaboration required are deeper and richer than before, and there is a need for a greater variety of forums, reporting standards and collaborative structures of a more permanent sort for organizations to thrive in turbulent environments, these essential elements are often simply not there, unless they are fostered by an enabling corporate culture.

In today's "game without a master" it may be quite inefficient to indulge in myopic competitive strategies and, even though citizens may end up being relatively badly served by such strategies, ideological commitments, cultural barriers or power struggles may prevent the emergence of what dispassionate observers would regard as "reasonable compromises" (Paquet 2004b). As Flyvberg (1998) puts it: "in open confrontation, rationality yields to power".

Transparency, better information and more inclusive forms of deliberation—all made possible by corporate culture—will be helpful in engendering better conductivity, defined as "the capability to effectively transmit high-quality knowledge throughout the organization". Corporate culture, as the sum of opinions, shared mindsets, values and norms within an organization, obviously catalyzes this capability (Saint-Onge and Armstrong 2004).

AT THE ETHICAL LEVEL
The cultural environment not only provides guideposts for effective action, but it also helps to define the

corridor of acceptable behaviour. The culture of the organization defines the way in which issues are framed, and constitutes a set of lenses imposed on situations that define constraints on the ways in which the agent or the group is allowed to act.

Corporate culture may be more or less permissive, may encourage more or less delinquency, may entice or tolerate more or less aggressive use of moral imagination and so on. This "elusive reality" identifies the sort of foci an organizational culture might encourage or discourage, and therefore defines what the survival strategy is: the individual must either adopt the privileged view, or choose to leave.

In no organization can it be said that all assumptions can be questioned, and all members can allow themselves to tinker with all mechanisms, structures and norms. Indeed, it is generally the other way around. Most organizations have an "appreciative system" and those who do not share it are deviants or outsiders. Moreover, as Warren Bennis put it, "most organizations would rather risk obsolescence than make room for the non-conformist in their midst" (Bennis 1976: 40). Indeed, most institutions are more or less neurotic about such things.

The corporate culture defines the constraints and the degrees of freedom that the organization avails to its members in developing strategies within a certain corridor, and the support or non-support for efforts to extend the width of the corridor of acceptable behaviour. It provides references or focal points in relationships by which acceptable behaviour might be defined. This process of ethical decision-making, which is a form of learning, entails a protocol of triangulation through which the context, the corporate culture and some basic assumptions are brought together in an effort to determine the corridor of acceptable performance.

None of these elements is rock solid. The critical appreciation of the context is always somewhat perfectible;

the corporate culture is more or less fully and accurately gaugeable, and always evolving; and the reference assumptions are more or less debatable. In this triangulation corporate culture plays a fundamental role: it helps in harmonizing context and fundamental assumptions.

The process of social learning is based on a continuous "negotiation" among agents to ascertain the boundaries of the corridor of acceptable performance. It cannot be operationalized without an appreciation of context in historical perspective, and this in turn calls for continuous "reconstruction" and reinterpretation of the meaning of the past. Finally, it is a process based on a need for moral "imagination" to extend the corridor of acceptable performance by developing new prototypes or extending existing ones. Triangulation work develops a sort of cumulative wisdom or connoisseurship that produces, over time, a "reflex" that generates a response "in a blink" (Gladwell 2005).

The ways in which the corporate culture affects the cognitive and ethical performance of an organization are not easily observable from outside the organization. Unless one is allowed to probe the decision-making process of the organization extensively, it is difficult to put forward even modest general propositions. Yet if one accepts that the dramatic/compulsive syndrome is dominant in Canada (and a casual awareness of the history of Nortel and Bombardier, to name but two, appears to support such a view), it becomes clear that this has had an impact on both the cognitive and ethical performance of these firms. Their business history is replete with impulsively bold ventures, overcentralization and obsessive behaviour that have neither served the organizations well, nor provided the sort of decision-making that has left stakeholders and observers satisfied with excessive reliance on rigid rules and narcissism, at times when the realities might have called for faster adaptation and less ritualized evaluation.

PRODUCTIVITY, INNOVATION
AND RESILIENCE: AN ECHO
OF CORPORATE CULTURE

In the best cases the sort of heightened conductivity and stronger ethical moorings provided by the corporate culture are crucial dimensions that underpin much of an organization's performance. These dimensions are anchored in organizational capital and collective mindsets, and the corporate culture they echo is often tacit and difficult to articulate or codify. Yet these dimensions and their underpinning are the foundation of productivity, innovation and resilience.

INTERPERSONAL ENABLING RESOURCES

Social and economic progress is generated by productivity growth and innovation, when individuals and organizations actively apply their entrepreneurial intelligence, ingenuity and imagination to better coordinate existing activities, or to fill gaps in such coordination in the name of making better use of existing resources. Rarely is this a matter depending on a single individual. Most of the time it is the result of the collaboration of many individuals who must have a modicum of trust in one another if they are to co-operate. This poses a major challenge for governance, which connotes effective coordination when knowledge, power and resources are widely distributed.

Ingenuity, entrepreneurship and trust are social capabilities that constitute factors of production just as land, labour and capital do. But they are special factors of production: "interpersonal enabling resources" are at the core of what Alfred Marshall called "organizational capital". The supply of technical ingenuity depends on an adequate supply of underpinning institutions supporting the production and maintenance of such capacities, *and* on adequate pressure to make active use of these "enabling resources".

This organizational and institutional support takes the form of public goods such as effective market signals,

wise funding agencies, industrial associations, agoras
where research institutions and industrial concerns can
co-operate, working networks, effective governments as
facilitators and catalysts, and so on. These public goods
provide material and psychological infrastructures to
entrepreneurs and innovators, facilitate contact among
them, help to create coalitions and provide constructive
coercion.

Corporate culture plays a key role at this level.
Pressure to take action may emerge from competition,
and the working of the free market in response to scar-
cities and bottlenecks. These forces press concerns into
improving continually and innovating in order to survive,
but their capacity to respond depends on "interpersonal
enabling resources".

Economists have been rather reluctant to probe the
murky terrain of these "interpersonal enabling resources"
(Foa 1971). It has often been left to political scientists,
such as Thomas Homer-Dixon (1995), or maverick economists, such as Harvey Leibenstein (1978), to explore
this socio-psychological and organizational underground.
Their work has shown that there are identifiable forces,
institutions and contexts that tend to promote greater
degrees of entrepreneurship, trust and ingenuity.

These interpersonal enabling resources give rise
to important increasing returns (Ben-Porath 1980).
Identifying "relational goods" and "relational assets"
(Hinde 1995; Gui 2000) is not unimportant, but what is
even more important is the full weight of these increasing returns and the inherent dynamics they underpin
(Laurent and Paquet 1998).

CONDUCTIVITY

Corporate culture is built on these particularistic and
symbolic interpersonal resources and assets. Their syncretic impact injects increasing returns in the dynamics of
productivity, innovation and resilience. Corporate governance is a nexus of multiplex relations that underpin

a capacity to transform, a capability to go beyond the limits of the organization, and an alignment of individual and corporate norms into a key enabler of enhanced organizational performance.

Corporate culture comprises not only artefacts, customs, ceremonies and rituals, experiences, behavioural norms, and beliefs and assumptions (Schein 2001) — although these dimensions do matter — but also the dynamic capabilities brought forth by such elements in interaction, which, when they are appropriately aligned, can make the difference. Here, as in so many other circumstances, the whole is greater than the sum of the parts.

These capabilities are identified by Saint-Onge and Armstrong (2004; 127ff) as: (1) a high-level of self-initiation and capacity by all to overcome an entitlement mindset, and to take responsibility for one's own performance and learning; (2) a high level of trust that permeates all relationships; (3) a culture of interdependence in which partners interact with one another with a view to creating new capabilities; and (4) an ability to translate self-initiation, trust and interdependence into partnerships.

The hyperconductive organization or economy is fuelled by a corporate culture that provides the requisite glue *and* solvent for the organization to have integrity. It ensures that ongoing organizational intelligence (fuelling stewardship) (1) detects patterns; (2) responds with speed; (3) generates capability; and (4) creates partnership; all this by: (5) infusing meaning (Saint-Onge and Armstrong 2004: 188). The corporate culture, through its cognitive and ethical signals, enables the right abilities, the right capacities and the right alignments to emerge, or prevents them from emerging. Anything that stalls or blocks the Boisot (1995) learning cycle, or prevents the emergence of the capabilities and leadership abilities identified by Saint-Onge and Armstrong, reduces conductivity, weakens governance and leads to inferior performance.

The extent to which the Canadian corporate culture has been individualist, inner-directed, oriented to the short-term and focused on achievement, has probably contributed significantly to a less than optimal investment in organizational capital, and to a poorer organizational alignment of capabilities. The fact that the new mantra on the Canadian corporate scene concerns the "search for a culture of integrity", while the mantra in the US concerns a drive toward a "culture of confidence" (at least according to CHL Global Associates 2006), may be revealing. Canadian companies do not sense that they have been able to align their capabilities sufficiently well to yield all the added value they know they can generate.

Too often, the dramatic/compulsive Canadian organizations have dealt only with surface adjustments, for the sake of appearances, and have done so in ways that have been so overcentralized that there has been no significant mobilization of the living forces of the organizations. Indeed, what happened when Paul Stern was at the helm of Nortel shows how quickly a fruitful alignment of the capabilities of an organization can get unstuck. Canadian companies have tended to wallow in the safety of evasive thinking (expressed in vision and mission statements), instead of tackling more tangible commitments (partnerships).

IN CORPORATE CULTURE THERE ARE MANY AMERICAS

In the Americas, as we have discussed above, corporate cultures vary dramatically across countries and companies, and it is not clear that any one corporate culture is readily exportable across boundaries. A corporate culture is built on much that is corporate memory and unwritten, and on much that is historical and contextual and also unwritten. It also remains to a large extent in the realm of the opaque. What is dramatically lacking is basic knowledge of the particular fabric of corporate cultures, and the toxicity of their idiosyncrasies. Even when such knowledge exists, it is not always clear how one can make use of such knowledge and it does not appear to lead to any easy solutions.

We know that only about thirty-six percent of Canadian executives regard their companies as having strong adaptive cultures; some fifty-five percent define their companies as weak (plagued with top-down managerial arrogance, fear of risk-taking, inward focus and bureaucracy); and, while sixty-four percent say that corporate culture is important, seventy-two percent say that their organization's culture is not what they desire for the future (Wahl 2005). Yet nobody seems to know what might be done about these problems or how to go about doing it.

Moreover, culture cannot be modified instantly. Even when strategies are sketched that might pay off over the long haul, in seven to ten years, it is difficult for these efforts to gain support. Most CEOs have a shorter time horizon and lose interest. The cost of such myopia and impatience in the face of profoundly complex issues is quite high (Tasar 2000).

This is why most corporations have accomplished so little of substance on this front. Most have been satisfied to install a plaque on the wall in the head-office foyer in the hope that such an incantation might magically provoke a cultural revolution. This is no substitute for transforming assumptions, morals and beliefs so as to create the sort of organizational intelligence capable of detecting patterns, responding with speed, generating capability, creating partnership and infusing meaning.

For those searching for the root causes of the corporate culture problem in the Americas, a glance at the indices compiled by Geert Hofstede is quite enlightening (www.geert-hofstede.com). Such analyses are bound to discourage "solutionists", for the diagnosis calls for nothing less than a revolution in our collective minds. In Canada and the United States the major assets are:

(1) relatively high degrees of individualism and self-reliance; (2) a relatively high degree of equality, or a lack of rigidity preventing upward mobility; and (3) a lack of what Geert Hofstede calls the long-term orientation (long-term commitment and respect for tradition). This allows a greater possibility of change. One must note, however, that Canada does not rank as high on individualism as the United States does, and even ranks lower than the United Kingdom or Australia. This may be an echo effect of the welfare state era. Another major difference between Canada and the United States that has been mentioned earlier is the dramatically greater degree of risk aversion in Canada. On this count, Canada closely resembles countries in Latin America where the degree of risk aversion is quite high.

In the southern portion of the hemisphere, the structure of power is relatively much more unequal, individualism is quite low and risk aversion is quite high. The implications of this sort of cleavage between the two Americas are important.

The national cultures of the North and the South are sufficiently contrasted for one to suggest that the chasm cannot be overcome with anything less than a cultural revolution. This revolution would entail a modification of the institutional order, with a change in the structure of power, a major surge in individualism, a dramatic shedding of the aversion to risk, and the abandonment of many of the traditions and rigid long-term commitments that have become impediments to change. This transformation would not come easily, for important vested interests are likely to be displaced by it. Canada shares some of these handicaps (especially the high degree of risk aversion), and might therefore play a significant role in partnering in the gradualist strategy that appears to be in the making. Indeed, partnerships are the fabric of risk-sharing and may represent, for both Canada and countries in Latin America, a way to jointly overcome this handicap.

More than anything else, the debates about the Free Trade Area of the Americas initiative has revealed the differences in the degree of readiness of the different countries of Latin America. Countries such as Chile (in the Andean Community), Uruguay and Paraguay (in Mercosur) or Costa Rica and El Salvador (in Central America), are clearly regions where a cultural revolution may be most likely to succeed. Some of the basics are in place or almost in place, including price stability, budget discipline, external debt, currency stability, market-oriented policies, reliance on trade taxes and functioning democracy. Partnerships are easier to hammer out when countries do not have ambitions to play a hegemonic role in their portion of the Americas. Canada may therefore already have "natural partners" emerging to the south. It is through these "windows of opportunity" that change is likely to proceed, that integration is prone to progress piece by piece, and that societal change (and therefore a change in corporate culture) might be initiated (Paquet 2000; 2005b).

Canada might be able to accompany and nurture such a strategy without having to bear the odium of being seen, as the United States often is, as promoting an "imperialism of free trade" that could easily lead to some "tyranny of free trade" if the non-dominant countries were to prove unable to mobilize their capabilities effectively and fully.

Canada's help may at first take the form of support for simple *bricolage*. It is much easier to tinker with the surface reality of corporate governance, along the lines proposed by the OECD (2003). Tinkering with voting rights, financial reporting, procedural dimensions of corporate boards and the like, is dealing with "social technologies". Such changes are more readily debated and can lead rather smoothly to structural changes. Via that indirect and oblique route, the "theory" (the notion of what business persons are in) might be transformed. Schön (1971) has shown that technology, structure and theory are fundamentally intertwined: any change in one triggers changes in the others. Corporate culture is at the core of "theory". Bricolage at the level of social technology is likely to be much less threatening (and therefore not to be fought so harshly), and so is more likely to lead less painfully to a change in both structures and theory.

The central question is one of patience. In the history of the world fifteen years (five to six thousand days), the time it might take to transform organizational culture, is a rather short time. For those, such as democratically elected politicians, who have a time horizon of three to four years, it may appear to be an eternity.

An oblique approach, focusing on those countries that have a greater degree of readiness, with special attention given to the social technologies of coordination through tweaked corporate governance, and positive benefits flowing quickly to those taking these initiatives, might well trigger massive changes in structures and theories as societal change proceeds.

CONCLUSION: CULTURE AS MINDSET AND SEXTANT

When faced with the unforeseen, corporate culture becomes extremely important. In such circumstances, the usual references and instruments are relatively unhelpful, for analysis provides no answer or solution. The best one may hope for is some pattern recognition, some broad appreciation of the context, the possibility of counting on some readinesses (Vickers 1965: 67ff).

Corporate culture's key function becomes meaning-making: "constructing a sense of what is, what actually exists, and, of that, what is important" (Drath and Palus 1994: 9). The most general tool for meaning-making is culture: it helps to create names, interpretations and commitments, and it creates a framework for interpretation and understanding. While corporate cultures in the Americas are quite different, one would have to be blind not to see that a "cultural conversation" is going on, that this conversation is forging new ways of making meaning, and that a converging dissensus is crystallizing.

For the time being, the checkerboard of countries in the Americas, the bombastic defence in each of the culture they happen to be stuck with for the moment, and the lesser or greater distance they all proclaim *vis-à-vis* the United States, appear to augur badly for any diagnosis of cultural convergence. That is why the expression "converging dissensus" is so apt. It symbolically affords to all countries a sort of security zone that will bring some comfort, while, under the surface, the slow process of convergence proceeds.

This silent convergence cannot be acknowledged without automatically endangering it, so it is denied. So it should be. Yet the double-looped learning process is at work, the cultural filter is doing its screening and sorting to the tune of an old jazz ballad — "the difficult I'll do right now, the impossible may take a little while" — and the steady diet of conflicts is slowly producing valuable ties and a scintilla of trust. Little by little, piece by piece, the convergence will proceed, even if one is forced, as Albert O. Hirschman says, to "modestly respect its unpredictability", for "change can only happen as a result of surprise, otherwise it could not occur at all, for it would be suppressed by the forces that are in favour of the status quo" (Hirschman 1995: 136).

PART II

Weak Infrastructure and Inadequate Scaffolding

Introduction

Crippling epistemologies are the major impediments to a full appreciation of circumstances, but they are not the only ones. Even if one could imagine a world in which there were no intellectual, educational and cultural filters, it is simplistic to assume that there might be an immaculate conception of effective governance in the absence of some basic infrastructure capital and appropriate scaffolding. The second layer of impediments to good governance and the second important source of failures of governance is therefore the sort of weaknesses one may legitimately ascribe to engineering failures: weak informational infrastructure, poor underpinnings for accountability and inadequate organization design.

It is difficult to ascribe mental prisons to individuals. The full weight of culture explains the crippling epistemologies. The contraptions preventing the emergence of good governance structures at this second level are more the result of political failures.

There has been a mammoth political inadequacy, almost as toxic as the epistemological one, at the source of the persistence of extraordinarily poor infrastructural information capital, and accountability and design machineries. Part of it can obviously be ascribed to the sort of cognitive dissonance that has cascaded from crippling epistemologies: pathetically reductive ways of seeing and listening; an education system that has never allowed the development of a rich appreciative system; a culture that has never encouraged probing. However, some of it can be ascribed to an additional failure of due diligence, the failure to take the steps that are obviously required to ensure that adequate infrastructure capital is in place.

In fundamental ways, there has been neglect in ensuring that the minimal requirements would be met on the informational infrastructure front, on the accountability front and on the organization design front. Social science research has done little to help in defining what these basic infrastructural supports should be, and without them it has not been able to make much of an impact.

It is surprising that there has been so little concern about the informational infrastructure necessary to ensure that basic credible, relevant and timely information is available in crucial issue domains. As a result, the forum has been easily hijacked by those peddling misinformation, crass theatrics and grossly partisan opinion-venting. This has given little space to critical thinking and has served the citizenry rather poorly. Since there has been no effort to create effective forums and to stimulate critical deliberation, much of this disinformation has come to crystallize as basic reference.

There has been no interest either in developing mechanisms of intelligent accountability that would underpin greater responsibility, serve as learning mechanisms and steer organizations in the direction of more effectiveness. Excessive unintelligent accountability has simply allowed organizations to suffer a double handicap: they are unduly constrained in their routine activities, but they are prevented from experimenting for fear of being indicted for straying too far from the routine. The result has been a stunting of the social learning process.

Not only has single-looped learning (revising the means) been stunted, but second-looped learning (revising the objectives) has been obliterated by the lack of any concern about organization design. Even when signs of dysfunction materialize, there is no one who is either aware of any responsibility or charged with responsibility for initiating any redesign corrective. In fact, the design function is nobody's business.

This second layer of dysfunction, obviously deeply rooted in epistemological failures, is tantamount to poor architecture and bad engineering being compounded with a flawed knowledge base. It may explain the additional difficulties experienced on the governance front, but it requires a different set of correctives.

Chapter 4 identifies the weaknesses of the cognitive infrastructure at three levels: the lack of credible, relevant and timely information; the lack of effective forums for deliberation and negotiation; and the lack of the margin of manoeuvre necessary for experimentation.

Chapter 5 exposes the lack of intelligence in the accountability apparatus in an age that celebrates accountability, but seems to be incapable of inventing ways to avoid falling prey to the simplistic cosmology of the *ex post facto* "gotcha" mentality. Transforming it into an *ex ante* experimentalist and social learning perspective is the only way out of unintelligent accountability.

Chapter 6 underlines the immense consequences of the neglect of the organization design function as a crucial flaw in the social learning process. This is an occasion to throw some light, not only on how it might be done, but also, and more importantly, on the need to develop new modes of inquiry bent on disclosing new worlds and not just on disproving hypotheses.

CHAPTER 4

Weak cognitive infrastructure

(written with Ruth Hubbard)

The wooden horse cannot be eaten.
— ALEXANDRE VIALATTE

It is not sufficient for government to experiment with
new mechanisms or collaborative arrangements, such
as P3s, to deliver public goods that they have provided
directly, or to partition public services into different
regimes. Even though these are clearly useful devices,
they cannot suffice. An experimentalist philosophy aimed
at building open-source, serious-play governance in
Canada must have the necessary infrastructure to enable
and/or ensure the required deliberation.

Such an infrastructure, both formal and informal,
exists in part today. We have a variety of loci where
multilogues are carried out on different issues. They
range from official political forums, such as the House
of Commons and the provincial/territorial legislatures,
to all sorts of committees and forums organized by
diverse groups in civil society. However, there is a great
deal of ad-hocery about many of these sites, and many
are rather exclusive, being under the control of powerful
vested interests. This can make many of them somewhat
ineffective in allowing free and honest deliberation, and
in achieving much effective influence.

Issues such as resolving the fiscal imbalance, a government's responsibilities and its ability to finance them, or redesigning inadequate health care or education systems may appear to be simple technocratic issues, but such a view is quite misleading. In a diverse and pluralistic world, in which the objectives pursued are many and evolving, and means–ends relationships are ill-defined and unstable, neither the experts nor the populace know what the optimal response to such "wicked problems" ought to be. Discussions with all actors, only partially informed and partially dispassionate as they are, about the institutional infrastructure most likely to ensure effectiveness, efficiency and fairness, are not just an option but a necessity, if appropriate trial-and-error exploration and social learning are to ensue. This sort of discussion is not likely to emerge organically in a world plagued with a great deal of ignorance about the root causes of existing problems. Pitched battles between interest groups, underhanded manoeuvres and shamefully misleading arguments are omnipresent.

Mass collaboration cannot materialize unless some reliable information is available, along with places where citizens can interact, deliberate and co-create ideas, arrangements and institutions. Whatever names one may want to give to these exchange sites, any ethnography of the institutional scenery in any country quickly reveals important gaps that prevent the "normal" processes of discussion, collaboration, learning and co-governance from proceeding and evolving as they should under ideal circumstances. Indeed, identifying such gaps has become a cottage industry (Tapscott and Williams 2007). Governance experts have already begun to provide tool kits intended to help in defining ways in which such institutions might be constructed (Ostrom 2005).

The central question, then, is to identify the exact nature of these institutional gaps, and to imagine which of these formal or informal forums, agoras and platforms might be put in place or allowed to emerge so that: (1) wherever discussions take place, they start with a credible base of information; (2) open forums exist, if needed, where conversations and debates can take place; and (3) such forums can be constructed in such a way as to enable both the necessary reliability, and the requisite innovation and exploration of new paths that have the potential to create new positive-sum games. Having in place the capacity to explore new possibilities and exploit the arrangements that are already in place is the challenge, and this sort of mix of exploration and exploitation is at the heart of successful social learning (March 1991).

In the case of a great number of important issues, there is, in Canada, not only a shortage of credible and objective information, but also of specific places and forums for discussion. In addition, the experimentation needed for unleashing the requisite creativity is suppressed more often than it is promoted. The situation may best be illustrated by the decision of the Supreme Court of Canada in the Chaoulli case. This decision stated that if a citizen is not adequately served by public-sector health care, that citizen has a right to seek such services elsewhere. The Supreme Court's decision did not state how this should happen, and one might have imagined that there would be discussion within and between the provinces and territories about the most effective way to react to it. Yet there is no broad forum where such discussion could take place. The result is that, while discussions have taken place in various provincial forums, they have been conducted *sotto voce* and in backrooms, instead of in an open and pan-Canadian forum. The consequence is that, while one would have welcomed all the experimentation that might have led to innovations that were potentially transferable to other jurisdictions, much of this potential effervescence did not materialize for lack of adequate forums.

In *Beyond Sovereignty*, David Elkins (1995) writes about the need for an *à la carte* kind of governance in Canada. The exploration of the possibilities of this new federalism has not materialized to any great extent. The various levels of government have clung to their respective powers, and the powerful groups that sustain them have staunchly and successfully defended the status quo, even where they have been conscious that productivity and innovation can materialize only through alliances and partnerships, whether private–public–civic or federal–provincial/territorial–municipal.

Yet there is a kind of underground liveliness, not only anchored in collaboration between levels of government, but also in the efforts of the private and not-for-profit sectors, that is starting to bear fruit. Examples such as the tri-level efforts to revive East Vancouver, the experiences of Alberta's "charter schools" or the approach to health care in Alma (Quebec) and Sault Ste. Marie (Ontario) are demonstrations that "small g governance" not only exists, but is also particularly effective. Some sub-national experiments, such as in Alberta's hospitals, where the waiting time for orthopaedic surgery fell by eight-five percent or more when the diagnostic work was transferred from surgeons to nurses with very specialized training, have been carried out spontaneously. More often than not, however, such initiatives have not succeeded in emerging and, when they have, they have not led to generalization of successful practices, as a result of a lack of infrastructural institutions providing better and more accurate information, appropriate agoras for discussion of such initiatives and ways to eliminate barriers to the adoption of new ways of doing things. There is a similar need for infrastructural institutions to enable debates that would force tough issues onto the table, notwithstanding the powerful vested interests that prefer the status quo.

NEW INSTITUTIONS I

The first great handicap that needs to be overcome is the lack of credible, relevant and timely information in a large number of issue domains. At present there is no source of basic and undisputed information for most issue domains. There is not always an obvious forum in which deliberation might take place, and when it does take place it tends to be polluted with disinformation, bluffs, misrepresentations or worse, aimed at appropriating as much money as possible regardless of the legitimacy of the claim. As a result, lots of energy is expended on grandstanding, deceiving and scheming, and "Danny-Williams-izing", instead of experimenting with more productive ways of delivering public services.

Information is a public good. It is the basis upon which citizens and governments make decisions, and it can and should stimulate additional experiments, as well as experiments that are more effective and more efficient. False or misleading information can only lead to empty debates and unreasonable decisions.

A good case in point is the issue of the fiscal imbalance. Ministers and bureaucrats at the federal level have been allowed to define it in whatever way their fantasy suggests in order to support their arguments. In fact, fiscal federalism is not unlike the Augean stables: it is in need of a good cleaning. What is required is an arrangement that would ensure that clear concepts are used; that norms about argumentation and minimal accounting standards are in place; and that transparent mechanisms are enforced to ensure that each player honours the commitments made.

No such institution exists. The Council of the Federation (provincial and territorial) and the Forum of the Federation (federal) are political creatures whose aims are, strictly speaking, to protect the interests of the provincial and territorial governments or the federal government respectively. These entities may, by fluke or happenstance, elucidate the debate, but this is not their main role. The fact that they do not include even the largest of the municipalities where a majority of Canadians now live is sufficient to ensure their ineffectiveness.

What Canada lacks is what I would like to call a Social and Economic Observatory, which would have

representatives from the federal, provincial and territorial, *and* municipal levels of government, as well as
from the private sector and civil society, and that would
have as its primary responsibility the job of clarifying
concepts and eliciting credible numbers, criticizing shaky
arguments, and separating the wheat from the chaff,
so that debates could proceed with a clear vocabulary,
reasoned and reasonable arguments, credible numbers
and well-established definitions of responsibilities. Such
a reference point would have the advantage of assur-
ing participants that they can negotiate with data and
evidence resting on a credible base, one with a kind of
ISO9000 guarantee of quality. An Observatory of this
sort could be supported by a secretariat in the same
way as the various round tables that have been created
over the past few years, and would report annually on
a certain number of evolving indicators and arguments.
The aim would be to illuminate technical debates and
clear out the underbrush from the thicket of arguments,
so that citizens and elected representatives could refer to
them with confidence in their debates.

Of course, such an institution would not be a panacea.
There is too much room in these debates for emotion and
affect, and too many tensions exist around problems of
equity, control and legitimacy for anyone to hope that
consensus can be found in algebraic formulas. It would,
however, clean up the terrain to a certain extent. One
would expect, at the very least, that certain norms of
basic logic might prevail and that theatrics (of the kind
favoured by Danny Williams) would generate requisite
admonition from the Observatory. If the Observatory
could at least cleanse the deliberations of Kafkaesque
arguments, it would have played an important role.

NEW INSTITUTIONS II

A second important handicap is a lack of effective
forums. Since deliberation and negotiation are needed
in order to arrive at any agreement, for a few key issues

there must be set places where the key participants can deliberate and negotiate. These arenas must be built around issue domains that are sufficiently circumscribed to enable significant exchanges, meaningful tradeoffs and firm commitments.

For the moment, such forums do not really exist in most controversial areas, such as health care, education or the social and technical infrastructure of cities. In some cases, summit-level meetings have been arranged, involving a high degree of theatrical intensity and bilateral discussions that have looked more like horse-trading than negotiation. Confrontations or behind-the-scene plots abound, but few forums exist where all the relevant players are present and can meaningfully debate important shared challenges. These discussions should obviously build on the results of the sectoral round tables (also multi-party) that have examined the terrain of operations, cleared out the underbrush and set out preliminary proposals. An Economic and Social Council, and the sectoral round tables that might underpin it, would *not* be a substitute for legislatures, but could deal administratively with a large number of problems that do not warrant the attention of houses of assembly or governments, and yet are of central importance. In other words, within a corridor defined by a political agreement among the parties, administrative discussions could be carried out and decisions usefully made.

At a more political level, and largely within existing jurisdictional boundaries, the role of parliamentary commissions could also be reframed so that they could deal with those issues that spill over the boundaries of mere administrative matters. They would be empowered to include a broader range of representatives of civil society, if and when the nature of the issue called for it. Experience of these assemblies, such as those that examined the electoral law in British Columbia or the separation of Quebec from the rest of Canada (Bélanger–Campeau), has shown how these kinds of forums can foster unconstrained deliberation and considerable social learning.

It is even possible to imagine that these forums, *if* they have, and are seen to have, clear legitimacy, and give voice to all, without exclusion, can deal with the thorny problems of public interest with the necessary diligence, and can expose hare-brained arguments. They could establish new approaches to accountability, to the extent that they were able to look back over the capacities of each of the various players to fulfill the commitments that they had made.

However, it is not possible to construct these deliberative instances that in theory would be able to use credible base documents without accepting the hard reality that it would be unwise to postulate angelic behaviour on the part of all participants. It is quite likely that some parties will use false information and far-fetched arguments, act as shameless opportunists and fail to keep their commitments. While being mindful of the need to resist the temptation to presume suspicion, so as not to undermine trust, such behaviour must be punished if the forum is to retain legitimacy (Gintis et al. 2005).

Action by the Observatory or the Council, or its constituent round tables, to hold up to public scorn any participants that have used erroneous data, defended specious arguments or failed to meet their commitments, would carry consequences. The press could also play an important role in denouncing bad faith by one or more of the parties, or the greed of any participants defending unreasonable positions. Would the accord between Paul Martin and Danny Williams (about Newfoundland continuing to receive equalization payments even when its riches from oil development have pushed its income level into have-province territory) have been allowed to take place if it had been debated in this kind of common forum? It is very unlikely, because it would have been seen for what it was and denounced as unreasonable extortion.

These punishment mechanisms might appear to be feeble, but actually they would not be. As the Gomery Commission showed, highlighting errors, trickery and lies carries consequences. Would we have had to wait for the Supreme Court to break the ideological stranglehold of the "state or nothing" view of acute-care heath insurance in Canada if we had had forums where the issue could have been debated? How many citizens would accept a law that allows someone to buy an MRI for their dog but not for their child, if there had been forums where these travesties and anomalies could have been publicly denounced?

NEW INSTITUTIONS III

It is not enough to have basic information and strong debating forums. There must also be instances where "safe spaces" can be created within which experimentation is permitted and incentives are provided so that pilot projects can try out the new forms of organization that seem necessary. An infinite amount of talking may not necessarily produce any actual action. Implementation is the Achilles heel of social architecture.

During the Great Depression, World War II and the thirty golden years that followed, Canada granted itself permission to experiment. For example, Canadians would probably not have the public health care insurance system that exists today if it had not been for the Saskatchewan experience. The capacity to grant permission to experiment has been greatly weakened since then. The conservatism of acquired rights has largely blocked learning by doing. It has allowed powerful vested interests or ideologues to sell experimentation as a public enemy, because it often questions certain sacrosanct forms of social protection, notwithstanding their unwanted and even deplorable consequences.

At the moment, experimentation is seen as risky and anyone who dares not to conform to what is usual is quickly vilified. There are taboos everywhere in key fields such as health care and education, even though Canadian performance clearly leaves a lot to be desired. Any experimental proposal is quickly killed by the antics of state-centric ideologues, or by key elites anxious to maintain their grip on power, hiding behind arguments about the "public good". Political correctness is a new despotism. Nevertheless, opportunities to experiment continue to present themselves. With a little institutional help to provide safe spaces for experimentation on a few key issues of national importance, progress toward better results for Canadians can be accelerated.

One example might be, once again, the recent Chaoulli decision, as discussed above. Quebec had to react and Alberta was interested in exploring other avenues. Canadians could have been invited to work out various ways of responding to the Supreme Court's decision and also authorized to creatively seek alternative approaches at the margins of today's conventions. Canadians could have had a veritable explosion of experiments, many of which would have been extremely interesting and several of which might have been imitated elsewhere in the country. Instead, the combination of the legislative rigidity of the *Canada Health Act*, the threat of federal financial penalties to cash-strapped governments, and a propensity to use misleading and/or false information, permitted key elites to denounce the decision as a cardinal sin and the idea of a mixed private–public health care scheme as an abomination. There was no place for "serious play" (Schrage 2000), where the rules of the game could be suspended long enough to try things out. Possibilities for innovation in key issue domains could also emerge naturally from debates underpinned by various public consultations and carried out by legislatures, the Senate and parliamentary commissions or other working groups of officials, which could serve as regular prospecting tools for Canadian federalism. An experimentalist mindset would say that, when confronted by certain dilemmas where no obvious solutions exist, but only a series of possibilities that need to be tested, it might be reasonable to set out to explore them.

In such cases, governments and other significant players might reasonably be asked to allow and even encourage experimentation to take place, so that the pluses and minuses, the costs and benefits, could be determined in each particular case. It would not be a matter of imposing anything on anyone in particular, but of allowing experimentation and protecting those willing to experiment from being taken to court for violating some law. This kind of permission could be sought from the Council of Institutions by any interested group. It would be a way for Canadian federalism to be allowed to explore its full potential for experimentation. This Council of Institutions would have to be an adventurous kind of institution, for it would be asked no less than to authorize a kind of Mardi Gras, a temporary suspension of existing rules in the name of promising experiments. James G. March (1988) has made the case for this sort of experimentation. Such latitude to experiment would stimulate experiments that would never be realized otherwise.

Another less formal and less bold path would be the use of incentives to enable pilot projects. This approach has been used by both the federal government and the provincial government of Ontario to entice communities to harness new technologies. As a result, both at the federal level ("Smart Communities") and in Ontario ("Connect Ontario"), strategies have been put in place to open the field to communities or groupings of communities wanting to explore the possibilities of new technologies for a specific period. Explorations such as these have a double role: (1) to urge all interested parties to put forward new solutions to thorny problems so that people are led to discuss big questions that have never been discussed in public to date; and (2) to explore, if anyone feels ready to do so, various pathways to get out of the dead ends in which Canadian federalism seems stuck in certain regions, cities or provinces.

CONCLUSION

The few examples we have given in no way exhaust the range of possibilities opened up by an experimentalist, open-source approach to institutional change. They are illustrations of the sort of institutional repair that could prove to add significant value. They also represent three different ways of stimulating mass collaboration.

The central challenge of "small g governance" is the mastery of mass collaboration. If, as Harlan Cleveland (2002) argues, there is "nobody in charge", and if effective coordination when power, resources and information are widely distributed is the objective, the levers are clear: credible information to start with; the most effective platforms for participation and collaboration; and the highest and best use by the mega-community of tipping points that would get the largest number of people to enter the game, directly or indirectly, and engage in prototyping and "serious play".

A modicum of reliable information is necessary if actors are going to choose plausible strategies that make sense, and the heuristics (trial and error) would be domain-specific. That is the reason why arenas, forums and agoras have to be reliable as well. Otherwise deliberation and discussion drift into evasive babbling, and deliberation becomes meaningless. Fundamentally, however, such deliberation must evolve the sort of "ecological rationality" that matches the heuristics and the environment within which it operates (Gigerenzer and Selten 2001). Clearly this is something that can and will differ by issue domain.

CHAPTER 5

Unintelligent accountability

> *It is necessary to be intelligent*
> *to know that one is not.*
> — GEORGES BRASSENS

In his book *La contre-démocratie* (2006), Pierre Rosanvallon suggests that modern democracies such as Canada have entered an age of mistrust. A greater surveillance of officials, an emphasis on resisting, vetoing and sabotaging their actions, and a great deal of adjudication and judicialization to modulate state action have swept across modern western societies in recent years. In such a world, decision-making tends to become strained and neurotic. It is based more than ever before on hunches and impressions, rather than facts. Governments address a broad array of disparate projects in desultory fashion without much rigour or critical thinking. Leading echelons centralize power and are characterized by narcissistic needs, a desire for attention and visibility, and action for action's sake. They display an unreflective decision style.

The *Canadian Charter of Rights and Freedoms* may be regarded both as part of this process and as something that has given it a harder edge in Canada than elsewhere. The impact of the Charter has been all the more insidious given that Canadians in general, unlike the interest groups that have made a career of making use of it, have only the vaguest idea of what the Charter is or of what it has done for and to them. Moreover, the social interpretations of the Charter are quite different in English Canada, where they tend to be anti-communitarian, and in French Canada, where they tend to be communitarian (Burelle 2007).

This is the background into which the sponsorship grenade was lobbed. As Sharon Sutherland has put it:

> [S]ponsorship was a dream scandal for a political opposition: it stemmed from lack of probity; losses were not material (big enough to matter) year by year, so were allowed to run on and on while attention was concentrated on the potential for material losses elsewhere; politicians were involved; the events were so old, beginning in 1993, that a huge net had to be thrown out to recreate any kind of proper history of what had occurred; and through all these factors, the impression was created among the public of absolute carelessness, blindness and impunity (2006: 30).

The sponsorship issue was blown out of proportion by a number of parties, from the Office of the Auditor General and the Prime Minister's Office down, all of which had an interest in focusing the attention of the citizenry on that particular juicy issue in order to deflect attention from matters of greater materiality that deserved much more public scrutiny, including the ineffectiveness of the Office of the Auditor General in detecting more material frauds; the toxic effect of the centralized mindset of the federal government; and the growing malaise in the public service.

The Gomery Inquiry satisfied all those parties interested in focusing exclusively on narrow financial misdeeds and ignoring many of the contextual problems that were the root causes of the misdeeds (Hubbard and Paquet 2007). Yet the Gomery circus ended up generating a dynamic of its own that increased the level of distrust even further. The subsequent government felt obliged, because of the public concern whipped up in the process, to be seen as reacting robustly to this concern, to the point of over-reacting (as some would say) by imposing an omnibus accountability bill.

Thus "accountability" became the new mantra. "Accountability" is a weasel word: it sells well to a crowd that has thrived on growing distrust and seems to want heads to roll, but it runs the risk of becoming a toxic idea when unintelligent accountability is inflicted upon a political system. Not all accountability systems are intelligent. I would like to explore the world of accountability by probing the word, gauging the context in which it is used, identifying some of the mental prisons that affect that context, arguing for intelligent action and suggesting what it might entail in terms of social architecture. Then I would like to explain why I am somewhat pessimistic about significant improvement in the short and medium terms.

THE WORD "ACCOUNTABILITY"

One cannot understand the concept of accountability or its flip side, the concept of ethics, without elucidating the notion of burden of office, because both of these subsidiary concepts are offshoots of that quite elusive notion (Paquet 1997). In a democracy, each citizen is an official, a person with duties and obligations. He or she has stewarding work to do and is not merely a consumer of governance, but a producer of governance. Indeed, it is only because citizens *qua* citizens have duties and obligations that they are entitled to rights that ensure they are fully equipped with the capacity to meet their obligations.

There is not much meaningful debate about the nature of this burden of office and, when there is, agreement

does not necessarily ensue (Tussman 1989). The elusive-
ness of the notion is, unfortunately, unavoidable. It is a
consequence of the fact that the concept of burden of
office is based on sets of expectations and justifications
that are quite difficult to define consensually. Another
way to put it is to say that the concept is an essentially
contested one.

W. B. Gallie (1964: 161) identified five conditions for a
concept to be essentially contested, and therefore to lead,
inevitably, to endless disputes. It must be: (1) appraisive,
in the sense that it accredits some kind of valued achievement; (2) this achievement must be complex in character,
and its worth must be attributed to the achievement as a
whole; but it must be (3) variously describable in its parts,
with the possibility of various components being assigned
more or less importance; and it must be (4) open in character, to the extent that it admits considerable modification in the light of changing circumstances. Moreover, for
it to qualify as an essentially contested concept, (5) each
party must recognize that its own use of the concept is
contested by other parties. A good example of this kind
of concept might be the idea of "championship" in figure
skating, which can be judged in a number of different
ways, with differential attention being paid to method,
strategy, style and so on.

My argument is that the notion of burden of office,
like the concept of justice, is an essentially contested concept, and that it is impossible to find a general principle
to determine which party is using the concept in "the
right way". As a result, the notions of accountability
and ethics are also in some way infected: the fuzziness
of the former concept translates into some haziness in
the definition of the latter two.

Accountability refers to the requirement to "answer
for the discharge of a duty or for conduct". This presup-
poses an agreement on (1) what constitutes an acceptable performance and (2) what constitutes an acceptable
language of justification for the actors in defending

their conduct (Day and Klein 1987). Ethics is a form
of goodness of fit between the standards defined by
the burden of office and those called for by the circumstances. This judgement is embodied in action. Moral
issues are resolved in the same way that problems faced
by an industrial designer are resolved: in both cases the
challenge is to find a form that fits the circumstances,
given the constraints. When a designer interacts with a
situation, this interactive process triggers the generation
of goodness of fit between two intangibles: a form that
has not yet been designed, and a context that cannot be
properly and fully described, because it is still evolving
(Alexander 1964). The essentially contested nature of the
notion of burden of office makes it impossible for ethical
conduct to escape a certain degree of fuzziness.

The fact that the notion of burden of office is essentially contested does not, of course, prevent different
parties from claiming that their use of the concept is
the only one that can command honest and informed
approval. Consequently there are different views about
accountability and ethical behaviour. This is perilous,
because, as the essential contestedness of the concept
transpires, there is always a real danger that those in
authority may grow impatient with trying to persuade
all the other parties, and be led to "a ruthless decision to
cut the cackle, to damn the heretics and to exterminate
the unwanted" (Gallie 1964: 189). The result is that
conversation and deliberation are then interrupted, and
democracy is in danger.

Another danger is that the use of the words "accountability" or "ethics" may convey to the uninformed a
misplaced sense of concreteness, when, in fact, they connote a wide range of realities. In English one gets a sense
of the fluffiness of the concept of accountability when it
is seen as part of a family of related words, constituting
a sort of archipelago of fuzzy words: "accountability",
"responsibility", "answerability", "liability", "blam-
ability" and the like.

THE CONTEXT OF ACCOUNTABILITY

Both accountability and ethics are conditioned by context, and the context has evolved significantly. The degree of relevant uncertainty and turbulence has increased as the intensity of interaction has grown. Over the past twenty-five years, modern democracies have experienced a broad range of reforms in the organization of all sectors — private, public and social. This has resulted not only from pressures generated by globalization and accelerated technological change, but also, and most importantly, as a result of greater cultural diversity, heightened and diverse citizens' expectations, crises in public finances new ideologies and so forth.

These pressures have eroded many basic assumptions upon which the more traditional forms of governing were built. The most important of these eroded assumptions are: (1) the notion that the state must dominate governing (state-centricity) because the public sector can be presumed to do most things more effectively than the other two; (2) a fixation on "one size fits all" uniformity in the delivery of public services; and (3) the notion that a firewall must exist between the public sector and the rest of society. As a result, Canadian society has evolved into something that can most usefully be thought of as a complex adaptive system (CAS), an interacting and evolving set of some thirty million individuals bound together by technologies and structures.

This CAS has four main characteristics. First, it is open, meaning that it receives material and immaterial resources from the external environment. It is forced to continually adapt to its environment and is therefore shaped to a fair degree by its context. As a whole it is like a living organism, capable of scanning the context and managing its interdependence with the environment.

Second, because it is open, the system must adapt to its environment, modifying its social and technical texture in response to the changes in the environment, if it wishes to maintain a certain goodness of fit with the context and to be adopted by it. (Adoption here means that the environment bestows on the organism a higher probability of survival and prosperity if a higher degree of goodness of fit prevails.) The goodness of fit between the context and the social system generates high performance, while misfits produce lower levels of performance.

Third, an open and adaptive system must modify its technologies, processes and structures in an effort to respond strategically and effectively to the environment. This entails a process of differentiation of the system to respond to the different challenges encountered.

Fourth, in a complex system in which the interactions among the millions of individuals and their organizations generate a dynamic of their own, every agent is forced not only to detect patterns in the torrent of inputs it receives from the outside, but also to convert them into changes in the internal structure. Such is the complexity of these interactions that agents cannot analyze them *ex ante*. For high performance to ensue for the system, they must discover new rules and new behaviours that generate the requisite coordination and integration as they go along (Holland 1995). This puts a premium on experimentation.

This contextual evolution has triggered nothing less than a refoundation of the process of governing, which has been drifting away from a regime that we have labelled "Big G government" — a state-centric, centralized, massively redistributive regime — toward a regime that is more decentralized, polycentric (with the state acting much more as moderator or catalyst), network-based and only prudently redistributive, and that we have labelled "small g governance". The political culture of western democracies has been transformed as the result of a change in the texture of the environment, becoming more effervescent, and demanding more subtle and more fluid governance.

Canadian society has, therefore, become differentiated and integrated in a particular manner over time, and its governance has had to evolve accordingly. To enable the system to maintain itself, to aggrandize and to innovate, governance must be as varied and diverse as the environment and the interactions it is trying to deal with. This is the "law of requisite variety", first formulated by Ross Ashby (Ashby 1956), though it has received many other formulations. The canonical one is: for appropriate regulation, the variety of the regulator must be equal to or greater than the variety of the system being regulated. In other words, the capacity of a system to evolve and to learn effectively, and thus to govern itself in an effective manner, depends on its capacity to adjust its governing to more complex forms of differentiation and integration, to be able to deal with the variety of challenges and opportunities in novel ways, while maintaining its coherence through time by retaining or shedding characteristics that are sources of good fits or misfits respectively.

In such a world, accountability is no longer linear but has become 360-degree accountability, because the burden of office entails meeting the evolving expectations, not only of hierarchical superiors, but also of partners, clients, allies, acquaintances and the like. The consequent increase in the level of complexity of the notion of accountability has been exponential. Accountability has become a nexus of moral contracts with this wide and diverse array of close and remote collaborators.

Yet, at a time when more flexibility, and a greater capacity to experiment and to innovate, both appear to be required, the dynamic conservatism of the interest groups that have developed their power bases in the pre-existing structures has also grown immensely. The notion of acquired rights has become a reference point, and the success of the interest groups in consolidating their position has led to the introduction of significant social rigidities, often to the point of rendering societies somewhat arterio-sclerotic and immensely resistant to change (Kindleberger 1978; Olson 1982).

This latter process of ossification has been particularly important in countries such as Canada that have fostered a process of judicialization and adjudication, in part, in Canada's case, through the proclamation of the *Charter of Rights and Freedoms*. This process has allowed many groups to express their preferences in a language of rights and to use the Charter in the courts to stall the process of change (Paquet 2007). The tension between the need for flexibility and the reluctance to allow for flexibility, has resulted in a process of evolution that has been much slower than many would have liked. Despite the impediments generated by the activism of interest groups, there has been a slow drift from "Big G government" to "small g governance", but this drift has been forcefully resisted, especially by federal bureaucrats, adjudicators and commissars, whose centralized mindset has led them to take full advantage of incidents and mishaps to call for additional controls and the strengthening of top–down governing.

Accordingly, the emergence of Möbius-web governance has been stalled, and any experimentalism that might lead in this direction has been discouraged. Möbius-web governance is characterized by mixed formal and informal structures, and by processes that are multi-directional (vertical, horizontal and transversal) and overlapping over several levels to form "a singular weblike process" (Rosenau 2003: 397).

MENTAL PRISONS

Given officials' reluctance to recognize that top–down hierarchical control might not work, the stage has been set for the reign of unintelligent accountability. This is not the place to provide an exhaustive analysis of all the mental prisons and ideological trappings that have prevented the emergence of intelligent accountability, but it is possible to identify a few of the main ones.

The first mental prison is the denial of complexity. If there is one important lesson to be learned from the analysis of complex environments, it is that it is unwarranted to assume that for every unwanted consequence there is always one originator at the source, and that deterring him/her by threat of punishment will solve the problem. Such an assumption is often erroneous. In complex adaptive systems, the degree of interaction is such that it is often impossible to ascribe responsibility to any one person or group. The propensity to regard any situation as calling for the discovery and incrimination of one or many culpable parties, is one of the most common biases generated by the accountability industry. The Gomery Inquiry was not asked to identify guilty parties, yet it could not resist the temptation to do so and may be said to have done it in an amateurish manner (Paquet 2006d).

Intervening in a naïve Skinnerian stimulus–response manner in complex human organizations, in the name of rationalism but on the basis of a very primitive and reductionist view of the world, can only lead to extraordinarily bad unintended consequences. M. M. Harmon has sharply criticized the "rationalist" discourse on government by arguing that the notion of responsibility with "ethical correctness and the conformity of action with authoritative ends" is "necessarily flawed in a fundamental way" (Harmon 1995: 5). Paradox is everywhere in public administration. For Harmon, the usual rationalist representation of accountability and ethics is an "irresponsible masquerade" that cannot escape the paradoxes it attempts to abolish (Harmon 1995: 65).

This is probably the most dangerous mental prison, since it is part of the intellectual capital of a large number of public institutions. It leads one to substitute a reductive mental construct for a much more complicated reality, and to merrily pretend to deal with the issues when one is merely tinkering with a cartoonish model of the world.

The second mental prison is the fixation on a very limited subset of "gotcha" accountabilities. Not only is the context such that the causal flow may be impossible to ascertain, but, in the complex world in which we now

live, officials are confronted with: (1) many interfaces
with different stakeholders, each with different claims
to authority (hierarchical superior, professional colleague, client and so on); (2) many types of accounts
demanded (political, managerial, legal, professional and
others); and (3) considerable complexity, heterogeneity
and uncertainty in the circumstances surrounding the
activities for which one is said to be accountable. This
results in a great deal of fuzziness in the definition of
accountability.

There is a great temptation to focus only on some
sub-aspects of this nexus of accountabilities, especially
those that lend themselves to quantitative marshal-
ling, and to generate black-and-white conclusions and
indictments on the basis of a very partial and reductive
appraisal. This mix of quantophrenia and Manichaeism
is toxic and often leads to conclusions deduced from
flat-earth type assumptions. The Office of the Auditor
General has shown a propensity to indulge in "gotcha" activities, calling certain practices unacceptable
on the basis of very narrow and contestable financial
accountability standards, without much attention being
paid to other key dimensions, such as performance
(Paquet 1999b).

The third mental prison is the false belief in openness and transparency as panaceas. It matters little that
considerable evidence has shown that transparency is no
panacea when it comes to deception, and that openness
and transparency may be immensely costly in terms of
hampering good governance and effective performance.
Onora O'Neill has forcefully argued that, although openness and transparency may replace deference and secrecy,
they do not necessarily generate trust, or limit deception
and deliberate misinformation (O'Neill 2002: 70). This
has not stopped the auditing phalanx from pursuing
strategies almost entirely based on a call for what Warren
Bennis (1976: 116) calls "well-intended goldfish-bowl
rules ... [that] have unintended results worse than the

evils they seek to forestall". They are likely to produce more secrecy, not less (only more carefully concealed), and, on top of it, so hamstring already overburdened administrators as to throw their tasks into deeper confusion. For secrecy is one thing; confidentiality is another. No organization can function effectively without certain amounts of confidentiality in the proposals, steps and discussions leading up to its decisions — which decisions should then, of course, be open, and generally will be.

The fourth mental prison is reluctance to experiment and innovate. Most organizations have considerable capital invested in routine and any transformation is bound to expropriate the privileged positions or advantages of a number of parties. As a result change is too often seen as a zero-sum game, where everyone presumes that the only possible gains will be to the detriment of other parties. Thus it is easy to understand why the dice are loaded against change. Very often the gains as a result of change remain only potentialities, while the losses are mostly obvious and measurable. This is why Albert Hirschman could write that "change can only happen as a result of surprise, otherwise it could not occur at all, for it would be suppressed by the forces that are in favour of the status quo" (Hirschman 1995: 136). So the propensity to innovate is weakened.

What is required to break out of this particular mental prison is to transform the view of change as a zero-sum game into a positive-sum game perspective (Wright 2000). This opens the way to collaborative exploration and, through experimentalism, rekindles a new form of dynamic solidarity and the emergence of "experimentalist accountability" through mechanisms of performance monitoring, comparative benchmarking, pooled experiences of diverse and often rivalrous groups, and practical deliberation focused on the need to respond to urgent problems that call for mobilizing some discovery procedure (Sabel 2001).

These mental prisons (and there are many more) are important because they stunt the whole process of social learning. They lock accountability into a backward-looking mode and they reduce a multi-dimensional world to a few measurable dimensions. This can produce pathologies through an undue simplification of the "fundamental, unresolved and perhaps unresolvable tensions" that characterize human behaviour (Hirschman 1986: 158).

THE DEED

Avoiding such pathologies cannot suffice. What is called for is a reframing of the notion of accountability in a manner that ensures that all the relevant stakeholders are fully engaged, and that all the important standards are evoked in the creative dialogue and the creative practice from which viable compromises emerge. This means 360-degree intelligent accountability, a form of accountability that avoids these mental prisons, is forward-looking, exploratory and experimentalist in focus, and feeds effective and creative social learning. Onora O'Neill has proposed the beginning of an answer in her Reith Lectures:

> Intelligent accountability, I suspect, requires more attention to good governance and fewer fantasies about total control. Good governance is possible only if institutions are allowed some margin for self-governance of a form appropriate to their particular tasks, within a framework of financial and other reporting. Such reporting, I believe, is not improved by being wholly standardized or relentlessly detailed, and since much that has to be accounted for is not easily measured it cannot be boiled down to a set of stock performance indicators. Those who are called to account should give an *account* of what they have done, and of their successes and failures, to others who have sufficient time and experience to assess the evidence and report on it. Real accountability provides substantive

and knowledgeable independent judgement of an institution's or professional's work (O'Neill 2002: 58).

We must recognize that: (1) the modern context is complex and not easily reducible to simplistic cause–effect dyadic relationships; (2) selective standardized measures of control are not effective and may even generate, as unintended consequences, a reduction in the level of trust; (3) openness, transparency and quantophrenia may not be the unconditional goods that they are supposed to be; and (4) it is absurd to pretend to manage our complex systems as if they were populated either by angelic Cartesian wantons or by a bunch of knaves and crooks. What ensues is a new focus on earning trust in the long run; a rejection of naïve devices such as openness and transparency as pseudo-levers; and much more attention being paid, in the short run, to targets such as deception and misinformation. This may appear to be unduly negative in the short run, but I feel that it is absolutely necessary. Experts such as Paul Thomas (2007) have put more emphasis on building trust. I agree with Thomas that the many ways in which one may build trust in the long term are quite important, but, in the short run, some focus on the major impediments to good governance is crucial. This is why one needs to focus explicitly on some of the negative sides of the issue, for the usual accountability apparatus does not appear to deal with major impediments, including deception and misinformation.

DEALING WITH DECEPTION

There is an extraordinary reluctance in the public service to deal with the notion of disloyalty. Most public servants are in denial: for them, such a thing seems to be inconceivable. Yet many, both in the public service and in the media, appear to have a licence to deceive.

What is disloyalty? It is knowingly and deliberately breaking the moral contracts defining the burden of office. There is general agreement that disloyalty may have increased over the past ten or twenty years. Many have ascribed this phenomenon to genuine disagreement ensuing from the greater complexity of policy issues and to the possible multiplicity of interpretations of these issues. These ratiocinations do not suffice to explain the observed phenomena.

A culture of disloyalty has been developing. It is more than passive disloyalty, a dwarfing interpretation of what is expected and required as part of the burden of office, and verges on active disloyalty through deliberate undermining of superiors and/or betraying the trust of partners and citizens (Hubbard and Paquet 2007b). Whether the deception is passive or active, it "is not a marginal moral failure. Deceivers do not treat others as moral equals; they exempt themselves from obligations that they rely on others to live up to" (O'Neill 2002: 71).

Unless this sort of behaviour, which amounts to betrayal and treachery, is seriously punished, there is no way that trust can ever be rebuilt. Yet the capacity and willingness of the public service to shield deceivers from any punishment, and even to reward such behaviour by lateral promotions, especially out of the country, stand as a constant reinforcement of this sort of behaviour. In fact, it has become obvious that the public service has neither the capacity nor the will to police that sort of behaviour, especially in its upper ranks, any more than the RCMP, or CISIS or some noble professions (such as the law) have been able to. It is obvious that a lay authority must develop an oversight role to deal with such activities. This is not an easy matter to deal with, and there will be accusations of McCarthyism by self-righteous public servants; but unless deception is robustly deterred, the whole institution of the public service as an independent and non-partisan organization is in peril. It is not sufficient for the mechanisms of accountability to promote openness, transparency and layers of control, in the naïve hope that the democratic accountability of government, the ministerial accountability of the cabinet and the managerial accountability of senior public servants will automatically and organically ensue.

The new ethos that has been constructed around the so-called accountability of public servants to assure the integrity of policies and programmes, has created a great deal of confusion. It has opened the possibility of senior public servants arrogating the power to decide what is in the public interest and determining when their duty to serve the elected government loyally is trumped by their own interpretation of their accountability. Deception will thrive unless: (1) this interface is clarified anew; (2) a principle of precedence is clearly defined among these loyalties; (3) the burden of office is reaffirmed as calling for active and creative support for the policies chosen by the elected government; and (4) stiff punishment is imposed for deception or failure to provide the best possible support.

These are necessary but clearly not sufficient conditions for trust to be rebuilt. Serious deliberation is required if unacceptable distortions are to be avoided. For instance, loyalty to the elected government should not be construed as condoning moral numbness and Eichmannism. The notion of loyalty is not an unconditional good either. In the words of Joseph Tussman, "loyalty is a dog without moral judgement" (Tussman 1989: 66). Public servants have a duty, as part of their burden of office, to provide the best advice to their political masters as fully as possible. If, having fully exercised their "voice" option to no avail, they feel that they cannot allow themselves to be identified or associated with certain policies being implemented, and have given up on working patiently for change within the system, they must "exit" and risk becoming outsiders (Bennis 1976: 54), rather than feeling that they have a licence to deceive or a duty to be actively disloyal to their political masters. In the same manner, all the other suggestions require clarifying discussion.

DEALING WITH MISINFORMATION

Equally important, and often more difficult to pin down, is misinformation, because it is a more diffuse problem, often ascribable to many actors in any social system. It is also much more difficult to expose because of the difficulty of assessing to what extent, in particular circumstances, information has been allowed to be circulated, even when it was incomplete, or whether disinformation was purposely circulated to deceive.

Misinformation often originates from official organizations and institutions, but it is also generated by the media and special interest groups. The only way to counter this flow of disinformation is by active checking. This is very difficult, quite time-consuming and not always possible for the ordinary citizen. Some have argued that the media are supposed to provide critical assessments of the information they distribute, but this is quite naïve. Despite the many newspapers and broadcasters that have charters and codes calling for impartiality, accuracy, fairness, giving a full view, editorial independence, respect for privacy, standards of taste and decency, and so on and so forth, the media remain "erratically reliable and unassessable" (O'Neill 2002: 77 and 89–90).

Super-bureaucrats, who are purportedly the super-defenders of the highest standards on this front, do not necessarily fare better. From time to time gross disinformation has been detected and exposed. Some will remember, for example, the deliberate misinformation concocted by James Coyne when he was Governor of the Bank of Canada (see Gordon 1961). The personal costs borne by H. Scott Gordon as a result of his drive to expose Coyne's misinformation, offer a cautionary tale. Gordon's original letter was signed by twenty-nine economists and the short book he wrote soon after demonstrated very effectively that there had been deception on Coyne's part; but after the event Gordon was marginalized and shunned by the federal bureaucracy. His part-time career as a mediator in public service affairs was brought to a halt, and his views were ignored by a royal commission on monetary affairs even though he was one of the best-known Canadian experts in this area. He later left Canada to pursue a successful career in the United States. This cautionary tale illustrates the perils of exposing deception and misinformation generated by officialdom in the public sector in Canada. The affair did lead to the removal of Coyne from his post, but only because Gordon brought it all to light. Nothing indicates that the defence mechanisms of the public sector have been in any way weakened over the past fifty years, and I know of many fabricators of misinformation and deception in the media whose careers have been consolidated by such actions, and who remain at their pulpits to this day.

The lack of critical thinking and the deliberate confusion among genres in the information industry, which presents factual reports, babbling by opinionated and less than fully informed columnists, and irresponsible rants by ideologically tainted journalists as if they are all information, leaves the public at the mercy of people who literally have a licence to deceive. Given the fact that citizens are exposed on a daily basis to this sort of distortion, it is not surprising that, as a result of such a diet, a high level of democratic incompetence exists among the citizenry.

THE SOCIAL ARCHITECTURE REQUIRED

Can one put in place, as a stop-gap measure, some institutional changes that might directly address deception and misinformation, the two major sources of distrust? Distrust is not simply a loss of trust, like a loss of grace, because things went wrong. Distrust is often built into our institutions, and is a cultural norm followed, consciously or not, by most. As such it represents a strategy of risk management. The only way to escape the cycle of distrust is through discussion leading to persuasion

and change (Earle and Cvetkovich 1995: 5). To respond
to the pressure for openness, transparency and the like,
some social carpentering is in order and might be most
useful. Although none of the contraptions that I will suggest should be regarded as panaceas, they would signal
a determination to deal with these two major sources of
dysfunction. The new mechanisms likely to reduce distrust should be seen as part of a new social architecture
likely to tilt the present accountability regime somewhat,
from a focus on conforming and a backward-looking
perspective, to a focus on performance and a forward-
looking outlook.

Not much can be done to improve Canada's performance until one can increase the general level of collaboration and co-operation within and among sectors.
Such arrangements require not necessarily trust, but at
least accurate information. There must also be forums
in which to debate, and there need to be real margins
of manoeuvrability to experiment and to innovate.
Currently the necessary infrastructure that would guarantee high-quality information, ensure vibrant forums,
and grant permission to experiment and innovate does
not exist in Canada. A number of new institutions are
necessary: a monitoring agency that would assess the
quality and reliability of information; forums where
governments, the private sector and the non-profit sector could debate important national issues in particular
domains; and a council that would make promising
experimentation possible even when it appears to trans-
gress the existing rules (Hubbard and Paquet 2006).

Many other mechanisms may also be required to
institute some form of "soft" accountability built on
earned trust. They will require time and a reframing of
the very notion of accountability, from a narrow focus
on rear-view-mirror financial audits in a world of knaves,
where exacting top–down controls are mandatory, and
blaming is the objective if one is to ensure conformity,
toward a broad focus on forward-looking assessments of

moral contracts at 360 degrees, with a view to fostering experimentation and social learning in a world geared to better performance.

In the very short term, however, the matter of deception requires direct action. A lay oversight agency might be charged, first, with the task of defining the contours of the nexus of "accountability moral contracts" based on a sound definition of the different officials' burden of office (Parliament, executive, public service). The composition of such a lay oversight committee might evolve over time, but it should initially be a credible blue-ribbon group whose members are seen as being above reproach (I would suggest, for example, Ed Broadbent, Monique Bégin, Claude Castonguay, Preston Manning and Gordon Robertson, though others would disagree). This group would help to clarify the major interfaces, and define the future mission and role of such a committee. Such a committee would be quite different in mandate and focus from the sort of committee suggested by Tom Axworthy to prepare an accountability code, but the composition envisaged for both committees is not dissimilar (Axworthy 2005). This oversight committee at first would attempt to clarify the reasonable expectations one might have of the different actors and the nature of the moral contracts likely to echo the contours of these burdens of office. It would also act in the early phase in a mediation mode, to ascertain the boundaries defining what can only be considered to be deception. Its opinions would be made public and might help to determine the nature of legitimate expectations in different cases. As with oversight committees in other areas, the purpose would not be to blame, but to improve performance. It would not adjudicate, but merely issue opinions. In that way it might break the existing mould where the senior bureaucracy acts as a solipsistic entity and relies unduly on ineffective self-regulation in these matters.

In the matter of misinformation, active checking and critical thinking pose a much more difficult challenge. In

Chapter 4, Ruth Hubbard and I suggested the creation of a Social and Economic Observatory to ensure the dissemination of reliable information, but this observatory could not be expected to perform the whole complex Herculean task. It may serve, however, as a basis for the development of some critical appraisal of the available information. Such an observatory could also play an important role, not only in quality control but in creating a culture of critical thinking about the interpretation and misuse of data. Still, one must realize that, important though such an institution may be in the short run, it is likely to take ten years or more to change the existing culture of gullibility prevailing among the Canadian citizenry.

It is worth underlining the observations that Onora O'Neill (2002) has derived from her scrutiny of the media. They are the source of much disinformation and deception, and it is unlikely, according to her, that a surge of critical thinking and self-assessment will materialize organically. In the long run nothing will replace making all information assessable, as well as the emergence of a new spirit that would challenge the licence to misinform and deceive.

A SOCIAL LEARNING FRAMEWORK

A sextant may be useful in this voyage of discovery of forward-looking and experimentalist accountability. Forward-looking experimentalist accountability is geared to social learning, based on an appreciation of the difference between what is expected and what happens, and embraces this "error" as a way to evaluate and adjust action. This learning can occur only under certain conditions: (1) if the conversation with the situation is conducted within a context where the ethos is sufficiently rich and supportive (the sum of characteristic usages, ideas and codes by which a group is differentiated is strong enough to allow a meaningful conversation to be carried out); and (2) if the conversation, deliberation and accumulation of judgements are conducted with tact and civility, with a capacity to span boundaries and to synthesize multiple logics.

This sort of learning does not necessarily congeal in formalized rules. Its cumulative result remains very much tacit knowledge, a capacity to deal effectively with matters of practice in a timely manner, with a full appreciation of the local and the particular context. Such accumulated tacit knowledge is predicated on the fact that through experience we learn a great deal and that at any time we know more than we can tell (Polanyi 1966). This is the way knowledge evolves in common law: case by case and often in a tacit way. (There is considerable opposition to this approach in traditional political science and public administration circles, where power dimensions trump all others and make non-hierarchical relations difficult to understand. This general suspicion of the very notion of governance is evident from almost every page in, for example, Hermet et al. 2005.)

The new accountability cannot be defined in a single direction, or with reference to only one stakeholder. That would amount to assuming that only one dimension is of consequence, and that all other forms of accountability can be regarded as irrelevant or in some sense secondary. Any framework worth using must, therefore, have the following five components:

(1) a focus on risk and exposure rather than pro-grammes, carried out with social learning and performance in mind, and not compliance and conformity, and regarded as a tool for change, and therefore as founded in experiments and innovation;

(2) a 360-degree process pertaining to all the stakeholders surrounding the official;

(3) considerable prudence in balancing the push or supply forces (living up to one's perception of one's burden of office) and the pull or demand forces (the need to meet the expectations and demands of the various other stakeholders);

(4) operation at many levels (legal, organizational, professional, political and so on); and

(5) implementation through layers of compatible moral contracts.

The basis for the first two components has been developed above. The third component of our framework was proposed by Robert Nozick (1981), and it is rooted in the tension between the push and the pull forces, or as an economist would put it, the supply and demand sides. Accountability will be satisfactory when the push forces are greater than, or equal to, the pull forces. This can be easily applied to a vast network of relationships among many different stakeholders in very many dimensions.

For the fourth component we may turn to M. J. Dubnik (1996), who has used the Nozick push-and-pull framework and applied it to four types of institutional forms in order to illustrate eight species of accountability. On the pull or demand side, one finds an array of institutional factors that frame the challenges faced by any official confronted with multiple, diverse and often conflicting expectations. On the push or supply side, are the more personal ways of interpreting the burden of office that materializes in traits such as an internalized sense of obligation, obedience, fidelity or loyalty, and amenability (the desire to actively pursue the public interest). Table 5.1 summarizes these species of accountability.

The fifth component of the framework is borrowed from Thomas Donaldson and Thomas W. Dunfee's (1994) integrative social contracts theory, which defines different layers or lattices of moral contracts as tools to ensure "good" performance for an organization. The moral contracts are at three levels: hypernorms, such as the obligation to respect the dignity of each person, that apply to all concerns; conditions under which the different communities operate; and microsocial contracts pertaining to expectations at the operating level.

In summary, then, the framework would be based on exposure to new risks, and focused on performance, forward-looking experimentalist accountability; pull and push *à la* Nozick (1981); various settings *à la* Dubnik (1996); and layers of moral contracts *à la* Donaldson and Dunfee (1994). It would reveal the great complexity of standards in vogue, even in organizations with traditional hierarchical structures. However, in new, more modular and network-like organizations where coordination and partnering are the order of the day, the number of relevant stakeholders increases significantly, issue domains get differentiated, and a multiplication of micro moral contracts becomes necessary to ordain the relationships among stakeholders, especially as "collaborative exploration" (Sabel 2001: 133) blossoms.

This makes the accountability challenge even more daunting. In this sort of world, each actor and group is accountable to a variety of stakeholders. A multitude of standards, not all compatible, and some even contradictory, are in play in different issue domains and with different time horizons. Accordingly, some priority rules must be elicited. Moreover, external pressures force organizations to explore new arrangements in order to survive.

Two major challenges confront those trying to use such a framework: (1) what are the basic principles that should guide the creation of the necessary conditions for

TABLE 5.1 Species of accountability

	Conduct of accountability (external pull)	*Accountability of conduct (internal push)*
Legal	Liabilities	Obligations
Organizational	Answerability	Obedience
Professional	Responsibility	Fidelity
Political	Responsiveness	Amenability

Source: Dubnik 1996

good performance-oriented, forward-looking and experimentalist accountability?; and (2) what priority rules should prevail when the different moral contracts appear to be incompatible? It is impossible to deal thoroughly with these issues here, but one may at least set the stage for further discussion by providing some guideposts.

On the first front (basic principles), we can use the prudent principles developed over the past ten years or so, in a variety of settings, as complex alternative service delivery arrangements that have been instituted to replace the traditional paternalistic state-centric systems (Tassé 1996; Office of the Auditor General 1999; Posner 2006). The minimum conditions of accountability that most appear to agree on are:

- clear rules and understanding as to who is responsible for what;
- balanced expectations and capacities;
- adequate authority and resources;
- adequate reporting mechanisms;
- reasonable review and adjustment mechanisms;
- appropriate transparency; and
- full recognition that different accountability regimes are necessary, depending on the nature of the government's role as master, partner or third party.

These guiding principles may help to ensure an adequate infrastructure that aims to avoid misinformation and deception.

On the second front (priority rules), it is not as easy to come up with guideposts. I would simply indicate that a lot of work has been done to develop the foundations of the principle of precedence to be used to determine ways in which the different accountabilities should be ranked and the different priorities ordered. For instance, the principle of precedence has been used effectively by Harry Frankfurt (1988: Chapter 8) and David Braybrooke (1987) to differentiate between needs and preferences. It also has some moral force in the definition of "capabilities" or "freedoms" that have to be given some priority to ensure development in a world of limited resources (Sen 1999a).

Any such prioritization process may lead to quite different results from place to place and from time to time, and it needs to be continually discussed and revised in the experimentalist world *à la* John Dewey (1927). Yet there is a general reluctance to discuss the foundations of such a process of hierarchization. The fact that it is not completely theorized does not mean that such criteria are not used. Governments *de facto* invent such schemes when determining what services will be removed from the official schedule of services offered as public goods to the citizenry. These choices are often controversial, but the idea, for example, that basic health needs should take precedence over cosmetic surgery — so that, if resource scarcity requires that one of these be removed from the schedule of services provided free of charge, it should be the latter and not the former — would probably not only receive wide support, even though citizens are not usually consulted on such matters, but would be perceived by politicians as easy to justify in public debates.

CONCLUSION

Intelligent, forward-looking and experimentalist accountability is quite a challenge. That is why those who prefer to simplify complex issues have had a field day. As H. L. Mencken wrote: "for every problem there is a solution which is simple, clean and wrong". Unintelligent accountability, in the form of standardized, narrowly defined, quantophrenic, top–down, formal rules, has descended upon us like a plague. This new credo has its own corps of Swiss Guards, a phalanx of rear-view-mirror, blame-seeking auditors, who have great difficulty in disentangling the difference between challenge and calumny simply because these two words have the same etymological root.

I have offered intelligent accountability as an alternative. It is based on a better understanding of the notion of burden of office and its context; it is of necessity "soft"; and, if it is to be effective, it must be forward-looking, and geared to experimentalism, social learning and better performance. Intelligent accountability, unfortunately, cannot count on panaceas such as openness or transparency to do all the work. It must proceed by attacking the viruses of deception and misinformation first, and then focus on building trust and improving governance.

At the core of this second and longer-term task is the crucial notion of moral contracts, which would have to be negotiated by officials with their 360-degree stakeholders, and often in different ways in different issue domains, if forward-looking experimentalist accountability is to generate social learning and innovation. In the long run this line of inquiry can only build on such elusive notions as trust, conscience, loyalty and burden of office, notions that are known to provoke hives and hot flashes in the quantophrenic professions.

That is why it is important to begin the requisite "re-education" immediately, with the therapeutic use of irony. Allow me to start this process by injecting the word "conscience" into our discussion with auditors through the marvellous definitions that Mencken proposed: "conscience is the inner voice that warns us that somebody may be looking", or, if you prefer, "conscience is a mother-in-law whose visit never ends" (www.quotationspage.com/quote/34477.html). Can one find a quantophrenic formula for this elusive notion?

Norman Malcolm (1984: 57–58) recounts the one incident in the life of Ludwig Wittgenstein that showed him the limits of his theory and led him to elaborate an entirely different philosophical system in the second part of his life:

> Wittgenstein and Sraffa ... argued together a great deal over the ideas of the *Tractatus*. One day (they were

riding, I think, on a train) when Wittgenstein was insist-
ing that a proposition and that which it describes must
have the same "logical form," the same "logical multiplicity," Sraffa made a gesture, familiar to Neapolitans
as meaning something like disgust or contempt, of brush-
ing the underside of his chin with an outward sweep
of the fingertips of one hand. And he asked: "What is
the logical form of *that*?" Sraffa's example produced in
Wittgenstein the feeling that there was an absurdity in
the insistence that a proposition and what it describes
must have the same form. This broke the hold on him
of the conception that a proposition must literally be a
"picture" of the reality it describes.

When can we expect something as revolutionary as
Sraffa's gesture to materialize, and from where is it likely
to come?

CHAPTER 6

Organization design neglected

> *... bringing people together to*
> *make something different happen ...*
> —HARLAN CLEVELAND (2002: 000)

Organization design is to governance what engineering is to science: the essential process of operationalization without which good reflective work is bound to remain fruitless. Yet this design work is poorly understood and quite difficult to execute, and is therefore not well done. It is the Achilles' heel of governance, the weak point not very carefully attended to, and it is likely to be the source of failures of governance and of poor performance.

For various reasons this weakness is more important nowadays than it used to be. Forty years ago it was merrily asserted that "structure follows strategy" and structure was seen as a mechanism through which strategy would be realized (Chandler 1962). This may have been the case in the relatively placid environments of earlier times, but in turbulent environments such as the ones the world is experiencing these days it is no longer true.

In today's contexts *ex ante* strategizing is, in a wide range of instances, quickly made obsolete by transformations in the context. Making the highest and best use of an existing organization's properties and capacities is often the best that strategists can do. Consequently, the nature of organizations has come to play a more determining role in the decisions that are made and the strategies that are chosen. In the short run, ideally, a designer must try to shape the relatively more "inert" dimensions of an organization, in such a way that they will tend to provide the greatest leverage and the widest margin of manoeuvrability when strategic decisions have to be made. If this is not done, an organization may be trapped by its flawed design into drifting in very unpromising directions. In the longer run, an organization's design must be adjusted, through social learning, to keep the organization in line with new missions and contexts. In fact, this does not necessarily occur.

An organization's design is often inherited from tradition and history, or is the result of improvisation by newcomers eager to make their mark on the organization they have just recently joined. In both cases there is often not a good fit between the design, the mission and the context. However, because of the prevailing myth that strategy should determine structure, back-of-envelope strategies are often hastily drafted, and the ensuing job of carpentering the appropriate organization, regarded as part of routine management, is delegated to junior executives as part of the implementation of the willed strategy. It is hardly surprising that what ensues is not of great significance. It is only when catastrophes hit the organization that redesign takes a front seat. Yet in such critical times, again, panic strikes, improvisation prevails and what is presented as organization design is nothing more than trite tinkering with the organization chart, on the basis of something too often sketched in an amateurish way.

A second reason why the design function is often performed badly is that it is not widely understood that organizations are not static fixtures but living entities. Very much like buildings, they evolve, despite their constraining structures, as their occupants take hold of them, and transform their functions and missions in ways that were never planned. The only difference is that evolution occurs at a much faster pace in organizations, and often in more dramatic ways, as a result of the unintended consequences of all sorts of interactions, planned and unplanned. Consequently, organizations suffer from various forms of fibrillation, arteriosclerosis or the like, signalling that the old organizational form is no longer adjusted to the challenges of the day. As a result of these tensions, the organization evolves, but often in ways that go undetected, so a chasm develops between the formal shape of the organization on paper and its real-life counterpart, and a new and quite different organization emerges under the veneer of the formally acknowledged one.

A third reason why effective organization design fails to materialize is that this sort of architectural work requires a different way of thinking. It cannot be guided by the sole sort of logic that dominates science, the search for general knowledge and the subsequent test of its validity, but instead is guided by an inquiry into systems that do not yet exist, where the logic is that of disclosing and crafting a new "world", with the sole purpose of ascertaining if it works and ensuring that it does (Romme 2003: 558).

For all these reasons the significant role that organization design (including redesign) plays in the work of governance is not appreciated as fully as it should be. It is my view that it will not acquire the status it deserves unless the design function is better understood, the epistemological difficulties it creates are better gauged, and the intellectual toolbox required to do the job is better developed and used.

In a first stab at these issues, I shall define an organization as an assemblage that merrily ignores the notion of scale. Consequently, it connotes anything from the usual private, public or social concerns, to cities or issue domains (health, education), to governments, nation

states and transnational regimes. Obviously, the nature of
the actors, the relationships and ligatures, the procedures
and the norms are different in different assemblages, but
there are fundamental commonalities in their design.

DESIGNING A LIVING ORGANIZATION

An organization may be outlined with the useful acronym
"PARC," that is, as a mix of people, or P (stakeholders
of all sorts, with their skills, talents and responsibilities);
architecture, or A (relationships of all sorts, defined
by organization charts and the like); routines, or R
(processes, policies and procedures); and culture, or C
(shared values, beliefs, language, norms and mindsets)
(Roberts 2004). At any time these components are
assembled within organizations in various ways and
bound together by ligatures making them into a more
or less coherent whole. Any shock disturbance in any
of these components, whether it originates from within
or from outside, whether it modifies a physical or a
symbolic dimension, obviously triggers some realignment in all the other dimensions. Thus the organization
continually evolves.

Organizations, therefore, are assemblages constantly
undermined, both on the surface and below, as a result
of the action of new or transformed stakeholders, new
emerging relationships, new procedures, or changes in the
material or symbolic order. The role of the organization
designer is to intervene in real time in an existing assemblage to improve the four-dimensional configuration of
the organization's PARC, in a manner that generates better dynamic performance and resilience, given the nature
of the environment in which the organization operates,
but also taking its turbulence and its evolution into
account. The four dimensions have to be tweaked in a
creative way to provide effective dynamic coordination.

This sort of work requires: (1) a new vocabulary,
because critical description is crucial at the diagnostic

phase; (2) a new form of knowledge, a new type of exploratory activity and a new process of creative thinking based on experimentalism; and (3) a new type of competence to do this work. Moreover, it requires (4) windows of opportunity to "tinker" with the organization with a modicum of chances of success, at a time and in a way that prevents these efforts from being neutralized by the dynamic conservatism of those who benefit from the existing order. This often requires exceptional circumstances. Otherwise, the pressures of those confronted with real and substantial losses in the short term will trump the timid actions of those hoping for uncertain future benefits from a new order. However, this process will lead to nothing substantial unless one has been able to develop (5) an intellectual toolbox of levers that can guide the work of crafting new organizations and can be used in such design work. However, because organization design is akin to creating a new world, none of the above will suffice unless the design process (6) truly discloses a coherent world (a body), and contributes to imparting it with a style (a soul) that provides it with a sextant and focal points that underpin its being able to sustain effective coordination and change.

Given these conditions for successful organization design, it is hardly surprising that such work is so often eschewed and that so many organizations are so poorly designed. It is much easier for governors and managers to focus their attention on less daunting tasks, and to allow poorly designed organizations to survive, even though organization design may be the most important determinant of the success of an organization.

The six basic elements outlined above are probed, in a provisional way, in the subsequent sections of this chapter. Two caveats are in order. First, it should be clear that it is difficult to capture the full flavour of organization design as process in action with a simple reductive focus on only one aspect of design, the architecture of the organization. The design process cannot be meaningfully reduced to tinkering with an organization chart, which is nothing but a glimpse at a temporary quasi-equilibrium that results from tensions between strategy and structure, accountability and adaptability, vertical hierarchy and horizontal networks, self-interest and mission success, among other dyads pulling and pushing the organization in different directions (Simons 2005: 8ff). Only unrepentant utopians believe that if a structure is imposed, the other dimensions will adjust (Boguslaw 1965). In fact, organization design has to be concerned with all the dimensions of PARC if it is to succeed. Yet the temptation to focus on structure alone is omnipresent. People and routines can be perceived as matters that can be handled by management, while culture is too often regarded as an elusive and treacherous terrain where self-styled pragmatists do not dare to go. (Two recent cases in which I was personally involved, the mandate reviews of the National Capital Commission of Canada and of the RCMP, offer examples of occasions for critical organization redesign where these other dimensions were dutifully avoided, either by the government, in the former case, or by the mandate review board, in the latter case.)

Second, it should also be clear that the design process being deployed in historical time, is shaped by a significant amount of multifaceted interaction with the environment, is fraught with accidents along the way and is bound to suffer from the effects of unintended consequences. One would need to film this interactive process to gain a sense of its dynamics: the interaction between a plan that cannot be fully spelled out, because it is evolving, and a context that cannot be fully described, because it is also continuously changing.

Organization design connotes the capacity to reflect systematically, rigorously and cumulatively in action as the inquiry proceeds, and as one experiments by trial and error in crafting an organizational form involving all the components of PARC in order to ensure dynamic performance and resilience.

PRECONDITIONS FOR SUCCESSFUL DESIGN WORK

The preconditions for successful design may be examined under two headings: description and epistemology, and competences and opportunities.

DESCRIPTION AND EPISTEMOLOGY

In order to intervene effectively in the design of organizations in real time, it is necessary to have some basic vocabulary that enables one to describe the context and the texture of the organization. Since both context and texture evolve, one must have a vocabulary that can adequately keep track of such change and its dynamic. Such descriptive work is built on a theory of knowledge or an epistemology. Knowledge is justified true belief, and epistemology deals with the criteria that justify such belief and make it count as knowledge (Hardin 2002). Without a sound epistemology, many unjustified beliefs may come to be regarded as knowledge and the vocabulary to describe what we know becomes deficient.

An epistemology crippled by ideology, ignorance or incompetence is bound to generate an inadequate vocabulary to describe new realities, and to produce massively distorted knowledge and information. Yet the poverty of the art of description and the dangers of crippled epistemologies are rarely acknowledged, even though they are fundamentally important (Hardin 2002; Sen 1999b).

Organizations and institutions are meso-phenomena that too often are poorly described and apprehended, because observers insist on looking at them through micro-perspectives that focus exclusively on individuals as absolutes and deny the importance of relationships among entities. They are equally poorly understood by using approaches that focus exclusively on macro-systems and totalities as absolutes. Organization design requires a vocabulary and an approach that focus on the meso-level.

Manuel DeLanda (2006) has provided such a perspective, based on the notion of "assemblage". Assemblages are populations of entities, none of which is seen as the fundamental building block. Any assemblage has properties and capacities. Properties are what an assemblage brings to one context or another, while capacities refer to potentialities to affect or to be affected by other entities in other contexts. Capacities are as real as the properties of an assemblage, but one cannot identify them except as they come into play in particular cases, circumstances or interactions (DeLanda 2006: 11). The identity of any assemblage is the result of its properties and capacities as they come to life in different territorial or other arrangements or processes, but it remains precarious since such processes may be easily destabilized (DeLanda 2006: 28).

An example of assemblage might be an ecosystem, but also an organization, a city, a government, a nation. Any of these, in turn, can be a part of a broader assemblage, but may also be decomposed into smaller assemblages defined by mechanisms that involve complex mixtures of causes, reasons and motives. The fact that these assemblages are in a continual process of change has led some to compare them to "publics" (in John Dewey's parlance), and to suggest that budding social movements, for instance, may be regarded as akin to "emergent assemblages" (Dewey 1927; Angus 2001).

The language of assemblages is well-adapted to the realities of organization design, but it also highlights its difficulty. One may tinker with the various mechanisms (causes, reasons, motives) at any level, but such tinkering does not have linear causal effects, since the same cause does not always trigger the same effect. Tinkering may mix properties, but it also modifies and catalyzes the capacities of the different entities it plays with, thereby (wittingly or not) triggering changes in the world of reasons and motives. The results may include surprising and unintended consequences.

The importance of culture and identity in the design of an organizational world cannot be overemphasized. They represent subtle ways in which coordination is effected in much more complex ways than the simple Skinnerian stimulus–response mechanism. Unfortunately, these dimensions are underemphasized and therefore under-played in the design process because of the richer epis-temology it requires. Group identity in the military, for instance, or cultural bonds in solidarity organizations can play crucial roles in generating effective coordination, but identity and culture are more difficult to craft than Skinnerian mechanisms, so unfortunately they tend to be discarded by hurried reformers as the result of a crippled epistemology, a lack of vocabulary to describe gaps at that level and a certain ignorance about effective ways to craft these elusive dimensions of organizations (Kreps 1990; Hardin 2002; Akerlof and Kranton 2005).

This underlines the daunting challenge of designing flawless assemblages. Charles E. Lindblom (1990: 39) is rather pessimistic about this, and has suggested that such attempts to arrange or rearrange volitions in various coherent and well-performing assemblages are unlikely to succeed. Others, such as Donald A. Schön and Martin Rein (1994), are more hopeful that coherence may emerge through a process of conversation with the situ-ation and with the multiple actors who have different frames of reference that can be reconciled. From these interfaces may emerge, in their view, a process of inquiry, discovery and learning that reduces contention, and elic-its a pragmatic resolution *in situ*.

COMPETENCES AND OPPORTUNITIES

Donald N. Michael (1980; 1993) has suggested that such work can only be done if new competences are acquired. Michael groups these new competences under three rubrics:

- developing ways to deal with organizations as learn-ing systems (seeking resilience rather than control, embracing error, spanning boundaries);

- learning interpersonal skills (active communication, open communication, intuition and feeling as data and valued information); and
- creating an effective corporate climate (dedication to partnership, inspiring mutual responsibility).

As I have indicated elsewhere (Paquet 2006c), these competences and skills have a great deal to do with *savoir-faire* and *savoir-être*, and learning by doing. Such competences, based on practical knowledge, have tended to be greatly underrated in a world where technical rationality has become hegemonic, on the assumption that knowledge flows from underlying disciplines to applied science to actual performance of services to clients and society (Schön 1983; 1987).

Substituting a two-way approach for this one-way street, emphasizing knowing in action and reflection in action (where knowledge emerges equally well from groping with situations and from surprises leading to on-the-spot experiments and knowledge creation), is, at least ideally, the way professionals are, or should be, educated (Simon 1981: Chapter 5). It emphasizes the development of skills and a capacity for a conversation with the situation through reflective practice (residency, articling and the like). It may be seen as the only way to impart practical knowledge in a manner that aims at nothing less than transformation and behaviour modification, for some of those skills are literally embodied. *Savoir-fair* cannot be learned and developed without a change in *savoir-être*, in identity. It has proved extremely difficult to ensure the requisite training and coaching in these new competences, for they require the development of perception skills, diagnostic skills and the like. This explains the explosion of parallel training ventures dealing with those areas that are dramatically neglected by the formal education enterprise.

However, no matter how effective one might become in developing this sort of delta knowledge and related skills (Gilles and Paquet 1989), and even though the mechanisms to ensure the requisite practices are available, that cannot suffice. Considerable opportunism is also required. Albert Hirschman suggests that none of the efforts to make use of this type of knowledge will work unless the right opportunity to intervene emerges, a moment when the forces of dynamic conservatism will be taken by surprise and somewhat neutralized, "for change can only happen as a result of surprise, otherwise it could not occur at all, for it would be suppressed by the forces in favour of the status quo" (Hirschman 1995: 136).

Such windows of opportunity exist in moments of transition between governments, or on the occasion of external shocks that threaten the survival of organizations. Yet these are often moments when organizations turn out to be particularly ill-equipped to take advantage of them.

ORGANIZATION DESIGN AS PROCESS
The design process is a loose protocol, and is as difficult and elusive as the pragmatic inquiry of professionals. It must be anchored somewhat if it is to serve as a launching pad for experiments and "serious play" (Schrage 2000) as basic components of the social learning process.

THE SIMONS-TYPE MODEL AS A POSSIBLE TEMPLATE
A loose protocol or analytical framework is nothing more than a sort of preliminary arrangement of the objects of the inquiry. It provides, not a theory of design, but merely a set of questions that underpin the appreciation of the situation, and help in the structuring of the process of constructing performing and resilient organizations. Robert Simons (2005) has proposed a template based on four basic questions that might be reformulated in the following way:

- Stakeholder definition: what are the best possible assemblages (those that are the most effective and

resilient, and likely to serve the organization's partners, clients and other stakeholders best)?

- Performance variables: what are the most effective
diagnostic control systems (the various mechanisms
likely to best monitor the organization and to suggest ways to excite them)?

- Creative tension resolution: what are the best mechanisms to resolve the creative tensions between the
frames of mind of the different layers and rings of
partners in the organization, and to catalyze interactive networks?

- Commitment to others: what are the mechanisms
of shared responsibilities and commitment to others that will ensure some coherence for the organization, and the requisite mix of reliability and
innovation?

The answers to these questions are meant to help in
defining the four basic dimensions of the Simons framework: (1) the span of control (who should decide?);
(2) the span of accountability (tradeoffs in performance
measures when it comes to rendering accounts); (3) the
span of influence (the full nature of the interactions and
the degree of mobilization they entail); and (4) the span
of support (the full range of shared responsibilities).
Simons suggests that proper alignment for an organization requires that the spans of control (hard) and support
(soft) on the supply side of resources, be adequate to
meet the obligations imposed by the spans of accountability (hard) and influence (soft) on the demand side
of resources.

Finally, Simons suggests that, in order to avoid indulging in what he calls "endless permutations and combi-
nations of design variables" (Simons 2005: 28), there
should be a focus on certain basic patterns or archetypes
of good organization design that appear to have proved
successful in a wide range of situations. These might
be patterns focused on specific pivotal values or focal

points such as low price, service relationships or expert knowledge. This latter point may be unduly reductive. While it may provide shortcuts in the case of standard private, public or social organizations, there is obviously a danger in thus limiting the quest for the right sort of assemblages that may be regarded as worthy of attention in such issue domains as education nor health care, where no single focal point or set of pivotal values can be identified *ex ante*.

A more useful, creative and pragmatic (if more adventurous) way may be to recognize that the right organization design is unlikely to be available ready-made and off the shelf, or off a paradigm. It must not only be invented, creatively etched on the basis of the properties and capabilities available, but also taking context and circumstances into account. The organization must be designed in the way a good architect designs a house: in keeping with the wishes of the users, the constraints of the environment and the material available to work with. It is obviously easier to limit the number of models when dealing with a house than when dealing with a district or a borough.

In the case of organization design, the designer is obviously constrained by the PARC dimensions. It would be unreasonable to ignore any of these dimensions. One must often build the architecture around indispensable or tenured people, around routines that are essential to ensure reliability and taking account of cultural factors that cannot be easily transformed in the very short run. A district may have to be built around an escarpment, for instance. The central challenge is to find the right balance of reliability and innovation. This may need to take different forms and may entail different balances in the different segments of an organization. Audit and marketing may require different balances. Whatever the constraints, the focus needs to be on the design of business and on the recognition that this requires nothing less than a new way of thinking (Martin 2004; 2007).

EXPERIMENTALISM AND SERIOUS PLAY IN A DYNAMIC WORLD

A promising way to develop the requisite organizational form is not to impose it "cold" onto an assemblage, but to allow it to emerge once the nature of relevant prototypes has been ascertained on the basis of the non-negotiable constraints. The key to this evolution on the basis of prototypes is:

- a drift toward open source governance (a form of governance that enables each partner, as much as possible, to have access to the "code" and to tinker freely with the way the system works, within certain well-accepted constraints) (Sabel 2001); and
- priority for "serious play" (a premium on experimentation with the imperfect prototypes that might be improved by retooling, restructuring and reframing innovatively and productively) (Schrage 2000).

By partitioning the overall terrain into issues domains and communities of meaning or communities of fate (assemblages of people united in their common concern for shared problems, or a shared passion for a topic or set of issues), it is possible to identify a vast number of sub-games, each requiring specific treatment. Each issue domain is multifaceted and is dealt with on an ad hoc basis, with a view to allowing the design of its own stewardship to emerge.

This open system takes into account the people with a substantial stake in the issue domain, the resources available and the culture in place, and allows experiments to shape the required mix of principles and norms, and of rules and decision-making procedures, likely to promote the preferred mix of efficiency, resilience and learning. A template likely to be of use across the board may not be available yet, but that does not mean that a workable one cannot be elicited here and now (Sabel 2004).

However, it is not sufficient to ensure open access. One must also ensure that the appropriate motivations are nurtured so that all citizens are willing and able to engage in serious play, and to become truly producers of governance through tinkering with the governance apparatus, within certain limits. This in turn requires that the requisite amounts of collaboration and trust prevail, and calls for a reconfiguration of governance, taking communities of meaning seriously. Such an approach might not only suggest that very different arrangements are likely to emerge from place to place, but would underline the importance of regarding any such arrangement as essentially temporary. The ground is in motion and diversity is likely to acquire new faces, so different patterns of organization design are likely to emerge.

Consequently, governance should not only rely on a much more flexible toolbox, but also require that any formal or binding arrangement be revisited, played with and adjusted to take the evolving diversity of circumstances into account. It should open the door to the design of more complex and innovative arrangements likely to deal more effectively with deep diversity.

Prototyping appears to be the main activity underpinning serious play:

- identifying some top requirements as quickly as possible;
- putting a provisional medium of co-development in place;
- allowing as many interested parties as possible to get involved as partners in improving the arrangement;
- encouraging iterative prototyping; and
- thereby encouraging all, through playing with prototypes, to get a better understanding of the problems, of their priorities and of themselves (Schrage 2000: 199ff).

The purpose of the exercise is to create a dialogue, a creative interaction, between people and prototypes. This may be more important than creating a dialogue between people. It is predicated on a culture of active participation that would need to be nurtured.

The sort of democratization of design that would ensue, and the sort of playfulness and adventure that would be required for serious play with prototypes, are essential for the process to succeed, and they apply equally well to narrow or broad organizational concerns.

ORGANIZATION DESIGN OUTCOMES

Organization design uses a variety of mechanisms to help to institute a living organization that has the capacity to be reliable and innovative, and to not only be resilient, but also to learn. It aims at coherence, but mainly at dynamism. This cannot be accomplished simply by tinkering with the hard dimensions of organizations (their architecture and routines); it must also modify their behaviour and culture. Moreover, depending on circumstances, this sort of intervention may have to be sequenced carefully if it is to be successful.

BACK TO PARC

The four PARC dimensions mentioned above are crucial in achieving a good fit and in reducing agency costs. Two dimensions, architecture and routines, are in the nature of plumbing, while people and culture deal with softer dimensions. The sort of assemblages likely to succeed will differ widely, depending not only on the context but also on the general nature and thrust of each organization. Yet the style of organization design most likely to succeed will call for disaggregation (Roberts 2004: 180ff), a choice of architecture and routines underpinned by wise incentive–reward systems for people, and supported by changes in the culture.

The main challenge is rooted in the fact that such disaggregation involves, of necessity, a growth of multitasking and it is difficult to resolve the problem of motivation in such circumstances. It is not easy to induce partners to allocate attention, time and effort, in appropriate and timely ways among tasks, when they differ significantly and are not equally well-measured.

This is an especially daunting task in the case of the exploration/exploitation split that often underpins the innovation/reliability challenge (March 1991). It is impossible to tackle this challenge without explicit efforts to transform the culture of the organization. The simple partitioning of tasks or efforts is unlikely to work. The following principles have proved useful:

- maximum participation to ensure the tapping of all relevant knowledge and more collaboration;
- subsidiarity, or the delegation of decision-making to the most local level possible;
- some competition to squeeze out organizational slack and promote innovation; and
- "multi-stability", requiring the partitioning of the organization into sub-systems so as to delegate to the one most able to handle a shock or perturbation the task of doing so, without the other sub-systems being forced to transform (Paquet 2005b: Chapter 8).

As for the most useful mechanisms, they have been:

- the setting up of ever more inclusive forums for effective multilogue;
- the negotiation of moral contracts defining clearly yet informally the mutual expectations of the different partners;
- the design of learning loops, enabling partners to not only revise their choices of means as the experience unfolds, but also to revise the very ends pursued through reframing the organization when it proves necessary; and

- the invention of fail-safe mechanisms to ensure that
  the multilogue does not degenerate into meaningless consensuses and to prevent saboteurs from
  derailing the collective effort.

However, there is no simple recipe or cookie-cutter
approach to organization design. Each case presents a
particular and singular challenge. What is involved is a
process of quasi-disintegration or partitioning, followed
by a process of quasi-reintegration based on the principle
of loose coupling, with the help of particular ligatures
in order to allow the organization to emerge and evolve
smoothly. The only basis of operation is a protocol to
ensure that a rich enough vocabulary and epistemology are
in use, that relevant competences have been developed, that
key questions are answered, that the right conditions for
prototyping serious play are in place, and that the whole
range of PARC levers and ligatures is kept in mind.

GETTING THE RIGHT FIT AND SEQUENCE

This may all seem too much like consulting a Michelin guide
the day before one is to embark on a long voyage—too rich
in detail, and thus too daunting and discouraging for the
interested traveller. Yet any design task may require a guide
to the guide, the modicum of a plan, similar to what a good
reporter has in front of him before conducting an interview.
The designer must be ready to prototype and to tinker as
the process unfolds, but no organization will permit him or
her to do so unless some action plan has been presented,
providing some sense of the nature of the experiment.

David Nadler and Michael Tushman (1997) have suggested a blueprint and a sequence for design that might
serve as a security blanket. Their work might be stylized
as follows (taking liberties with their sequencing and
taking the analysis above into account):

- organizational assessment: functioning, performance gaps;

- design criteria: what the new design should accomplish;
- groupings: options for general grouping;
- coordination requirements: information processing needs;
- linking: linking mechanisms (formal and informal);
- properties and capabilities of the ensuing assemblages;
- provisional analysis of impact;
- simulation of the way in which the design would play out in different circumstances through proto-typing and serious play;
- operational design required: detailed planning of implementation, supporting key power groups, rewarding desired behaviour, monitoring transition;
- organizational culture (values, beliefs and norms) as means and ends;
- social learning loops, mechanisms as a way to adapt.

The process of organization design is not linear, but is rather an iterative inquiry, a trial and error experiment, a search process. It is the sort of reflection in action that Donald Schön (1983; 1987) aptly described as a conversation with the situation that leads to discovery. At the core of this process is the inquiring mind, the designer paying attention to the evolving environment, a double-looped learning through which ends and means are continually revised as the experiment proceeds, in the same way that an Inuit artist scrapes away at a reindeer antler with a knife, examining it first from one angle and then from another, before crying out, "Ah, a seal!" (Schön and Rein 1994: 166–167).

In this inquiry it has often proved easier to tinker with the technology than with the structure, and easier to tin-ker with the structure than with the culture of an orga-nization (Schön 1971). However, it would be unwise to assume that any particular sequence will always work.

DISCLOSING NEW WORLDS AND IMPARTING STYLE

The core task of organization design is to disclose new worlds. Organizations are worlds: each is a totality of interrelated pieces of equipment to carry out a specific task (such as hammering in a nail); these tasks are undertaken for some purpose or purposes (such as building a house); and these activities confer identities upon those accomplishing them (such as being a carpenter) (Spinosa et al. 1997: 17). This is the sense in which one may refer to the world of medicine, or of business or of academe.

However, there is more to organizations than the interconnection of equipment, purposes and identities. Spinosa et al. (1997) use the word "style" to refer to the ways in which all the practices are coordinated and fit together in an organization. Style is what coordinates action, what makes certain kinds of activities and things matter. In a way, style is an echo of culture: it pertains not only to the way coordination is effected, but also to the way change is effected.

In their study Spinosa et al. (1997) (and also Max Boisot [1995] and many others) show how economic, social and political entrepreneurs are those who spot disharmonies between what seem to be the prevailing rules and what appear to be the sort of practices that are likely to be effective. They detect anomalies. Those anomalies create puzzles. The reaction to puzzles is often to ignore them and pursue ongoing tasks as usual, instead of recognizing that the anomalies create mysteries and that what are called for are ways of understanding mysteries, in a search for "guidelines for solving a mystery by organized exploration of possibilities" (Martin 2004: 7).

This is where sensitive individuals become more aware of marginal practices or alternative ways to retool, restructure and reframe their activities, according to principles previously not necessarily regarded as of central interest. They tend to become involved in lateral thinking, articulating the problem differently, cross-appropriating ways of doing things elsewhere and adjusting them to the task at hand, and reframing the very notion of the business one is in along different lines. This is the world of prototyping, experimentation, serious play, organization design. Innovative persons in all areas, economic, political, social, become organization designers and redefine the styles of their organizations.

The difficulty is that higher education is not organized to foster this type of world-disclosing activity or inquiry based on empathy (for one always designs for somebody else); holistic problem-solving (solution-focused strategies, looking for what works) and prototyping (not waiting until one has the best solution, but starting with anything promising, prototyping it, getting feedback, playing with it and learning in that way) (Tim Brown quoted in Martin 2004: 11). As a result, the skills required are not necessarily cultivated (Paquet 2006c). This explains why design work is often done so poorly.

CONCLUSION

It remains unclear whether this failure is to be ascribed mainly to the way higher education has stunted the learning process, to the neglect of delta knowledge and design rationality, the prevailing organizational culture or simply the underdevelopment of organization design studies. It is likely that all these forces have played a role in the crystallization of this crippling epistemology.

It is difficult, however, to underestimate the toxic effect of positivism and scientism on the social sciences, including management studies. These forces, denounced by F. A. Hayek (1952) nearly sixty years ago, have proved even more toxic than he anticipated. A great deal of research in management and governance has been vitiated by this virus (Paquet 1987), and, most importantly, alternative ways of strengthening governance education have been grossly neglected. Management and governance studies have been trapped in the doldrums of technical rationality, and it was only in the 1980s, with the work of Donald Schön (1983; 1988), that alternative trails were opened. Yet these trails have not been as fully explored as they should have been and much of what one may call the pathologies of governance must be properly ascribed to these foundational flaws (Paquet 2004b; 2005c).

Bemoaning this derailment may be caricatured as strictly an academic concern, of no interest to those living outside the higher education enterprise. In a way this is true, but on the ground the situation is a bit different. Reflective practitioners have succeeded, despite the higher education establishment, in providing a momentum, and generating and cultivating entrepreneurship, creative democratic action, and solidarity. Yet scientism still inhabits the corridors of academe, and the tolerance for this perversion will continue to inflict damage on future generations unless some radical transformation is engineered in governance studies.

One should not, however, assume that all is rotten in the state of Denmark. Governance, ethics, organizational culture and organization design have begun to permeate management schools. Such subversive studies are beginning to show signs of being a source of rejuvenation in administrative studies, asking different and open questions, forcefully underlining the professional nature of management and recognizing that there is more to governance than has been accepted or understood.

Nevertheless, with few exceptions in the academic community, design inquiry is left to practitioners and management consultants, and, as a result, "the body of design knowledge appears to be fragmented and dispersed" (Romme 2003: 569), and to a greater extent than in other bodies of knowledge. The time may be ripe for a revolution, for, as Chalmers Johnson (1964: 22) put it: "multiple dysfunctions plus elite intransigence cause revolution".

PART III

Less than Effective Bricolage

Introduction

Can one infer that failures of governance are logically bound to follow from crippling epistemologies and inadequate scaffolding? Not automatically and not always, but, as a matter of probability, most certainly. It cannot be expected that an effective apparatus of governance will ensue from a poor knowledge base, and flawed organizational and institutional arrangements. Are failures ascribable to those particular inadequacies, or to other extraneous factors? This cannot be established without a careful look at some case studies. In this third part of the book I shall attempt to make the case that the two sets of forces critically examined in the first two parts are of paramount importance in such failures. I shall do this in three different ways.

Chapter 7 (which was largely written in 1996, but is still very relevant) tries to make the general case that crippling epistemologies have led to an overly stylized and sanitized notion of the public policy process that has proved unduly naïve, and that the lack of adequate evaluative procedures has compounded the problem even further, generating a public policy process that has proved quite ill-suited to dealing with the complex issues of the day. These flaws have stunted social learning and have prevented the emergence of public policy interventions of the sort that seem to be required.

The simplistic linear template imposed on the policy process by instrumental rationality does not match the messiness of the "wicked problems" being confronted in those complex "affairs" that John Dewey (1927) was so fond of tackling and disentangling. What has made this simplistic view so resilient in policy circles, is the occluding of the whole context, and the failure to have any concern for the minimum informational and evaluative apparatus necessary to ensure effective learning feedback. Such lack of concern has led not only to allowing this missing apparatus to go unnoticed, but, even when it has existed, to its actions becoming totally irrelevant, when not actually perverse.

These general points are made starkly in Chapter 7, but they are developed in more elaborate and nuanced ways in the two chapters that follow. In both science policy and foreign affairs, the degree of complexity of the issues is enormous, power, resources and information are in many hands, and the only way to effectively steward the country and the social system is to find ways to generate the requisite degree of mass collaboration. Yet in both settings, action has been crippled by a very simplistic understanding of the forces at work and by the lack of an appropriate apparatus to ensure the requisite collaboration.

Chapter 8 reviews the science policy conundrum that has been with us since the dawn of modern economies, when knowledge and information became prominent and determining factors of production. This may have been the case from time immemorial, but it became a crucially critical dimension after World War II. The heroic efforts of Senator Maurice Lamontagne and his colleagues, to communicate to the government the central importance of a science policy in a knowledge-based economy failed miserably in the 1970s. The dual burden of poor understanding of the issues and poor institutional design, do much to explain the failures on this front, and dealing with this burden is of paramount importance in kick-starting an effective process of social learning. Nevertheless, it is fair to say that, fifteen years after the paper on which this chapter is based was first published, the situation remains as depressing as it was in 1994.

Chapter 9 deals with foreign affairs, where matters are equally complex and the prospect for avoiding failures of governance is equally bleak. In this case, the emergence of the sort of governing that appears to be required in a pluralist society is prevented by the mélange of crippling epistemology (the refusal to acknowledge the reduced importance of the nation state in foreign affairs or the new role of other actors); dynamic conservatism of the institutional apparatus in place at the national level (the existence of a Republic of International Affairs Apparatchiks not dissimilar to the Republic of Science in science policy); and defective organizational design (flawed consultation mechanisms).

The sort of experimentalist approach that appears to be called for is prevented from emerging, both because it is regarded as intellectually unacceptable (there is no need to experiment, someone is in charge) and because the vested interests in the existing structures are so powerful that they can effectively thwart any effort to make the foreign policy process more open. In both issue domains, but for different reasons, prevailing cosmologies and inadequate scaffolding are engineering failures of governance that are likely to continue.

CHAPTER 7

Nothing is more rational than a rationalization

> *The policy development process is . . .*
> *a process of transforming what is desirable*
> *into what is feasible, which is part of the work*
> *that we sometimes shy away from.*
> — JOCELYNE BOURGON

We should greet with exhilaration the announcement that, as the result of scientism and the new religion of accountabilism (Weinberger 2007), a wave of rationality is blowing through government operations and the policy development process in Canada. It is all the more exciting when the announcement comes, not from some academic Moses carrying simplistic tables down from some Mount Sinai, but rather from practical men of affairs, with a great deal of moral authority in the public policy community, and couched in crisp financial-statement prose. It is all the more promising when this new cosmology has already been tested in Alberta and carries the imprimatur of public officials in Ottawa, who have been newly converted to this gospel and see in it a promise of refurbishing the whole system of federal governance. The new mental image of public policy marksmanship is so vivid and so palpable that we cannot deny its power. More reason in human affairs, at long last!

Against this background, my words of caution may sound hollow or even somewhat blasphemous. So in order to ensure that there is no misunderstanding, some clarification is in order. These words of caution should not be interpreted as expressing opposition to rational policy making that is based on the maximization of precise measured goals within a world of well-defined constraints, if and when that is possible. Many aspects of public policy can benefit greatly from such an approach and such a thrust. These comments are simply a fore-warning that much of the public policy apparatus may not be amenable to such analysis, and that any efforts to force round policy pegs into Cartesian analytical square holes could have unintended and undesirable consequences.

I wish to draw attention to the fact that "reason is wholly instrumental. It cannot tell us where to go; at best it can tell us how to get there ... all reason can do is help us reach agreed-on goals more efficiently" (Simon 1983: 7 and 106). This leaves us far short of being able to easily handle the real world's "wicked problems" of public policy, problems where goals are either not known or ambiguous, and means–ends relationships are poorly understood (Rittel and Webber 1973).

In my view, a significant portion of public policy issues deal with such wicked problems. Therefore, a simple framework built on performance measured in terms of the maximization of precisely measured goals, within a world of equally precisely defined constraints, may be elegant, but it would not be very helpful to navigation. Thus I would caution the designers of the new cosmology and accounting/monitoring schemas that they should guard against being unreasonably optimistic about the results they can expect, that their proselytiz-ing may have unfortunate unintended consequences. It should be clear that this cautionary tale is not meant to discourage vigorous and enthusiastic experimentation, but rather to introduce to the debate a much needed

sense of limits, at a time when the zeal of the newly converted might lead them to proceed without the requisite
modicum of care.

The most important limitation of the new hyper-rational
cosmology is that it is based on a set of assumptions that
do not appear to describe the public policy scene well, as
one observes it from the academic mezzanine. Perhaps this
perception can be entirely ascribed to the vantage point.
Perhaps the public policy game is altogether a much more
rational affair than it appears to be. However, it may also
be that the stylization of public policy underpinning the
new cosmology is a great simplification of reality, and that
some words of caution might be useful.

WICKED PROBLEMS AND SOCIAL
LEARNING

Governance is about guiding: it is the process through
which an organization or a society is nudged in certain
directions. Fifty years ago in Canada, governance was
debated in the language of management science. It was
presumed that public, private and social organizations
alike were directed by leaders who had a good understanding of their environment, of the future trends in that
environment if nothing were done to modify it, of the
inexorable rules of the game they had to put up with and
of the goals pursued by their own organizations. Those
were the days when the challenges of policy sciences were
still Newtonian. We lived in a world of deterministic,
well-behaved mechanical processes, where causality was
simple because the whole was the sum of the parts. Given
the well-defined goals of organizations, and the more or
less placid environment, the challenge was to design the
control mechanisms likely to get organizations to where
they wanted to be.

Many issues were, and still are, tractable with this
approach, but many are not. In the past thirty years
or so, the pace of change has accelerated and the issues
have grown more complex. Private, public and social

organizations have all been confronted more and more with "wicked problems" (as defined above). To deal with these wicked problems, a new way of thinking about governance is required. In this quantum world there is no objective reality, the uncertainty principle looms large, events are at best probable, and the whole is a network of synergies and interactions among the different parts of the system that is quite different from the sum of the parts (Becker 1991). This has forced the system of governance to evolve accordingly. It has been transformed through a number of rounds of adaptation over the years so that it can provide the requisite flexibility and suppleness in action. The ultimate result of these changes is a composite system built on unreliable control mechanisms and pursuing ill-defined goals in a universe that is chronically in a state of flux.

In this world, organizations can govern themselves by becoming capable of learning both new goals and new means as they proceed. This can be done only by tapping the knowledge and information in the possession of the citizens or members of the organization, and by allowing them to invent ways out of the predicaments they are in. Such a system would deprive the leader of any illusion that he or she has a monopoly on the governing of the organization. For the organization to learn fast, everyone must take part in the conversation, and bring forward each bit of knowledge and wisdom that he or she has that has a bearing on the issue (Paquet 1992; Webber 1993; Piore 1995). We are in a world of "governing by learning" (Michael 1993).

This process of social learning requires new structures, more modular and network-like, and integrated informal moral contracts, but it is only one half of the learning process. The other half is the work of leaders as facilitators. Instead of building on the assumption that the leader is omniscient and can guide an organization autocratically from the top down, the new process of "distributed governance" builds on social learning and on the steward's capacity to nudge through a critical dialogue with stakeholders, ensuring that everyone learns about the nature of the problem and about the consequences of various possible alternative initiatives (Paquet 1996a).

The citizenry learns in this manner to limit unreasonable demands. Managers and administrators learn to listen and consult. Other stakeholders learn enough about one another's views and interests to gauge the range of compromise solutions that are likely to prove acceptable. Distributed governance predicated on social learning, builds on the answers to four questions posed to all stakeholders: is it feasible? is it socially acceptable? is it too destabilizing politically? can it be implemented? (Friedmann and Abonyi 1976).

This is the world of public policy that I am familiar with, one in which the essential fuzziness of goals and targets, and the essential uncertainty of means–ends relationships, force us to adopt a social learning mode, a strategy of learning by doing, learning by monitoring (Stiglitz 1987). This is a world that Denis Desautels, who was Auditor General of Canada from 1991 to 2001, also appears to recognize as something of central importance in the public policy world when he underlines the centrality of organizational learning, the fact that "managers have to learn from experience" (Desautels 1997, 6).

Whatever may be done to improve this process of learning must therefore be applauded. The more outcome-oriented the focus of the conversation, and the more timely and performance-related the reporting and monitoring process, then the more effective is the accountability framework as a learning device, or, to adopt the phrase used by Desautels in many speeches, "as a corrective mechanism" (Desautels 1997, 10). He suggests that much can be accomplished by a process of clarification of goals, objectives, expectations and responsibilities, and through timely and credible reporting in a manner that provides feedback for corrective action.

Desautels is also prudent, however. He adds very quickly that this is not sufficient to ensure effective accountability. The second blade of the scissors is a significant cultural change, a willingness to learn when things do not go as well as expected. This cultural change would even include a reconsideration of the traditional views on the respective roles and responsibilities of ministers (politicians) and deputy ministers (public servants). This rather prudent way of setting the stage is very much in line with my own perspective.

THREE WORDS OF CAUTION

The public policy process is a social system designed to regulate the broader complex system within which it is embedded. It purports to ensure the provision of certain public goods, to establish and maintain a set of frameworks of rules within which the system can function smoothly and effectively, and to effect the cross-subsidization and redistribution required to achieve legitimately defined meritorious objectives.

As with any other social system, the public policy process is composed of three elements: structure, technology and theory. The structure consists of the set of roles and responsibilities of, and relations among, the actors involved in this process (citizens, stakeholders, officials and so on). The technology refers to the tools used by these actors. The theory is the view held by members about the process, its purposes, environment and future. These dimensions hang together, and any change in one affects the others (Schön 1971).

Governing is learning, and the capacity to transform is a measure of organizational learning: the speed with which the public policy process is able to ensure the requisite restructuring, retooling and reframing in order to enhance its "triple-E" performance. Triple-E performance pertains to the capacity to ensure effectiveness (doing the right thing), efficiency (doing it right) and economy (doing it frugally), while carefully maintaining due process and fairness, not only in the outcomes, but also in the process through which these outcomes are generated. The hyper-rational cosmology has approached this very complex public policy process in a rather parsimonious way. It has focused mainly on the processes of clarifying goals and of reporting and monitoring improvements, being intent on increasing the transparency and the efficiency of the public policy process.

This approach is most useful at the service delivery end of the public policy funnel—ranging from taking account of the socio-technical environment to be regulated, through the mediating lenses of ideology, culture, institutions and the structure of power, to programme definition and service delivery—(for example, measuring how much time it takes to have cheques mailed and delivered). It is less clear what this improvement in clarification and reporting contributes, or may contribute, at the other end of the funnel—at the environment scanning and policy formation end of the spectrum. Indeed, many public administration scholars and practitioners are bluntly sceptical about the very possibility of usefully modelling the whole public policy process on this managerial template (Savoie 1995).

It is therefore easy to understand why the new gospel has focused mostly on tinkering with technology in the first instance: on sharpening service delivery systems and evaluating narrowly defined programmes. However, the prophets of the new cosmology promise that the improvement of clarification and reporting will soon lead to questions about the rationale of the different programmes, and about the appropriateness of the allocation of roles and relationships in programmes. They have even promised that through an aggregation of these local and partial measures (as building blocks) they will soon produce macro-indicators of performance for whole departments, and even for whole provincial or federal governments. Indeed, they have already produced prototypes of such measures. This is where the new hyper-rational cosmology runs into difficulties, by unduly simplifying the complexity of the whole public policy process, and by stylizing the whole process on the model of the service delivery problem.

We have identified three ways in which the new cosmology might unwittingly generate unfortunate consequences if attention is not paid to the potential pitfalls generated by this sort of simplification: danger, seduction and quagmire.

OVERSANITIZING THE PUBLIC POLICY PROCESS

The first word of caution is about the danger of an overly sanitized stylization of the public policy process. There are a number of stylizations of the public policy process currently in circulation. They span the whole range from the rational decision-making model to the garbage can model, with all sorts of mixed stylizations in between. The social learning model is one of those middle-of-the-road stylizations, presenting the public policy process as a groping trial-and-error procedure.

The new cosmology has assumed a view of the public policy process that is very close to the rational decision-making model. The goals are presumed to be known and certain, the means–ends relationships clear and the business plans transparent. This stylization sideswipes many of the complexities of the multi-stakeholder power game that underpins much of public policy formation. It flies in the face not only of the day-to-day experience of any Ottawa-watcher, but even of the stylization of the public policy process used by the Clerk of Privy Council (Smith and Taylor 1996).

The new cosmology adopts *holus bolus* the managerial view of the new public administration, and it excises political haggling and the socio-technical milieu from the world of public management. In this ethereal world, transparency is a virtue and every error is an occasion to learn, while in the real world this is not quite the case (Savoie 1995). This view of the public policy process tends to suggest: (a) the separability of policy forma-tion, programme design and delivery mechanism; (b) the sacred nature of the Westminster model of government and the consequent assumption that accountability to the minister must remain untouched as the process is amended; and (c) the assumption that explicit detailed contracts are sufficient to ensure that the policy intended by the senior executives (political and bureaucratic) will be carried out. The fact that it does not correspond to the real world does not appear to bother the ambitious architects of the new cosmology. They plan to construct very tall buildings on this very shaky ground. The result is the production of broad aggregates that may not be very meaningful syncretic summaries of the performance of a whole provincial government, because they are based on the light generated by only a few flickering flashes.

THE SEDUCTION OF QUANTOPHRENIA

The second word of caution is about the seduction of quantophrenia. The greatest appeal of the new cosmol-ogy is that it is not only built on an ideal type of public policy as rational decision-making, it is also a numerical model. Goals, targets, outcomes and results are quantifi-able, and performance indicators are to be computed to ensure that what has been promised can be compared to what has been realized.

As with the five-year plans of the former Soviet Union, the computable representation of reality, however cari-catural and problematic, acquires an all-important cen-trality because of its numerical magic. Reality becomes transmogrified into a numerical representation and performance into a set of flashes. This quantophrenic fixation gives a false impression of certainty and it fun-damentally misrepresents a notion of performance that is essentially fuzzy. In fact, performance in public policy making is an essentially contested concept (as discussed in Chapter 5). While the massaging of numbers probably provides intellectual satisfaction to the masseurs, it is also likely that public management will be drowned in meaningless numbers. The process could end up as an exercise in the management of a numerical representation of reality, rather than the management of reality.

One can only imagine the possibilities opened up by the fixation on numerical outcome measures related only in the most general way to the true performance of programmes. The fantasy land that surrounded the discussion of the five-year plans in the former Soviet Union may provide some insight into what the new numerological game holds in store for us.

PERFORMANCE VALUATION AND EVALUATION

The third word of caution is about the quagmire of performance valuation and evaluation, and the potential for stunting the social learning process. This concern should not be perceived as casting doubt on the skills and commitment of the Canadian Institute of Chartered Accountants or its Public Sector Accounting and Auditing Board. The profession works very hard at developing better evaluative measures. The problems are extremely complex, however, and there is a real danger that valuation in an essentially contested world might trigger perverse adjustments. When social indicators of performance become the new rules of the game, agents adjust their behaviour accordingly. Since whatever sets of indicators are chosen are bound to be partial and imperfect, social learning may be misguided, slowed down or even derailed. It is therefore crucially important not to fall prey to these new indicators, nor to be tempted to use them in complete isolation from the array of other evaluative instruments available, which have had a reasonable track record.

In an essentially contested world, valuation may reasonably take many directions. Therefore it is important that some consensus among the stakeholders be arrived at as to what the purpose of the exercise is supposed to be. This is what is done in the modern internal audit process. However, the very diversity of the valuation process that necessarily ensues makes any comparison of the evaluation process from one place to another, and from one moment to the next, rather difficult. Consequently, it is important to be able to intervene quickly with a meta-evaluation team that has a full grasp of the diverse corrective mechanisms and social learning protocols in use all over public management land. Without such a competence at the top—an audit capacity and a mandate to investigate major foul-ups—it might be extremely difficult to ensure that the learning process works. It is all the more important to have this central competence, given that the new cosmology suggests a battery of indicators and an ongoing monitoring mechanism, but nowhere makes it clear (1) how and through what process the ever-improving indicators will be generated, or (2) what is the nature of those crisis events that would call for an investigation by a meta-evaluation team.

The only way to ensure that a public policy system continues to learn new goals and new means as circumstances change, is to ensure that it is equipped with a dynamic capacity to transform. This is not nested in technology, structure or theory, but in the dynamic interaction among them. In this context, if we accept a Schumpeterian view of things, tinkering with technology—the most likely result of the adoption of the new cosmology (at least at the beginning)—must be seen as the disturbance of a delicate cognitive and learning organization.

The impact of this tinkering should be focused much less on static allocation of chores among sectors, and much more on the effectiveness of dynamic evolutionary learning (Paquet 1991; 1992b). This has important consequences for the public policy process because learning proceeds faster when the process is decentralized, delayered and participative, and operates through a network of units sensitive to local circumstances (Snow, Miles and Coleman 1992). It requires an organizational structure that is dramatically different from the one in place in hierarchical bureaucracies.

Whether one is led by tinkering with the technology of delivery to the redesign of traditional organizations into circular organizations (Ackoff 1994; Mintzberg 1996b), or into spherical structures that rotate competent self-managing teams and other resources around a common knowledge base (Miles and Snow 1995), any such restructuring triggered by new delivery mechanisms is bound to be the source of some reframing. For instance, the creation of a delivery mechanism more sensitive to local circumstances might generate a greater recognition of the variety of needs, and foster a reframing of policy away from a focus on rights and standardized rules defined centrally, to a focus on needs and tailor-made services defined at the periphery (Paquet 1994). The interaction among the different phases of the policy process demands continuous adjustments: this is what organizational learning is all about. If a new logic is introduced at the delivery phase, it will affect the whole process. Modifications in structure and technology may lead to reframing or to blockages and policy messes (Mintzberg 1996a). The grafting onto the public policy process of a battery of performance indicators, and of a gross and imperfect monitoring protocol, without the complementary change in organizational culture, will not produce a dramatic improvement in the process of social learning. Certainly, it does not automatically follow.

CONCLUSION

Does this mean that the new hyper-rational cosmology should not be promoted, or that we should not do everything we can to gain a better sense of what we are doing in the public policy process? Obviously not. Nor, on the other hand, does it mean that we should celebrate the new cosmology as a panacea. In a Schumpeterian world, the benchmarks for assessing the response to the basic governance question are effectiveness and social learning. Although we must strive to ensure maximum learning at the individual and organizational levels, it is most important not to overestimate the extent to which a crude numerical model of the public policy process might help to improve the system of governance.

Experimenting with such models is potentially important and this revolutionary potential should not be denied; but it is equally important not to be naive. The numerical model may well serve to lead to an efficient system of the most ineffective sort. It might also be misused, and serve to maintain federal control over many programmes that should be legitimately devolved to provincial and local governments. This might be done through engineering delivery mechanisms that give the impression that a programme is at arm's length from the federal government when in fact it remains entirely under its spell. That would only lead to more conflicts in a federal system like Canada's (Paquet 1996b).

A wise use of the new cosmology might generate some benefits, but if it is misapplied to a large segment of the public policy process or to the whole system, it might also generate extraordinary disadvantages. A blind search for economy and efficiency could stunt social learning and be destructive. It is therefore important that the new cosmology be considered, not as a panacea, but merely as an hypothesis. It should also be clear that the burden of proof lies on the shoulders of its defenders. On the other hand, old situationologists, like me, who still have faith in the qualitative ways of yesteryear, should at least agree, in the name of fair play, to keep an open mind and pledge never to fall into the sin of methodological cruelty.

CHAPTER 8

Science policy: circumstantial evidence

(written with John de la Mothe)

> *Some circumstantial evidence is very strong,*
> *as when you find a trout in the milk.*
> — HENRY DAVID THOREAU

A question has long haunted Canadians interested in problems of science and technology: how can Canadian activities in science and technology be coordinated so that Canadians can make the highest and best use of their brain power in the pursuit of social and economic prosperity? Over the years, many answers to this question have been offered. Some have been willing to bet that economic competition would provide the requisite drive, even for scientists and other researchers. Others have preferred science policy blueprints through which to plan the national science effort. Still others have sought some sort of compromise on a middle-of-the-road position, somewhere between the pure market and a central plan, some form of loose coordination that could be sold under the rubric of either scientific or economic pragmatism.

Neither faith in the coordinative abilities of perfect market competition nor the belief in a perfectly planned science agenda has provided viable policy alternatives. The market is woefully ill-equipped to take account of the subtle long-term and synergistic benefits of research, and therefore tends to induce significant underinvestment. Top–down government planning is painfully utopian, given that ours is a world laced with complexity and uncertainty. This is made especially clear when dealing, as we do in science and technology policy, with such ill-understood processes as innovation and creativity. Thus, despite the attractive aspects of each of these simple polar-opposite views, one is forced to opt for the third way: bottom–up approaches with a modicum of management or coordination geared toward ensuring minimum waste and maximum gains.

Since World War I, there have been geopolitical and economic pressures on the Canadian government to develop a coordinating function, to ensure that the national science effort is as effective as possible. Yet over the same period, strong science-based interests have defended the gospel of the absolute autonomy of the "Republic of Science" in Canada, resisting even the mention of the word "coordination". The result has been many years of national equivocation, punctuated by a series of unsuccessful attempts to find effective compromises between the need for relevance in matters where public funds are involved and the icon of excellence, which is served best, or so academics assert, by curiosity-oriented and "peer-reviewed" research. The challenge facing any science policy review is to find effective balances, on the one hand between the forces of the market and planning, and on the other hand between the imperative of relevance and that of excellence. Finding the right balance in both cases constitutes the riddle that has vexed our forefathers for some eighty years and that faces the government today.

In the next section of this chapter we shall sketch the interplay between policy objectives and circumstances that has woven a web of unsuccessful attempts at coordination. In the section after that we shall examine the roots of the failures in coping with the same task in the 1970s and 1980s. Then we shall examine the constraints and opportunities facing Canada in designing a science and technology policy today, and sketch the broad contours of a plausible strategy that is likely to constitute a suitable response to these haunting dilemmas. In conclusion we shall venture some suggestions for its smooth implementation.

BY WAY OF THE PAST

Volume 1 of the *Report of the Senate Special Committee on Science Policy*, chaired by the late Maurice Lamontagne, contains a synopsis of the efforts, from the early days of confederation onward, to design some form of science policy in Canada (Senate 1970: 1). There was a great deal happening, even in the 19th century, in Canadian science. The oldest government scientific organization, the Geological Survey of the Province of Canada, was created in 1841. It laid the foundation for the Canadian mining industry. Other government-instigated activities stimulated important work in agriculture, fisheries and forestry. Nevertheless, the Senate committee concluded that, despite clear evidence of scientific activities and development, "on the whole, the growth of Canadian science before World War I was a slow and cautious process" (Senate 1970: 20).

Of course, this should not be surprising. Canada was a young country that had a very limited scientific infrastructure in the years before 1914. In 1917, total expenditure by industry on research and development was less than 150,000 dollars, and a survey of more than 8,000 Canadian firms showed that only 37 had any facilities for research and development at all. Economies then were still very much tied to their natural resource endowments.

Necessity being the mother of invention, the advent of war brought with it the need for a formal science policy. Indeed, World War I involved Canadian scientists and engineers in novel government efforts to apply science both directly to the war effort itself — notably aerial warfare, chemical warfare, naval strategy and the development of automated weaponry — and to broader problems of industrial production. The growing awareness that science and technology might make a difference to social and economic development led industrialists and universities to press for the creation of the National Research Council (NRC) in 1916. Its function was not to carry out any scientific work itself but to survey, plan, advise on and coordinate the national science effort. Its initial budget was 91,600 dollars and it had one full-time member of staff. Only in the 1930s did it begin to develop its own laboratories. This was a mixed blessing for Canadian science policy, for tensions developed as a result. One was between the NRC's function as a central coordinating agency and its role as a government body operating its own laboratories. Another arose from the NRC's struggle with other parts of the bureaucracy for budgets and staff.

World War II posed a major challenge to Canada. Because the private-sector research base was not robust enough to meet the requirements of the war effort, the NRC was funded generously so that it could dramatically expand its operations. Its yearly budget increased from less than one million dollars to close to seven million dollars within months of the beginning of the war. More than twenty new labs were created and the NRC's staff complement grew to more than three hundred.

During Canada's fifteen years of prosperity between the end of World War II and 1960, economic growth proceeded briskly, and science and technology reaped the benefits. By 1947 total gross expenditure on research and development had risen to approximately eighty million dollars, but by 1960 it exceeded 300 million dollars. Such massive expenditure might appear to cry out for coordination, and yet unbridled growth tempered the wish for priority setting. The function of coordination that had been assigned in 1916 to the NRC, which was formally an advisory committee to the Privy Council, had all but disappeared. At the end of the 1940s, a scientific advisory panel was appointed to help the Privy Council Committee on Scientific and Industrial Research (PCCSIR), but the PCCSIR did not play any significant role. Indeed, it did not even meet during the 1950s. Priorities were set nonetheless, as the government *de facto* played a prominent role in the new funding and performance of science and technology work, and a second attempt was made at shaping science policy, this time through the policy of "big bucks". Additional expenditures were not directed toward fostering industry, but were instead directed mainly towards either fuelling the NRC's laboratories, which focused on pure science, or on "big science" projects. The latter were largely pursued by government enterprises in the name of national prestige or in response to an aspiration for Canadian self-sufficiency. The development of nuclear energy and military aircraft were two prominent government initiatives of this sort.

This sort of policy was costly and was not spectacularly successful, as was made very clear in the *Report of the Royal Commission on Government Organization* (the Glassco Commission) in 1963. It was once again recommended that some sort of machinery might usefully coordinate the national science effort, that such machinery should be under the authority of the Treasury Board and that it be given extensive powers. However, on the advice of the President of the NRC, C. J. Mackenzie, whom Prime Minister Lester B. Pearson consulted about the recommendations of the Glassco Commission, the proposed coordinating function was significantly scaled down and weakened. It was located in the Privy Council Office, as a Science Secretariat, in 1964. In 1966, this Secretariat was replaced by the Science Council of Canada, an advisory group of more or less independent persons that was charged with the task of comprehensively assessing

Canada's resources, requirements and potentialities
in science and technology. The Science Council was
never perceived by the bureaucracy as a tool to coordinate the national science effort, yet that did not stop
Omond Solandt, its first Chairman, from telling Senator
Lamontagne's committee in 1970 that the reason the
Council had undertaken to specify national goals was
simply that "somebody has to start".

There was now a plethora of quasi-coordinating
bodies: the NRC, which still retained some of its original role, an increasingly active PCCSIR, the Science
Secretariat, the Science Council of Canada, as well as the
Economic Council of Canada created in 1964. All these
bodies vied with each other for the newly recognized
role of national science coordinator, forming a confusing
maze of institutions interested, in one way or another,
in the question of science and technology coordination.
It was not clear to anyone, including the government,
exactly who was doing the coordinating work. Indeed,
one of the key findings of Senator Lamontagne's committee was that nobody was doing it. This did not seem
to bother either the scientific community, which did not
want any coordination, or the government, which did not
feel the need for any coordination in an age of plenty.
Riding the impressive post-war wave of prosperity, gross
expenditures on research and development in Canada
more than trebled between 1960 and 1970, reaching
one billion dollars.

STORMY WEATHER

By the 1970s, however, economic growth had come to
an abrupt end, not only in Canada but throughout the
industrial world. Stagflation, oil shocks, widespread
slowdown in the growth of productivity and rising structural unemployment, all pointed to a fundamental shift
in the nature of the economic process. As we now know,
a permanent shift had indeed begun, away from wealth
creation based on physical resources toward wealth

creation based on new knowledge, research, science, technology and innovation. This shift has affected everything from the character of job creation, employment, trade and investment flows to the nature of business decisions on development and location. Competitiveness in the 1970s was still dependent, to a significant degree, on resource prices and cost differentials, but comparative advantage was increasingly being defined by science and technology.

Senator Lamontagne's committee clearly recognized this and in its report it complained that, unlike most industrial countries, Canada had yet to articulate a science policy in keeping with the changing circumstances. Canada had evolved in a rather peculiar way and had come to occupy a unique position among industrial nations. It spent much more on scientific research than on technological development, and conducted much more work in government or academic laboratories than in industrial laboratories, with the result that the research and development efforts of the private sector were relatively weak. What the committee called Canada's "hidden science policy" had been consistent since 1919, even though it was an accidental policy defined and implemented by the leaders of the "Republic of Science" in their capacities as senior government officials (Senate 1970: 152).

The evidence presented to the committee clearly indicated that this approach was not well-suited to the challenges of the new knowledge-based economy, but no consensus emerged about what an effective policy machinery might be. There was some action in the early 1970s even so. More reliable statistical data on the national science effort were collected and published, and a new post of Minister of State for Science and Technology was created. Citizens began to recognize the economic value of high technology, and to press for more spending on research and development. At the same time, they were becoming acutely aware of the environmental and health risks associated with unaccountable research, and thus insisted on regulatory frameworks and safe-guards. Science had become a public issue.

The shift in the public's general perception of science, in Canada and elsewhere, began to place entirely new pressures on the scientific enterprise and on the coordinating ambitions of policy-makers (see Nelson 1977; Galbraith 1968; Winner 1977; Leiss 1990). Many countries responded by developing think tanks and policy groups within government and research institutes to assess future trends in technology, risk and the impact of science on society. Examples include the Office of Technology Assessment in Washington, DC, and the work by MIT and the Club of Rome that popularized the phrase "limits to growth". In Canada the Science Council turned its attention to this kind of broadbrush work rather than to direct policy advice, and produced a series of future-oriented studies, such as *Two Blades of Grass* (1970), a report on the future of agriculture; *Cities for Tomorrow* (1971); and *It's Not Too Late ... Yet* (1972), a report on pollution.

Greater awareness, better data and some *de facto* science policy machinery did not amount to much in the face of two major impediments. The first was the growing burden of financial and economic difficulties that forced the Canadian government to attend to urgent economic woes, and therefore neglect long-term objectives. At a time when most countries were increasing their real gross expenditures on research and development, Canadian expenditures declined in real terms for most of the 1970s. The second major stumbling block that prevented any major overhaul of the national science effort, was the moral authority of the "Republic of Science". This community of researchers, who vehemently eschewed the central planning of science and the setting of priorities for science by non-scientists, but still cried out for ever more untied public funds, effectively sabotaged any effort to implement the recommendations of Senator Lamontagne's committee.

It was, and has remained, a dominant view in Canadian scientific circles that any form of science policy that attempted to conduct effective integration, evaluation and planning would be deleterious. E. W. R. Steacie, then President of the NRC, said in 1958 that "we are, in fact, one of the few countries which has recognized the fundamental fact that the control of a scientific organization must be in the hands of scientists" (Stercie 1965: 119–120). This has remained the guiding principle of the "Republic of Science" in its fight against the "Republic of Management" (to use the language of Senator Lamontagne's committee). The fact that this is the prevailing view to this day, is evidenced in the speeches of the Canadian Nobel laureate John Polanyi.

Still, the evolving nature of the world economic process had begun to make an impact on the Canadian scene. With the explosive growth of new high-technology industries, the research and development performed and financed by business almost doubled in real terms between 1976 and 1981, and trebled by 1990. This fresh commitment of resources by business did not pass unnoticed in government circles. There was a renewed interest during the 1980s in a coordinating mechanism that might help to obtain as much "bang for the buck" as possible from this new business spending. There were numerous initiatives to influence the general direction of the Canadian science and technology effort: the Natural Sciences and Engineering Research Council, established in 1979, with its five-year plans; the House of Commons Select Committee on Research, Science and Technology, which began its meetings in 1986; the Council of Science and Technology Ministers; the matching grants policy for collaboration between universities and industry; the National Advisory Board on Science and Technology, set up in 1987; and the Centres of Excellence initiative, launched in 1990.

However, none of these initiatives provided the necessary machinery for effective coordination. The "concerted action model" proposed by Senator Lamontagne's committee in the 1970s, leaving the design and performance of research and devlopment programmes to departments and agencies, but providing a strong central machinery with enough authority to exercise a knowledgeable oversight function, still remains a dead letter.

The dispersed efforts of the federal government could not lead to anything but frustration. The private sector was finally engaged by the challenges of the new knowledge economy, but found its efforts either insufficient or wastefully scattered. Governments appeared ill-equipped to catalyze and steer science and technology initiatives. Indeed, far from having evolved in the direction of providing coordination, these diverse federal activities may even have exacerbated the dispersion by favouring uncoordinated prestige projects. The network of Centres of Excellence, the Canadian Space Agency and the Kaon Factory are all cases in point.

Senator Lamontagne's committee had identified the main sources of difficulty in producing a workable "concerted action model". First, there was the flawed structure of the Canadian economy, characterized by extensive foreign ownership, cowardly financial institutions and a risk-averse population unlikely to distill the entrepreneurial spirit that was thought to be required. Second, the important political clout of the "Republic of Science" and the power of dynamic conservatism that it mustered could not be overstated. Finally, there was the rampant attraction of prestige projects, which remain very seductive for governments in search of instant gratification. These traps remain.

A STRATEGY FOR THE 21st CENTURY

Anyone involved in the development of Canadian science and technology policy, or in reviewing such policy, must first recognize that Canada is a middle-power country. This is not readily acknowledged by those in the "Republic of Science" who still insist on Canada's involvement in every major area of research and its presence in every field of scientific endeavour as something of a *sine qua non*. Neither is it readily acknowledged by those in the bureaucracy who still think of Canada as a world leader, whose ambitions on the science and technology front must reflect this standing.

A FRAMEWORK

The failed attempts of the past have left Canada with a legacy that has not been fully understood. Many of the efforts at formulating a basis for science and technology policy were so extraordinarily constrained by diffidence toward the "Republic of Science" and by the ambitions of the bureaucracy, that policy was often couched in the most grandiose of terms while being fundamentally vacuous in operational terms. Science and technology have been depicted as holding the keys to full employment and prosperity, but this feat is supposed to materialize almost organically, without much explicit or deliberate intervention except in terms of broad targets, such as the ratio between gross expenditures on research and development, and gross domestic product. Such macroscopic views might be elegant, but, like the maps of the early days of cartography, they are not helpful to navigation. Attempts to translate such grandiose views into microeconomic surgical interventions by government always fail, both because of the great looseness of the reasoning that links the broad picture to specific applications, and because of the deep ideological opposition, both in the private sector and in academic circles, to such deliberate, selective and pointed interventions.

What is required in order to design meaningful science and technology policy is nothing less than a reframing of the basic questions, for science and technology policy cannot evolve unless a new social contract is forged among the stakeholders. However, such a contract does not yet appear to be in the offing because, for the time being at least, the stakeholders seem to share very few assumptions, either about the nature of the world we live in or about the ways in which they might most usefully work together.

To guide us in this process we have taken as our point of departure a generic definition of science and technology policy widely used in various recent debates: science and technology policy is a deliberate and coherent attempt to provide a basis for national decisions that influence the size, institutional structure, resources for, and creativity of scientific and technological research in relation to their applications and public consequences. From an examination of these six dimensions, it is possible to derive some preliminary considerations pertaining to the constraints and opportunities that characterize the Canadian scene.

As a middle-power country, Canada must first recognize that its resources are limited, and therefore that the size of its science and technology effort will also have to be limited. Hard choices are necessary, especially in an economy plagued with so much foreign ownership of its industries and so much accumulated debt among its governments.

The only meaningful guiding principles for arriving at such choices have to be rooted in the applications and public consequences of science and technology. These have to be the driving forces that help us in making hard choices. Beyond this, and at a time when dollars are in short supply, the government must recognize that it can affect creativity only in an oblique way. This leads us inexorably to focus on institutional structures.

The notion of institutional structure is very broad. It refers to the range of arrangements surrounding, underpinning and catalyzing the science and technology effort. Quite clearly, for instance, the educational system is one of the cornerstones of any science and technology effort. It provides breadth and capacity to the national research effort, for it generates the requisite background to partake in the scientific and technological conversations that are going on all over the world. Canada therefore needs a strong basic educational and research infrastructure in order to fuel its personnel and intelligence needs.

Over and beyond these baseline requirements, which may be regarded as the dues that must be paid before Canada can take part in international science and technology conversations, Canada has to identify the broad sectors, clusters or niches in which applications and public consequences might be the most positive. This must take both competences and needs into account. For instance, telecommunications and remote sensing might be key areas in which Canada has both significant competences and needs. Another niche might be cold ocean technologies.

No one stakeholder has complete and perfect knowledge of this terrain. The contours of a strategy that is best adapted to Canadian circumstances will emerge from extensive conversations (speaking, listening and thinking) with all those who have portions of this information: industrialists, scientists, engineers, entrepreneurs, bureaucrats, academics, futurists, managers, technologists, engineers, production personnel and so on.

This process of social learning need not converge at all, nor need it converge quickly, if any stakeholder proves unwilling to entertain alternative scenarios and to accept meaningful compromises. In this process of learning, the black-and-white politics of principles have to give way to the grey world of the politics of compromise. Compromise in the process of social learning is not a sign of weakness, but is instead an essential ingredient. In particular, when dealing with broad policy issues such as science and technology, it is essential to recognize that a more transactive process is required to tap into local knowledge. The social learning model is built on mutual learning by experts and clients. The objective is to create a wholly new situation in order to generate the possibility of going substantially beyond the initial hypotheses (Paquet 1991b; Williams 1979; Vos and Balfoort 1989).

HOPEFUL AVENUES

With these caveats and guidelines clearly in mind, the central questions the government must ask as it embarks on its science and technology policy review have to do with: (1) identifying the crucial needs of Canadian industry, and the basic strengths and weaknesses of Canadian science and technology; (2) eliciting the ways in which needs and competences might be best harmonized; and (3) assigning rights and responsibilities in a renewed social contract among all the stakeholders on the science and technology scene. This would call, in principle, for an OECD-type review of science policy in Canada, and a critical examination of the challenges that Canada will face as a result of recent economic and social developments, as well as a stock-taking of what is known about innovation, and about the management of science and technology. We would also need a good cartography of what we are starting with. This would enable us to sketch a workable strategy, as well as a protocol through which to put it into action.

This cannot be accomplished in this short chapter. Nonetheless, we can identify some avenues that appear to call for priority attention. Indeed, we are led to suggest a three-pronged approach to the strategic conferencing involved in the development of science and technology policy. We believe that such an approach may offer a focus for the search, and help to avoid many of the pitfalls experienced in the past as well as the difficulties outlined above.

First, we would like to emphasize the importance of focusing, as a matter of priority, on science and technology infrastructure as an enabling strategy. Second, we insist that the search tackle the problem, not on the basis of microeconomic analyses or macroeconomic policy, but with action at the meso-level, where effective link-ages can be made between broad objectives and action, and where the requisite amount of trust can be gener-ated and the most effective alliances can evolve. Third, it should be recognized from the outset that transversal coordination is a vastly preferable way to go. However, since this would require nothing less than a system-wide overhaul of the public service culture, an interim loose form of vertical coordination might be more feasible in the near term.

An infrastructure strategy draws attention to the fact that one of the main sources of dysfunction in economic growth is the chasm between technology and economic infrastructure. The government must provide the neces-sary social overhead capital that is likely to support and stimulate private-sector action, rather than meddling with day-to-day decisions. Yet government cannot be simply a supplier of some of the infrastructure. It must also actively promote the integration of all the various sources of existing infrastructure. Moreover, it must do so on the basis of a multi-staged strategy in which local clusters and industrial corridors are leveraged and facilitated, and thus integrated, by technology infra-structures. The potential spill-over effects including synergies, job creation, and linkages between users and producers, would be considerable (see Tassey 1992; Lundvall 1988).

What is required is to focus the strategic search on the middle-range phenomena where synergies and interac-tions are most visible, and where intervention is most likely to be effective. Clusters and networks, channels and synergies are the new meaningful "units of analysis". They constitute the level at which effective intervention can be achieved, and at which science and technology policy should be directed. It might be useful, for instance, to revisit certain ideas of the 1980s that have not been adequately studied or exploited, such as the metropolitan technology councils proposed by the Science Council of

Canada in 1984, or to give more attention to ongoing initiatives such as business networks, which have not yet received the attention they deserve.

Finally, in a perfect world it would appear absolutely ideal to be able to ensure the coordination of science and technology activities through those networks that bind all meaningful actors. However, the degree of distrust between actors is so high, and their reluctance to cooperate, unless dollars are up for grabs, is so rampant, that one cannot hope to have such "virtual structures" emerge or succeed in the short run.

A second-best solution would be to ask Industry Canada, jointly with International Trade Canada, to act as "quarterback" in a loose horizontal coordination game, since a necessarily heavy focus of science and technology policy must be on industry and economic growth. However, in a world where even senior departmental bureaucrats have been held at bay by their own science personnel, and dare not hold their own science-based units accountable to government priorities for fear of being perceived as barbarians at the gate, such an arrangement would entail extraordinary political and operational difficulties. We cannot see, in the short term, how such a coordinating effort could escape being seen as anything but tampering in the affairs of another department. This prevents the development of a serious science policy.

One is therefore forced to seek a third-best solution: loose vertical coordination. In order for the federal government to gain better knowledge of how it spends billions of dollars a year on science and technology and to understand why the present allocation of resources is (or is not) appropriate, a well-placed joint committee, perhaps between the Privy Council Office and the Treasury Board, is needed. Without the rapid establishment of such a formal structure and function, there is a real danger that in the next inevitable round of budget cuts the "hidden" science and technology budget will simply be devastated without any real sense of priority being allowed to prevail. As a result Canada could easily find itself in the worst of all worlds, having "rationalized" or eliminated half of its science and technology budget, but the wrong half.

CONCLUSION

Our three avenues may not appear to be very clearly benchmarked. The reason is simply that they cannot be defined *ex ante*. If there is any meaning to the ongoing social learning that underpins the public policy process (the process of learning implies both better means and better ends), it is that only a broad consultation of all the stakeholders can reveal the details and the broad potential of science and technology policy. Our sense is, therefore, that at this juncture in Canada's history these three avenues are the only ones that do not lead to yet another *cul de sac*.

How is one to implement the process of social learning? By transforming what might easily degenerate into a perfunctory consultation into a true strategic social learning exercise, based on extensive negotiations with stakeholders and designed to answer four basic questions: what is feasible? what is socially acceptable? what is not too destabilizing? and what can be implemented? A good example of this sort of process is Energy Options. Although the process was somewhat derailed when some experts effectively hijacked it, it illustrates the great benefits of the search process. The difficulties the Energy Options process experienced might even serve as a cautionary tale when launching a parallel process in the science and technology field (see Paquet 1989a). Stakeholders should not simply be allowed to reiterate their usual complaints or demands, but must be nudged by senior politicians and bureaucrats into a multilogue where every proposition would be discussed with these four basic questions in mind. It might not be as difficult as all that to ensure that the multilogue will converge on certain science and technology priorities and directions for the medium term.

All that will then remain is to translate these priorities into a series of retooling and restructuring tasks. There should be new mandates for the various science-based departments and agencies, such as the NRC, the Natural Sciences and Engineering Research Council and the Natural Resources Department. There should be a critical review of the role of the various programmes and operations related to science and technology, such as the network of science counsellors posted in Canada's embassies and high commissions. The goal should be to focus attention on government priorities, not departmental ones. A loose vertical coordination of all this activity must be assured through the guidance of an interim joint committee between the Privy Council Office and the Treasury Board.

To be sure, there would be bellyaching on the part of the "Republic of Science", outcries on the part of science-based departments and probably little cooperation from either group at first. However, as it became clear to all that they must choose to be part of the problem or part of the solution, and that being part of the problem might result in across-the-board budget cuts, there should be a meeting of minds on the need to take part in this learning exercise.

CHAPTER 9

Foreign policy: the many are smarter than the few

> *The cure for the ailments of democracy is more democracy.*
> — JOHN DEWEY

This chapter was first presented at a conference with a captivating, perplexing and exceedingly circumspect title: "Polycentric Governance?: Subnational Governments and Foreign Policy in an Age of Globalization". First, such a title plainly stated a fact of life: the presence and importance of subnational actors of all sorts (regional, sectoral, sectional) in the making of foreign policy, just as in the making of most domestic policies around the world. Second, it unexpectedly put a question mark after the expression "polycentric governance", as if it were merely a conjecture rather than a fact. Third, for reasons that were not made entirely clear, it appears to draw attention mainly to subnational "state" actors, to the exclusion of all others, thereby occluding whatever is not "public governance" *stricto sensu* (Ladeur 2004).

In light of this cautious problematic, this chapter is somewhat radical. It takes as a point of departure the concluding remarks made by James Rosenau in his book *Distant Proximities* (2003): that the world is confronted with the challenge of "Möbius-web governance", a multipolar/multidirectional, mixed formal/informal mode of governance that mobilizes the contribution of all actors, from the public, private and social sectors, as producers of governance. This eye-catching label was inspired by the Möbius strip, where the inside and outside are one and the same. Rosenau looks into this abyss, cosily nests this daunting mode of governance within a typology that also accommodates a variety of more traditional genres of governance (top–down, bottom–up, market, network, side by side), and then walks away, leaving this *terra incognita* for another voyage. This chapter makes the case for the effectiveness of a very bold version of such an approach: open-source Möbius-web governance.

The argument is built in four stages. First, I shall briefly underline some major developments of great consequence in world affairs: the relative decline in the role of the state and the state's disaggregation into subnational fragments; the parallel emergence of multi-sectoral and multi-level governing mechanisms; and the illiberal flavour of the state-centric culture of adjudication that attempts, in the face of new and complex situations, to grant ever more arbitration power to the state's supertechnocrats.

Second, I shall suggest that, while this rearguard action by states is unfolding, new units have coalesced at the infranational and cross-national levels that are new loci of productivity growth and innovation. These new nests of actors have not only important stakes in domestic and foreign policy in a Möbius-web world, but also much of the knowledge and power needed to take part in this governing process. These units and actors are often non-governmental or non-state units and actors. Indeed, they are often the result of cross-sectoral arrangements and mixing, and demand more and more access to the policy process at the domestic and international levels.

This is not the place to document the damage done by national governments' top–down, one-size-fits-all counter-approaches to these emerging forces, and by their propensity to coerce and adjudicate in order to maintain their hegemony. Suffice it to say that the new dynamic units are actively seeking ways to take part in the construction and maintenance of a multiplicity of regime-like arrangements that challenge the assumption of nation states and regional governments that they have the only legitimate and authorized voices in policy-making.

Third, I shall argue that open-source Möbius-web governance offers an opportunity to build a very resilient foreign policy, piecemeal and bottom up, through effective prototyping and "serious play" (terms that will have to be added to the vocabulary of international relations), and that the fear of chaos evoked by traditional state-centric Jacobins, fighting any effort to construct such a regime of governance, is much exaggerated.

Fourth, I shall examine the feasibility of such a transformation of the Canadian foreign policy process on the basis of both the experiences of the World Trade Organization and cognate international organizations, and the current discussions inside Canada about opening up the process. While international forums give plenty of evidence of an evolving open-source international policy-making process, it would not be unfair to say that the scene inside Canada is less promising. It is no different in this area from what exists in other Canadian policy forums: an arrogant old-guard big-government phalanx within the federal government still maintains that there is no need for any opening up of the process, that Canada must speak with one voice internationally, and that Ottawa is uniquely and solely equipped to determine what this unique message should be. While this techno-cratic voice is being challenged, it is still very powerful.

In conclusion, I shall argue that the conventional wisdom defended by this old guard is wrong-headed and dysfunctional, is unlikely to lead to an effective foreign policy process and most likely will inflict significant damage upon the fabric of Canadian society.

THE DISPERSIVE REVOLUTION

If one had to characterize the drifts in the world order experienced over the past thirty years or so, one could do worse than to refer to these transformations as the echoes of a dispersive revolution. The OECD's Forum for the Future has documented the long-term transformation of "geo-socio-technical systems" over this period and probed their contours over the years to come. Four reports have been published, on technology, economic growth, diversity and creativity, and governance (OECD 1998; 1999; 2000; 2001). The major challenge identified in these reports has to do with "geo-governance". Technological, economic and social dynamisms require new ways to ensure effective coordination in a world where power, resources and information are ever more widely and asymmetrically distributed.

In such a world the centre cannot hold, and there has been a significant implosion of all the traditional behemoths: centrally planned economies, totalitarian or "mass society" regimes, centralized information or innovation systems. All modern effective systems have tended to become more decentralized and distributed, organizationally, spatially or both (Paquet 2005a; 2005b). Moreover, the multiplex relationships holding these diverse centralized systems together and helping them to reinforce one another, have also fizzled out. The linkages between state, nation, elites and territory that provided much of the social glue have been shaken loose. While states and nations, and related notions of citizenship and identity, have traditionally been anchored in territory, they have of late become much more footloose and "deterritorialized". As a result, the hierarchical and authoritarian geo-governance nation-state structures that have prevailed for more than one hundred years have proved to be rather ineffective in meeting the coordinating needs of socio-technical systems that are continually stirred by new technological advances, external forces generated by globalization, greater social differentiation and a higher level of interdependence.

A dispersive revolution has led organizations to adapt to the new circumstances by various processes of disintegration of existing arrangements and quasi-reintegration in more diffuse patterns. The search for heightened capacities for speed, adaptiveness, flexibility and innovation, based on new forms of integration and coordination, has triggered the emergence, not only of new structures and tools, but also of a whole new way of thinking. Private, public and social concerns have ceased to be drivers of people, and have become "drivers of learning" (Wriston 1992: 119), learning organizations based on new forms of alliances and partnerships that are rooted in more horizontal relationships and moral contracts (Paquet 1992a; 2001). This dispersive revolution has led to the crystallization of new network business organizations, more subsidiarity-focused governments, and increasingly virtual, elective and malleable communities. Major challenges to governance have ensued, centring on how to acquire speed, flexibility and innovativeness while maintaining the necessary coordination, coherence and integrity.

These forces have been at work for quite some time, but their impact has been considerably heightened by the digital revolution. Internetworked technologies have transformed all levels of governance. As technology has made participation not only possible, but easier and less costly, businesses, governments and communities have been confronted with greater demands for participation. Citizens have become more active partners in governance. This has redefined the "public space" and even the notion of "publics". New publics have emerged and, through their prodding, new regimes of distributed governance, based on a wider variety of more fluid and always evolving groups of stakeholders, have developed deeper roots (Angus 2001; Tapscott and Agnew 1999). This expansion of the democratic sphere has elicited partial and temporary arrangements in response, involving meso-level summits, task forces, clubs and partnerships, regime groupings, networks of cities and the like, largely based on "soft power" (incentives and persuasion) and "soft laws" (flexibility, evolving moral contracts, memorandums of understanding). These contraptions may only partially and imperfectly meet the imperatives of effectiveness, transparency or legitimacy, but they have often been the best that could be practically accomplished.

Most nation states have responded to these pressures by agreeing to some modest degree of deconcentration of power and resources to subnational levels. However, devolution has often been designed to ensure that real power will not be diffused too much and will remain within reach of the centre. The rationale provided for such timid deconcentration and hesitation to proceed with effective decentralization is that centralization might need to be re-established quickly in times of global crisis. Yet it is difficult to rationalize such a reluctance to decentralize on this sole basis. There has also been reluctance to share power, and there is a tendency on the part of governments to declare, without a scintilla of evidence, but with considerable bravura, that any significant decentralization would impair their capacity to perform their duties in both normal and abnormal times.

Some subnational "states" have gleefully grabbed the limited opportunities to acquire new leverage, whether real or symbolic, while others have resisted these symbolic and fragile gifts from the centre, which might so easily be clawed back. The slight broadening of the oli-garchic base of the state and the temporary sharing of state power that has ensued, have therefore often been nothing but cosmetic reshuffling, since the true power bases remain the same and only surface realignment has been offered. However, because, in some cases, disaggregated states have ensued, opportunities for effective devolution and power-sharing have recently been seized more aggressively by a number of subnational states, to such an extent that one may speak of a new order emerging (Slaughter 2004).

Up to now, this evolution has largely remained, in most countries, a surface intergovernmental laundering of power: that is because, at many levels, these initiatives have failed to: (1) recognize and gauge sufficiently the complexity of the policy challenges lurking ahead that call for new types of concerted action; (2) acknowledge the fact that resources, knowledge and power are irretrievably distributed well beyond the ambit of the state; (3) accept the harsh reality that no one is omniscient or omnipotent; (4) factor in the fact that transnational, local and non-state actors are bound to become more important; and (5) understand that collaboration is the new categorical imperative.

It is particularly intriguing that the structures that have emerged in response to this dispersive revolution have taken quite different paths on the economic and political fronts. In the 20th century, increased regulation of capitalism and increased deregulation of democracy appear to have been the dominant trends (Zakaria 2003). This strategy has not been entirely successful: economic regulation has crippled economic growth and innovation, while, on the political front, there has been a growing fear of emergent publics and their demands. This has led many to argue that, in the 21st century, deregulating capitalism and regulating democracy even more might be the better way. Indeed, economic deregulation has now come to be the conventional wisdom, while the rising culture of adjudication that has emerged in recent years has given much more power to superbureaucrats, judges, central banks and commissars of all stripes, and has amounted to efforts at regulating democracy (Paquet 2006a).

Many eminent scholars who had always been diffident about devolution have celebrated this growth of undemocratic institutions, arguing that the professional technocrats in charge of these superinstitutions are more efficient than the amateurs elected as members of legislatures. These scholars have proposed the multiplication

of such adjudicatory institutions in various areas, such
as health or the environment (Blinder 1997; Dror 2001;
and Zakaria 2003: 248ff). Others (and I am one of
them) have denounced such creeping illiberal delegation
of various tasks to independent bodies as a seductive
but damnable way to try to overcome the ailments of
democracy by delegating more and more functions to
the technocracy (Paquet 2006a). For this latter group,
as for John Dewey (1927), the solution to democracy's
ailments is more democracy, not less.

GOVERNING IN A PLURALIST SOCIETY

The dispersive revolution, compounded by the increased
social diversity of the texture of modern communities, has consolidated the pluralist nature of society.
Globalization has accentuated the intermingling of populations, and most societies have become more multiethnic
and more multilingual. It has also generated a new
transnational competition that has affected groups of
actors quite differently, both within and across borders.
City regions have emerged and have become impressive
growth poles, with world markets. Meso-systems of
innovation have come to dominate the global industrial
landscape. New "communities of practice" have taken
shape, while others have dwindled. Such groups, national
and transnational, have forged a variegated fabric, and
public, private and social "communities of meaning",
often operating in circumscribed issue domains and/or
"territories", have emerged as meaningful stakeholders
(Paquet 2005b).

Shallow diversity could be tackled by political arrangements that one might lightly characterize as "boutique
pluralism", to adapt an expression used by Stanley Fish
(1999: Chapter 4). Boutique pluralism recognizes the
legitimacy of diversity and pays attention to it, but only
as long as it does not lead to any significant adjustment
in the prevailing order. In a general way, however, the
political process chooses to ignore these differences and

strips individuals of any characteristics except their citizenship, in an effort to find a legitimate way to aggregate preferences. It creates the citizen as rational being, erasing all differences in order to impose the "citizen without qualities" as the arbiter of all decisions (Paquet 2005b). Deep diversity is not so easily erased. In such a world, the citizen without qualities cannot claim to be the sole legitimate source of power. Differentiation is not circumstantial but essential. This calls for an explicit recognition that governance must take these differences seriously. The diffraction of society generated by deep diversity has two major effects. First, even with the best of intentions, it is quite difficult to ensure that all the varied points of view are fully acknowledged and appropriately weighted in collective decision-making. Aggregating such intractable value differences in macro-baskets, and allowing for some horse-trading, is clever, but it is not helpful. It may lead to certain expedient and opportunistic balancing acts at the higher level, but such aggregation of social choices does not necessarily lead to the best outcomes, or to consistent and fair choices, or even to choices that take diversity seriously.

Second, it generates different sorts of conflict between or among factions. These conflicts are not all necessarily of the same nature or resolvable in the same ways. For instance, one must distinguish between routine distributional issues that can be resolved by discussion and negotiation, and categorical conflicts that cannot be so resolved because things such as identities "cannot be changed by rational arguments" (Fleiner 2001).

Truly plural societies are societies that explicitly recognize that individuals and groups can legitimately have different value systems. To pursue their different objectives they require positive freedom: the capacity and opportunity to actively and effectively pursue these values, and to work proactively at the elimination of the constraints or "unfreedoms" that prevent them from doing so. Moreover, truly plural societies deny that there is any constantly overriding value (Kekes 1993: 19). This entails the inevitability of conflicts and the need to develop reasonable conflict-resolution mechanisms, based on some core working credo, however minimal and strictly procedural, that disputants may share. While the plurality of conceptions of the good life increases the range of valued possibilities, not all possibilities are reasonable. There is also a need for limits, and for the justification of such limits as excluding unreasonable possibilities, unreasonable ways of pursuing them or ways that might simply maximize destructive conflicts.

There is a quasi-doctrinaire dominant belief forming part of the prevalent ethos, that the state is the centre of the public sphere and the privileged locus, if not the only locus, where conflicts among groups are to be resolved. It is my view that in a modern, pluralist, knowledge-based society there is no privileged or transcendent locus of conflict resolution, and, therefore, that the valence of politics and the state is considerably overstated. It is more realistic to admit that horizontal, community relationships are as important as the vertical relationships between the citizen and the state. The reduction in the relative importance of the state and state-centred politics, disenchantment with the political, the drift toward a reduction of the intermediation role of the political, its reconfiguration in new sites, all this means a shift from "big G government" to "small g governance" (Paquet 1999a).

"Small g governance" can be defined as effective coordination when resources, information and power are widely distributed. This does not mean that "big G government" is imploding. There is no doubt that the world is changing with the pressures of globalization, deepening diversity and citizens' wanting to participate more, but the public sector continues to play a crucial role in sustaining a healthy society through the provision of infrastructure and social overhead capital that would not be produced otherwise. Such necessities make it easy for state technocrats to bombastically make the case for a strong state, and to claim that command and control are required to correct demonstrated market failures. This is a *non sequitur*. Public-sector intervention may be necessary, but it need not be from the centre, or without significant participation by, and collaboration among, private and social actors.

The many concurrent drifts, (1) from national to subnational actors (private, public or social), (2) from government to governance, and (3) from central government to regional/local government, are therefore often confounded in debates. It has proved much easier for state bureaucrats to persuade the citizenry that the agonistic choice is either centralization or chaos, than for their critics to persuade citizens that what is required is a very different institutional order in western-style democracies, an order anchored in a philosophy of subsidiarity that reduces the scope of centralized state action in normal times (Paquet 1999a; Hubbard and Paquet 2007a).

In this new world, as in a Möbius strip, there is no inside or outside. At all times agents operating domestically are forced to face various forms of competition from the outside and, in order to survive, must engage in a variety of evolving arrangements with agents abroad that have complementary assets. Since the issue domains are varied, and the constellations of actors involved in these various transnational arrangements are not identical, the nation state cannot always provide a standard security zone for all these agents, for whom the world is their oyster.

Centrally important is "preceptoral politics", with stewards from all sectors becoming facilitators, called upon to reframe our views of the public realm, to design organizations of mutual education and to set off the learning process necessary to elicit, if possible, a latent consensus about what can and cannot be done (Marquand 1988; Schön and Rein 1994). Such learning is unlikely to occur easily in today's deeply diverse society, whether through national-level institutions or through institutions that lie completely or even primarily within the public sector. It will in all likelihood be based on (1) middle-range (meso) institutions, possibly built upon the city regions and "communities of practice" that are emerging as new units of analysis for policy development (Hubbard and Paquet 2005); or (2) networks designed to promote communication and co-operation on issues that mobilize existing groups and communities at the local level, or forums that are likely to remobilize the commitment of the citizenry in organizations scaled to fit (Hubbard and Paquet 2007a).

This underpins a process of policy-making that is based on intelligence and innovation within issue domains, a dynamic monitoring by those closer to the issues, which feeds an innovative learning process and embraces all stakeholders. This new form of governance, based on continuing feedback and constant problem reformulation as experiences accumulate, also requires new partnerships between the public, private and social realms, and between elected officials, bureaucrats and players from other sectors. This is a world of moral contracts among members of networks, of negotiated norms that are much less rigid and less likely to foster adversarial relations than if the work is done through formal regulations and rules. As Morgan (1988: 163) puts it, "The general idea is that if it is possible to agree on the broad principles that particular sets of regulations strive to achieve, it should be possible to produce a flexible set of arrangements that satisfy the interested parties without hamstringing operations."

In this context the state is to become not only a less important actor, but also, and most importantly, an enabling learning organization, ensuring a constant dialogue with the citizenry and improving the communicative competence of its citizens. This requires some organizational development and institution-building, since one cannot rely exclusively on organic feedback. New instrumentalities are necessary if a capacity to learn at the centre, and a capacity for quick feedback and instantaneous action at the periphery, are to materialize.

These new instrumentalities do not need to fit nicely into only one of the private, public or civic sectors. The different logics of market, state and reciprocity may cohabit in the design of the most efficient arrangements. Indeed, they may be usefully commingled (Hubbard and Paquet 2002). Such commingling is increasingly becoming an accepted vehicle (Goldsmith and Eggers 2004). In this world, built on a multiplicity of flexible arrangements, governing by network is the rule and effective leadership might best be described, in the words of Harlan Cleveland (2002: xv), as "bringing people together to make something different happen."

This cannot be done by coercion, but will be arrived at mostly by negotiated agreements. For this sort of leadership of equals to work, rich communication, coordinating activities, relations-building and trust are all required. In this world of collaboration much depends on how people work together and how they communicate. Leaders are truly connectors, who instruct members of their "communities of practice" in a light way, often by example. This transforms the usual pattern of motivation: one can no longer be satisfied with monetary carrots and accountability sticks. Trust and professionalism are crucial when collaboration is central (Evans and Wolf 2005).

Public-sector leaders must maximize public value by concentrating on building core government capabilities and identifying what partners the state might benefit most from collaborating with, and in what ways. The public sector becomes itself a connector and an enabler, and not necessarily a doer (Paquet 2006b). This does not necessarily mean that the public interest will be neglected in any way. Governing by network does, however, wield a different sort of power: power with, instead of power over.

"Möbius-web governance" is a label one might use to connote this new ecology of governance. It is characterized by mixed formal and informal structures, and by processes that are multidirectional (vertical, horizontal and transversal). The dynamics of such hybrid and baroque arrangements are intricate, and overlap at several levels to form "a singular weblike process that, like a möbius, neither begins nor culminates at any level or at any point in time" (Rosenau 2003: 397). Such governance requires that authority be dispersed and decentralized.

FOREIGN POLICY AS PROTOTYPING AND SERIOUS PLAY

It would be wrong to suggest that this new world has only just sprung into existence: *natura non facit saltum*. The central governments of nation states have always paid some attention to subnational groups and subnational interests when shaping their foreign policies. Indeed, particular elites have traditionally been very influential in the formation of domestic and international policies alike. The process has been informal at times, but has also taken on some formal attire. Over the past twenty years, for instance, the Canadian government has customarily consulted sectoral parties with an interest in foreign trade policy. However, these consultations have been extremely limited and the experience of the Sectoral Advisory Groups on International Trade has had mixed results. Interactions between the federal government, on the one hand, and provincial, regional, city-regional and sectional interests, on the other, have remained rather more limited and confrontational than extensive and collaborative.

However, the acceleration of globalization and the deepening of diversity within advanced democracies, have put additional pressure on the system of late and have revealed that the apparatus in place may leave too much to be desired. First, consultation mechanisms are mostly controlled by the federal government. Second, the advisory nature of the relationship has meant that a voice was granted, but not necessarily a hearing. Third, the dynamics of deliberation is grossly excluded: groups are not really engaged in discussions as partners.

What lurks behind this situation is the remnant of a Hegelian-flavoured metaphysics. The State, tellingly spelled with a capital "S" and meaning, mostly, the federal state, is presumed to be the fundamental societal organism, with moral purposes that transcend those of its individual citizens. Therefore, depending on the coefficient of Hegelianism being harboured, tinkering with the State's decision-making is perceived as, more or less, *lèse-majesté*. For the soft Hegelians, there is more to the state than service provision, but this does not prevent them, at times, from legitimately seeking more efficiency and effectiveness in alternative, non-state delivery systems. For the hard Hegelians, tinkering with any aspect of the State that may reduce its scope, or ambit or power can only be regarded with suspicion. For them the task of finding ways for all interested parties to take part in the making of foreign policy will not only appear to be quite difficult, but will be regarded as nothing less than sacrilegious and utopian.

To borrow a phrase from Geoffrey Vickers (1983: xxvii) the concern here "is not with solving problems but with understanding situations". Problem-solving is never more than fifteen percent of effective stewardship. The rest requires a deeper understanding of realities that are often less than fully describable and less than well-structured, but that is the unconditional prerequisite before a solution can become effective. The task ahead for the makers of foreign policy requires a significant amount of experimentation and an acceptance that experiments will differ from sector or region to sector or region, and will often fail. The guideline for such experimentation, therefore, cannot be instant success, but minimum regret. Failures of governance cannot be corrected by simply adding on mechanical contraptions, any more than electricity has emerged from efforts at improving candles. In the end some reframing and some cultural change will be required.

The key to an evolution like this comprises: (1) a drift toward "open-source federalism", a form of federalism that enables each citizen and each group of citizens to have as much access as possible to the "code" and to tinker freely with the way the system works, within certain well-accepted constraints; (2) priority for "serious play", the development of a premium on innovation and experimentation with the view that, if a thousand flowers bloom, one might be able to better retool, restructure and reframe innovatively and productively (Schrage 2000); and (3) a full recognition of the wisdom of crowds.

OPEN SOURCE AND ISSUE DOMAINS

One of the central features of modernity is the existence of a plurality of conversations through which practical people hope to be able to reconcile and to articulate in some loose but comprehensive manner, some common mode of conversation. Federalism, if it is thought of as a regime, can be regarded as a social technology that has the capacity to build such a means of articulation. The original variegated fabric of Canada explains why traditional federalism was seized upon as a workable social technology. In the recent past, however, there has been an extraordinary growth of diversity of all sorts in our modern societies and the plurality of conversations has made most societies truly polyphonic.

In the face of such deep diversity, traditional federalism does not appear to be as powerful an instrument as many had hoped. It has mainly developed along territorial lines and has come to be fundamentally associated with a form of geographical essentialism that is "politically naïve, constitutionally undesirable and theoretically irrelevant" (Carter 1998: 55). Even when federalism has attempted to inject a "national" flavour into such geographical essentialism or has tried to transform itself into a multinational federalism, the results have not been great, because diversity has by now acquired such polymorphous dimensions that the simple categories of territory and nation have failed to grapple with deep diversity in any significant way (Paquet 2005b: Chapter 13).

To the extent that the terrain of operations has become so diverse and the array of actively interested stakeholders is now so varied, the best way to accommodate such terrains and such stakeholders is by dealing with them relatively separately, empowering them, and, as I have suggested above, giving them as much access as possible to the "code". Creating a collection of open-source approaches appears to be the answer.

By partitioning the terrain into issue domains and "communities of meaning", it is possible to identify a vast number of sub-games that require specific treatment. This partitioning does not exclude giving attention to territory and nation, and knitting them together into a relatively coherent whole, but it does not provide these global dimensions with some overarching dominant role. Each issue domain (such as health care, education or the environment) is multifaceted and must be dealt with on an ad hoc basis, with its own governance. This in turn calls for all the stakeholders to be allowed to tinker with the existing arrangements, within certain limits.

The expression "ecology of governance" has been proposed by Walt Anderson to identify this new fluid form of governance, with "many different systems and different kinds of systems interacting with one another, like the multiple organisms in an ecosystem" (Anderson 2001: 252). Such arrangements are not necessarily "neat, peaceful, stable or efficient ... but in a continual process of learning and changing and responding to feedback", and must remain at all times an open system that has the capacity to learn and to evolve: the model is not a cathedral but a bazaar (Raymond 1999). This open system shapes the required mix of principles and norms, rules and decision-making procedures likely to promote the preferred mix of efficiency, resilience and learning.

The template likely to be of use in this regime-based federalism may not be available yet, but it is not unworkable. Experiments in the private sector have established that uncentralized networks are workable arrangements, even in complex transnational organizations. The most interesting example is the "chaord" underpinning the operating structure of VISA (Hock 1995). Hock has shown that in attempting to govern something as complex as VISA's financial empire, for instance, the design problem was so momentous that a new form of uncentralized organization had to be created. This was seen as the only way to ensure durability and resilience in such a complex organization, exposed to a vast array of turbulent contextual circumstances, but also having to face the immense coordination challenge involved in orchestrating the work of more than 20,000 financial institutions in more than 200 countries trying to serve hundreds of millions of users.

This new form of organization would provide both the main purpose, and the mix of norms and mechanisms likely to underpin its realization, through bottom–up effervescence, within the context of some loose framework of guiding principles agreed to by all. Hock has given some examples of the principles, norms and rules that cannot be simply dichotomized, and has defined the sort of organization used to cope with these challenges in the construction and design of VISA (Hock 1995; 1999: 137–139):

- it must be equitably owned by all participants; no member should have an intrinsic advantage; all advantages should result from ability and initiative;
- power and function must be distributive to the maximum; no function and no power should be vested with any part that might be reasonably exercised by any lesser part;
- governance must be distributive; no individual or group of individuals should be able to dominate deliberations or control decisions;
- to the maximum degree possible, everything should be voluntary;

- it must be infinitely malleable, yet extremely durable; it should be capable of constant, self-generated modification without sacrificing its essential nature;
- it must embrace diversity and change; it must attract people comfortable with such an environment, and provide an environment in which they can thrive.

It will not be surprising that, much as in the case of VISA's "chaord", federalism, as a way of thinking and as a way of governing organizations, has been explicitly mentioned and its spirit echoed in a variety of guiding maxims that provide the culture of emerging organizations. Charles Handy (1992) has identified a few such principles:

- authority must be earned from those over whom it is exercised;
- people have both the right and the duty to sign their work;
- autonomy means managing empty spaces;
- twin (status and task) hierarchies are necessary and useful;
- what is good for me should be good for the corporation.

No single template is likely to become a rigid recipe for a mixed regime-based organization, but both "chaords" and federal systems are interesting illustrations of plausible and credible experiments. Both organizational forms are examples of institutional and organizational mixing. In a multidimensional world there is always some scope for modification of the parameters (Paquet 2005b).

The challenge is to show how such a system might effectively transform Canadian federalism into a foreign policy apparatus capable of better serving Canadians, while at the same time maintaining a degree of coherence and integrity that would enable it to function smoothly.

This is where the dynamics leading to permanent deliberation, and the evolving and always-in-transition features of the apparatus are central to the success of this
sort of arrangement.

PROTOTYPING AND SERIOUS PLAY

It is not sufficient to ensure open access. One must also
ensure that the appropriate motivations are nurtured so
that all are engaged in "serious play", the capacity for
citizens to truly become producers of governance through
tinkering with the stewardship apparatus within certain
limits. This, in turn, requires that the requisite amounts
of collaboration and trust prevail. It calls for a reconfiguration of federalism, taking "communities of meaning"
seriously and allowing their presence to weigh heavily
in the functioning of the federation. Such an approach
would not only suggest very different arrangements,
but would underline the importance of regarding any
such arrangement as fundamentally temporary, since
the ground is in motion and diversity is likely to acquire
new faces.

Consequently, federalism would not only rely on a
much more flexible toolbox, but would require that
any formal or binding arrangement be revisited, played
with and constantly adjusted to diverse circumstances. It
would open the door to the design of more complex and
innovative arrangements likely to deal less ineffectively
with deep diversity. Unfortunately, for the time being,
most schemes at the federal level are in denial in the face
of deep diversity. Factoring it in, even in a modest way,
might revolutionize and modernize federalism.

Playing with prototypes, or, in other words, serious
play, has not been encouraged in Canada. Yet since the
Supreme Court decision in the Chaoulli case, a decision
that stated *grosso modo* that citizens have the right to
seek private health care when the public system fails
them, different groups throughout Canada have begun
exploring different prototypes of arrangements that

would be in keeping with the Supreme Court ruling. They have timidly begun to play seriously. To do it well, a number of required steps have been identified. Tinkerers need to: (1) identify some top requirements as quickly as possible; (2) put in place a quick and dirty provisional medium of co-development with their partners; (3) allow as many interested parties as possible to get involved as partners in designing a better arrangement; (4) encourage iterative prototyping; and (5) thereby encourage all, through playing with prototypes, to get a better understanding of the problems, their priorities and themselves (Schrage 2000: 199ff).

The purpose of serious play is to create a dialogue, a creative interaction, between people and prototypes, which may be more important than creating dialogue between people alone. It is predicated on a culture of active participation. The sort of democratization of design that ensues, and the sorts of playfulness and adventurousness that are required for serious play with prototypes, may not yet be part of the culture, but they are emerging tendencies.

The zero-sum-game theatrics of present-day federalism, with its few actors trying to protect their vested interests, and a single position inflicted on all regions and groups whatever its dysfunctionality for some (*pace* the Kyoto Protocol), are not very promising. The interaction among a large number of interested parties around a prototype, each intent on designing a better one, is much more promising. Only such an extended multilogue has the possibility of transforming the zero-sum game into a positive-sum game. Yet one has to be sensitive to the fragility of these games. It takes little to sterilize the multilogue or to derail the conversation: declaring any assumption or hypothesis taboo or sacrosanct would suffice. One can only guess at the social costs of having declared the *Canada Health Act* sacrosanct, rather than taking it as a prototype, and allowing it to be tweaked and improved.

That this approach can be extended to the realm of foreign policy is regarded as impossible by some apostles of clarity and certainty. Yet if there is an area where, because of the lack of world government and the multiplicity of national rules, fuzziness and blurring are dominant characteristics, it is the world of external affairs. The fact that diplomats may find clarity and certainty convenient should not be allowed to stunt the creative process through which subnational actors of all sorts might be allowed to experiment with new arrangements. Some of the experiments in Europe, where subnational regional governments can negotiate treaties across national borders without having to obtain permission from the nation state, constitute a step in the right direction, but they are only a beginning, since they are restricted to subnational governments. One can imagine a whole array of experimentation, putting flats and sharps on "national understandings" and developing creative arrangements, under the sole constraint that they do not violate certain basic covenants. The timid experiments in Europe have allowed subnational governments to experiment in a limited terrain. There is no reason to believe that experimentation on the international scene by all subnational actors, subject to certain minimal rules, would not be possible or should not be encouraged (Paquet 2000).

THE WISDOM OF CROWDS

There is a palpable suspicion that one may have slipped into utopian thinking when large-scale evolutionary tinkering and play are proposed to replace top-down technocratic decision-making. While this sort of argument is continually trotted out, and at first may look as if it has some force, one needs to be only vaguely familiar with the *de facto* chaotic nature of the real decision-making processes in foreign policy to be disabused of the impression that Cartesian thinking effectively prevails. What is mostly on display is some ritualized rationality that provides little reassurance to critical observers.

The making of foreign policy evolves in the absence of fail-safe mechanisms and ultimate power-brokers. It has mostly been stylized in the language of game theory as two-level games or two-face games (Putnam 1988; Jung 2002). These are largely descriptive schemes, which are useful in sorting out the issues, but are most often indeterminate when it comes to predicting outcomes. Recognizing this sort of reality makes it much easier to question the pretentiousness of career nation-state bureaucrats when they pretend to analytically solve foreign policy issues.

The alternative is to recognize that foreign policy outcomes are broadly determined by evolution and by the emergence of "correlated conventions" that make the games evolutionarily stable (Skyrms 1996). Actors in the game context quickly learn that when they are able to coordinate on a correlated equilibrium, all parties do well. The exact nature of this equilibrium may not be predictable, but the trial-and-error process may be counted on to elicit it in the form of a convention. These correlated conventions emerge through evolution rather than through rational adjudication, and even those who are portrayed as "naïve, unsophisticated agents" "can coordinate themselves to achieve complex, mutually beneficial ends, even if they are not really sure, at the start, what those ends are or what it will take to accomplish them" (Surowiecki 2004: 107). Analysts are so mesmerized by the command-and-control way of arriving at an evolutionary stable convention, that they exclude all other approaches. Yet evolution and learning are the ways in which our species has come about: through unpredictable outcomes, generated by evolutionary stable strategies underpinning social learning.

It is my view that open-source prototyping involving a large number of actors, is a more effective way of evolving foreign policy than the present ritualized-rational way of doing it. This is the way regimes have evolved in the past and with much greater effectiveness than had been anticipated most of the time. It is the way Linux and Wikipedia are also evolving surprisingly well (*Economist*: April 1, 2006).

James Surowiecki (2004) has explored the diffuse process through which crowds elicit effective evolutionary stable strategies and breed surprising outcomes. He has shown that, under conditions of diversity, independence and decentralization, collective intelligence can emerge from crowds and effective coordination can ensue: "the many are smarter than the few". He has also shown, however, that attempts at aggregating information and the judgements of crowds through serious play and quasi-market mechanisms — such as the FutureMAP programme or the Policy Analysis Market — have been received with immense hostility in foreign policy quarters, as being "viscerally unappealing" (Surowiecki 2004: 79ff). It is fascinating that even a private-sector version of a refurbished Policy Analysis Market, without government involvement, ran into difficulty because of the hostility to using the collective intelligence of crowds and the dedication to reliance on experts, despite the evidence that the former performs better than the latter.

Still the pressure to open the system to broader participation and social learning is making headway in foreign policy development, albeit in an oblique and unplanned way. Two interesting examples are the evolving foreign policy of Quebec and the shambles surrounding the Kyoto Protocol. Both issues make Cartesians nervous, inducing them to denounce the chaos and the excesses to come, but they are unfolding anyway without any one person in charge.

LESSONS FROM ABOVE AND BELOW

The paradigmatic change emerging in the world of foreign policy, is a simple echo of the paradigmatic change in the whole world of the social sciences in general, and economics in particular. After years of romanticizing the beauty of planning and social engineering, social scientists have come to realize something that the physical sciences confronted one hundred years ago: cathedral-like models, *à la* Walras or Durkheim, have been replaced by bazaar-like evolutionary models.

One hundred years ago, physical scientists tore up the theoretical constructs that social scientists had just borrowed from them, and boldly entered the world of relativity, quantum mechanics, chaos theory and complexity theory. Now may be the time for the social sciences to follow suit (Beinhocker 2006). Indeed, this sort of work is under way, although it is not yet front and centre in universities. These are precious moments in the evolution of prevailing cosmologies, for perspectives are still fluid and have not yet congealed. This fluidity allows journalists and lay commentators to discuss matters on a par with experts and pseudo-specialists. Indeed, international affairs as a field of study may be regarded as an area that still has not allowed itself to be completely colonized by tribes of grand theorists. This is not for lack of trying on their part, but is due to the failure of their theoretical machines to produce anything but trite results.

Wisdom is distilled in this area by trial and error. Allow me to refer to two sets of lessons recently reported, one from above and the other from below. From above, the synthetic work of Sylvia Ostry has underlined the decline in deference to governments and elites in the functioning of international institutions traditionally charged with foreign policy (Ostry 2001). Some of the actions of non-state groups, both at Seattle in 1999 and at Quebec City in 2001, were orchestrated by non-governmental organizations and took on an operatic quality, but the theatrics should not hide the fact that other actors, such as multinational corporations, were very active behind the scenes in negotiations with governments, and that this has amounted to nothing less than a privatization of trade policy. Why bother with tedious intergovernmental negotiations when one can achieve the same goal privately? This has raised questions about the insignificance of being a trade minister when the issues at stake span almost the whole range of domestic policy portfolios and involve direct action by a range of stakeholders that is wider than ever before.

The presence of these new actors in the foreign-policy area, has led specialists to entertain the possibility of allowing all non-governmental actors to bring their cases directly to dispute settlement panels or policy forums, such as those of the World Trade Organization, and thus allow a culture of litigation (Ostry 2001) to emerge. The committees of some United Nations agencies already include representatives of trade unions, employers' organizations and other such social actors, giving reality to "what has been called hybrid governance, which involves a combination of 'hard law' (implemented by the coercive power of the government or intergovernmental institutions) and 'soft law', or codes of conduct which provide principles and norms for guidance and emulation" (Ostry 2001: 372).

From below, one must acknowledge the multiplicity of efforts by subnational governments and stakeholder groups of all sorts to enter the fray, and to make an impact on the making of foreign policy in different countries. This is centrally important in Canada, since the federal government does not have a monopoly on foreign affairs. Ever since 1937 and the Privy Council's decision on collective agreements, the provinces have not been bound to implement any international treaty signed by the federal government pertaining to matters of provincial jurisdiction (Paquin 2005).

This situation has forced Canada to specify, in its international treaty commitments, that it can respect only those treaty provisions that fall within the scope of its own competences. However, it is only *ex post*, reluctantly and minimally that provincial stakeholders have been allowed to take part in the making of foreign policy. Many other countries, including Germany, Switzerland, Belgium and Spain, have developed processes to allow greater participation in the process by subnational units, but Canada has been hesitant to borrow or adapt these mechanisms.

One might expect that since, even under constitutional duress, the Canadian federal government has been reluctant to open up the process of decision-making on foreign policy to subnational governments, it is clearly most unlikely to agree to open it up to other less formally empowered stakeholders. Consequently it is unlikely that Canadian federal apparatchiks would look kindly upon the possibility of opening up the process. What is most likely is that the policy-making powers of the federal government will slowly be eroded and that the federal policy machinery will adjust pragmatically, by making minimal overtures to ensure that no major embarrassing blockages ensue. This is most certainly not the most Cartesian way to respond to an optimization problem, but since the issue is not optimizing but satisficing with minimal debate, for fear that no permissive consensus might ensue, it will ensure that no major crisis materializes.

As for the presence of the other stakeholders, that is likely to materialize in specific meso-forums and to make a lot of impact without much fanfare. A good example of this sort of virtual forum, is the debate around softwood lumber. A large number of stakeholders from the public, private and social sectors have been heard, but in a serial and informal set of meetings at various sites, without any person acting as final decider. In some cases new virtual networks, such as "Cascadia", may take shape and acquire a certain degree of formality, but this need not be the case, for it is not clear that such virtual territorial units will be able to develop a consensus on most issues.

The process of slow-moving, permissive, minimal inclusion in various sectoral policy-making forums may not be ideal, and may not produce the most coherent overall foreign policy for Canada, but such an objective would be utopian in any case. As the response to the Kyoto Protocol has demonstrated, the degree of *anomie* in the Canadian system is already such that one has to be satisfied with aiming at a much less ambitious objective.

The considerable degree of diversity in Canada calls for a considerable degree of polyvalence and polymorphousness in its foreign policy. Anything less complex could only be oppressive for major segments of the country. Only multi-level, loosely coupled negotiating forums, where different arrays of stakeholders are present, can be expected to work. Over time these would generate a variety of slightly different arrangements coexisting within a broad corridor of compatible but different designs. Canada already has considerable experience in designing such patchwork quilts. As long as the external effects of such arrangements on third parties are minimal, there can be peaceful coexistence. It should therefore be possible to construct Canada's foreign policy piece by piece, as has been done up to now in any case, without undue damage, but with certain opportunity costs (Paquet 2000).

CONCLUSION

"Polycentric governance" is not an expression that refers simply to some pluralist coalition of states and subnational governments shaping policy in a multipolar world. It is a subversive new way of envisaging the making of foreign policy. New units of analysis, such as "communities of practice" (accountants) or "city regions", are not only present on the national scene, but have tentacles around the world. These units are subnational actors of extraordinary consequence, but they often have no formal presence and are somewhat occluded.

Few policy areas are less closely welded to the old nation state than foreign policy. Its very substance is rooted in the belief that the nation state is the basic unit of analysis. From this assumption stems a variety of bizarre corollaries: that the nation state has a soul and represents "national values"; that territorial integrity is so sacred that the "national community" (whatever that means) must speak with one voice; and so on and so forth. This view of the world is as antiquated as such units of measurement as the ell.

The reductive fascination with "national character" and national uniformity must be resisted. Countries are convenient boxes used to simplify the global mapping of cultures, but one should not fall prey to the logical fallacy of *ignoratio elenchi* and ascribe causal force to a principle of classification used for convenience. Measuring unemployment by regions does not allow one to ascribe the differences in observed rates of unemployment to "regional factors". Such a tautological argument invents a fictional "national character" as warranted when, in most cases, it is not (Heath 2003). Whether one can ever break loose from the mental prison of "national policy" is not in doubt. The problem is when and through what subversive stratagem.

It would be unwise not to recognize that there is a strong and dynamic conservatism at work. It is anchored in a conventional view of foreign policy as the preserve of a federal department. Since this department has a strong and vibrant tradition, not unlike that of the Zouaves or the Foreign Legion, it is likely to put up a big fight to maintain the traditional order. Yet the old guard is unlikely to win this fight. There are three reasons for this. First, univocal foreign policy, imposed from the top down, is likely to be shown to be seriously dysfunctional, given the polyphonic nature of the country. Second, it is bound to serve a variegated and diverse society rather badly. Third, and most importantly, it is bound to inflict significant damage on the fabric of the country. Our survival instinct should, therefore, guide us toward Möbius-web governance.

CONCLUSION

The difficulty of unlearning

*It isn't what we don't know that gives us trouble,
it's what we know that ain't so.*
— WILL ROGERS

There is a facile theory of learning that defines it as a smooth, continuous, cumulative and linear process of correcting errors in a seemingly effortless way. This view is both enlightening and perplexing. It assumes, rightly, that a great deal of learning is indeed the result of correcting errors, but it unduly simplifies the process and casts no light on the nexus of forces that determine how errors are detected, or not, and how they are corrected, or not.

In learning how to swim, an error is quite obvious when it amounts to not staying afloat, but it is less clear when it is a matter of modifying one's leg work to acquire the speed of an Olympian. In such cases, swimmers have often, over time, acquired bad habits that they are not even aware of but that cripple their performance. A coach has to identify these crippling habits, and get swimmers to unlearn their natural ways of using their feet and acquire a new *modus operandi*.

Such crippling habits are even more toxic when it comes to matters of the mind. One can conceivably develop a mindset that selectively blocks out some aspects of what is perceived and overemphasizes other aspects. Over time, this habitualized way of scanning the context may lead one to occlude certain aspects of what is going on and to select certain other aspects as being of determining importance. This use of a cultural filter becomes second nature and ceases to be perceived as a filter at all. This is what ideology entails. When such shackles develop, individuals and groups come to be crippled by reductive ways of perceiving. They are unaware of the mental prisons that prevent them from having a full perception of the assumptions they are making and therefore leave them unaware of the errors to be corrected. Consequently, they can hardly be expected to correct these errors. Some external shock is often necessary to make one aware of the errors one is making and to trigger the "unlearning" that is required before any new learning can become possible.

The failures of social learning exposed in this book can often be ascribed to such blockages. Some of these blockages are externally generated by power intrusions that trump rationality. They may originate from tradition (the democracy of the dead, as G. K. Chesterton (1908: ch. IV) called it), from built-in institutional constraints or from interventions by powerful interest groups or partisan politicians, but they may also stem from the cultural milieu, or from prevailing principles that seem unchallengeable in the given context, such as egalitarianism in the era of the welfare state. These forces define what is in and out of bounds, and impose taboos. They constitute a sort of censorship that may considerably weaken the process of exploration, learning and innovation.

Other blockages are more internally generated, more easily traceable to certain structures and rules that an organization or a group has chosen to work under, and that can be changed. For instance, they may stem from the perversities of an incentive–reward system in place. What is one to expect when a system rewards failure and

punishes success, other than a great deal of confusion
about what is expected and, consequently, an attenua-
tion of the drive to explore new ways and to innovate
(Hubbard and Paquet 2008)?

Most organizations are not only shackled by a variety
of such internal blockages, but they are significantly
enslaved by cultural factors that are immensely more
difficult to identify and to neutralize. These factors
crystallize in the form of a prevailing mindset that permeates the whole *modus operandi* of the organization and
cripples it in a tacit way.

In Part I, I have underlined the ways in which crippling epistemologies have led the post-secondary education system to fall prey to certain views — about useful
knowledge and about what is a meaningful contribution
to the production of new knowledge — that are so profoundly rooted in the mindsets of the institutions that
they appear to be unchallengeable. The fact that such
views have been incorporated into the rules of operation of post-secondary institutions has accentuated the
problem, and the dual impact of crippled epistemology
(Hardin 2002) and perverse incentive–reward systems
has been toxic in supporting a system of accreditation
that is fundamentally thwarted.

In Parts II and III, I have emphasized some broad
infrastructural weaknesses of information, evaluation,
accountability and design that appear to plague organizational arrangements in all sectors, at the macro, meso
and micro levels. I have also proposed some repairs.
Some of these are promising, but it should be clear that
the blockages that are the most difficult to overcome are
those stemming from crippling epistemologies.

Geoffrey Vickers (1972) nicely explains the notion of
a mental prison by arguing that the trap is a function of
the nature of the trapped. He gives the example of a lobster trap that takes account of the nature of the lobster's
limitations in movement and thinking. A lobster trap is a
square cage with a wire funnel at the top and some bait

inside. The lobster climbs onto the cage and discovers the upper part of the funnel, which is wider than the lower part. It touches the funnel with its antennae, to measure it, finds that its body fits, and goes down through the funnel into the trap. After eating the bait, the lobster uses its antennae again to touch the lower end of the funnel, and discovers that it is too narrow to enter. On the basis of its beliefs and its previous experience, the lobster stays inside the trap, waiting for the fisherman to catch it. Unlike a lobster, however, no human being would ever be caught in a lobster trap, because he or she would see how to escape from it.

The difficulty in overcoming limitations of this sort is that often the lack of awareness is consubstantial with the very identity assumed by persons or groups. The mental prisons are not merely present and unchallenged, they are defined as part and parcel of being and belonging. Consequently, unlearning—getting rid of the mental prison—is not even perceived as an option, for it would be tantamount to shedding a part of one's self. This sort of situation can only lead to cognitive dissonance and an active resistance to unlearning.

The case of many middle-range universities provides a cautionary tale. The collegiality disease is often regarded in the social sciences as a *sine qua non*, and can lead to the perpetuation of Kafkaesque programme requirements that fail to meet students' needs but cater to the professoriate's expertise. The fact that course contents serve students badly, but remain in place despite scathing evaluations from those students, is testimony to the powers of cognitive dissonance and to the capacity for rationalization. It seems natural to assume that students do not really know what is good for them and to discard their views.

Part of the force of active inertia that stunts the unlearning process, is a mix of unreliable information and guild-like organizations insulating producers from performance evaluation and other such factors. But the most important factors are: (1) the mental prisons that

constitute the underwater portion of the iceberg; and
(2) the phenomenal distaste for confronting obvious
pathologies, and for confrontation in general, on the
part of both those in positions of authority within the
different organizations, and of those who have fallen
into voluntary servitude and do not dare to challenge
pathologies unless it is a matter of survival. This sort of
consensual hypertolerance explains why indefensible situations persist through the sheer complicit and uncritical
lethargy of all parties.

MENTAL PRISONS: A WINDOW DISPLAY

A comprehensive review of the whole array of mental
prisons is beyond the scope of this section. I wish only
to draw attention to the most obvious families of mental prisons that generate false consciousness, result in
truncated perceptions or representations and entail a
non-dialectical form of knowledge.

The most obvious mental prisons are crippling epistemologies, such as narrow disciplinary perspectives, that
focus attention in a very reductive way on some limited
aspects of reality or motivations. They also underpin
the assumption that only certain forms of codifiable
knowledge (academic, quantophrenic) can be regarded
as meaningful knowledge.

A different family of mental prisons pertains to the
dissemination of knowledge: mental blocks that tend to
occlude or deny value to certain types of information
that might be disturbing to the prevalent system of beliefs
(cognitive dissonance, "political correctness"), or that do
not originate from members of certain accredited tribes
(credentialism). Obversely, one might underline the undue
sanctification of the ill-founded opinions of celebrities
or adjudicators (columnists, superbureaucrats), opinion-
moulders who have a grip on the public, and play a key
role in the propagation and accreditation of myths.

A third family of mental prisons emerges from the
sanctification of certain so-called principles that tend to

disempower critical thinking and prevent the interpretation of observed phenomena in anything but stylized ways that conform to taboos or irrational dominant dogmas. This tends to bestow a sacred character on meta-norms that make it difficult, if not impossible, to challenge what might normally be regarded as deviant from the point of view of common sense (excesses in human rights claims, certain versions of the precautionary principle).

Finally, there is the elevation of certain rules of operations to the status of non-negotiable dominant norms that command the suspension of judgement and of the challenge function in interpersonal exchange. Hypertolerance, collegiality and failure to confront, entail the refusal to call a spade a spade, and sanitize discourse to the point where evasive thinking allows the worst outcome to prevail for lack of willingness to tolerate any form of conflict. This is the world of soft consensus.

These blockages serve as stoppers on the normal use of critical thinking, but they are at their peak toxicity when they are associated, as suggested above, with some sense of identity or community. Opposing them becomes tantamount to challenging the very identity and sense of worth of the person or group. Any such challenge usually triggers a shutting down of all the normal processes of rational discourse, and the dominance of feelings of outrage and offended pride. Matters of reason are transformed into matters of honour.

SABOTAGE AND BRICOLAGE REQUIRED

The only way to effectively fight these diverse mental prisons, is to change the mindset and to unlearn some of the most fundamental patterns of behaviour that have been almost wired in by the dominant culture. Often this cannot be done directly and in a confrontational way, because the defence mechanisms are too robust. Attacks would generate a strong sense of revulsion and a mobilization of the outraged. How could one easily surrender to such attacks on one's voluntary servitude? It would call for reneging on one's sense of self.

The attack must therefore be launched obliquely, by way of a discussion of the process of social learning in general. This is where the notion of governance is so fundamentally subversive. It reframes the very definition of stewardship in a seemingly innocuous way, by focusing on coordination in the absence of a single omnipotent source of power.

It is an antidote to the toxic notion of the potentate, a magical entity supposedly embodying the fount of knowledge, and sparing members or citizens the need to know, think and act. Whether the potentate is an individual leader or the state is irrelevant. Governance starts with the assumption that no one person, or organization or institution has all the knowledge, an idea that can easily gain some support, and proceeds to argue that, to the extent that the active critical thinking of a larger number of meaningful stakeholders, framing issues differently, can be mobilized, more knowledge can be mustered, and it becomes less likely that a reductive and pathogenic view will prevail.

This provides the basis, and a *prima facie* case, for open sourcing as a strategy of massive collaboration. Such collaboration is unlikely to emerge, however, unless there is a point to it, the point being to add value. Knowledge for the sake of knowledge is unlikely to be sufficient. Nor is knowledge likely to emerge without some engineering of effective mechanisms of coordination through experimentation, and social learning through collaboration.

Bent Flyvberg (2001) has been bold enough to suggest some cautious and provisional methodological guidelines for forms of bricolage that can help in giving a focus to the sort of reformed social science that might be useful in such construction. He reminds phronetic researchers of the centrality of power at the core of their analyses;

the need to remain close to reality and practice; the need to pay close attention to small things and particular circumstances; the core importance of the historical context as a focal point, and of the dynamic question of how one engineers the collective action that seems to be required; the necessity at all times of focusing on agency and structure jointly, and of fully recognizing the polyphony of voices in the forum; and the centrality of meaningful dialogue in context in the face of conflicting frames of reference. In the words of Flyvberg (2001: 140), "the result of phronetic research is a pragmatically governed interpretation of the studied practices."

As I hinted earlier, any meaningful inquiry has to focus on the full complexity of the psychosocial context and cannot deny this complexity. It is not sufficient to wish for good things to occur, as if by immaculate conception. One has also to work at reducing the bad things that may emerge, predictably, from the pathologies identified earlier.

An inquiry that aims at uncovering the dynamics of harm is therefore called for. It is conducted in order to gain an appreciation of the dynamics at play sufficiently good that one might hope to be able, by appropriate bricolage, to sabotage the process generating unwelcome and unfair outcomes. In the words of M. K. Sparrow:

> ... scrutinizing the harms themselves, and discovering their dynamics and dependencies, leads to the possibility of sabotage. Cleverly conceived acts of sabotage, exploiting identified vulnerabilities of the object under attack, can be not only effective, but extremely resource-efficient too (2008: 27).

It is this mix of sabotage and bricolage that is likely to pay off, and not some grandiose endeavour that refuses to acknowledge or take fully into account the psychosocial dynamics at play.

Such inquiries are of necessity stunted when certain sources of knowledge are shut off. It is therefore easier to begin by (1) seeking support in principle for a form of reflexive governance based on social learning and anchored in open sources; and (2) developing some demonstration projects that desperately call for experimentation in circumscribed issue domains of particular interest, such as (in Canada) federalism, education or health care, issue domains where effective coordination, in situations where power, resources and information are widely distributed, is both required if harm reduction is to be meaningfully engineered and, by all accounts, not in place.

OPEN-SOURCE GOVERNANCE AND THE EMERGING "SMART MOB"

Any action plan has to build on a necessary first phase of deconstruction, revealing different intentions, projects and actions, critiquing them and acting upon the lessons learned. The second phase of reconstruction builds on reflexivity, as knowledge acquired gets integrated during the process, influences the design and unfolds in order to modify the outcome.

The reconstructed setting is the world of reflexive governance. In our complex, uncertain and surprise-generating world, governing entails a process of effective coordination of the activities of persons and groups with portions of power, resources and information. It entails much more than ensuring that fiduciary duties are dispatched in an orderly and ritualized way by bureaucratic authorities acting as sentinels to prevent things from going wrong. Neither will it be satisfactory to put mechanisms in place to analyze the external challenges and organize effective consensual strategies to cope with these external shocks hitting the open system.

What is required is the design of a capacity for the organization to learn, to reflect on its own experience, to make sense of it and to retool, restructure and even reframe the basic questions facing the organization, in order to generate effective ways to discern and grapple with the generative challenge of learning (Cleveland 2002; Chait et al. 2005). These requirements have been spelled out by practitioners of reflexive governance. They may be summarized as follows: knowledge integration and learning by doing; capacity for long-run anticipation of systemic effects; adaptiveness of strategies and institutions; iterative experimental and participatory definition of broad directions; and interactive strategy development (Voss et al. 2006).

At the foundation of these requirements is a bold capacity for critical thinking. This in turn requires a willingness to overcome the fear of conflict and its corollary, the failure to confront. How is this to be done? Donald Schön has reminded us that any social system

> contains structure, technology and theory. The structure is the set of roles and relations among individual members. The theory consists of the views held within the social system about its purposes, its operations, its environment and its future. Both reflect, and in turn influence, the prevailing technology of the system. These dimensions all hang together, so that any change in one produces change in the others (1971: 33).

The path of least resistance is obviously technology. This explains why there is so much interest in e-governance, for new technologies, introduced more or less surreptitiously, may indeed transform structure and theory more or less painlessly, if slowly. This is the gamble of those who have bet on technologies of information, communication and coordination as ways of modifying structures of governance.

This is not wrong, but it may not suffice, because of the weight of the mental prisons in place. Technologies may indeed be disruptive and trigger a cascade of changes, but there is no assurance that they will not be tamed or hijacked. It may turn out that a more effective approach would involve experimentation and the best use of demonstration projects. This is where the works of Walter Truett Anderson (2001), M. S. Y. Chwe (2001), Howard Rheingold (2002), Don Tapscott and Anthony D. Williams (2006), and Simon Parker and Niamh Gallagher (2007) can be most useful. All these works point to the transformative capacity of technology as an instrument to ensure effective coordination and mass collaboration, and thus as a lever to instigate a social revolution. In that sense, Rheingold is probably the boldest thinker, though others, such as Tapscott and Williams or Parker and Gallagher, have provided the engineering work to complement his visionary architectural work.

The philosophy of open source may be regarded as, at present, the most radical version of the new technology of governance that is proposed. It aims at making each member or citizen a potential producer of governance. It aims at transforming structure and theory much more fundamentally than has been envisaged by more timid versions of other models of governance, which maintain a much higher degree of state-centricity. Its very radical nature has generated an immense amount of resistance from those who have understood how fundamental a revolution it wishes to create. This has led to a significant obscurantist movement in reaction to the simple implication that we might be drifting away from "Big G government" and toward "small g governance". This hypothesis has been portrayed as a mix of idealism, neo-populism and anarchism that is both wildly unrealistic and, potentially, immensely destructive of the so-called social order. "Emergent publics" *à la* Ian Angus (2001) or "smart mobs" *à la* Rheingold (2002) have been caricatured as sources of nothing but the chimeras to be expected from such wild experiments. Such fear-mongering has been fed by a whole phalanx of politicians, bureaucrats and columnists, for whom the only choice is between state-centricity and chaos.

Despite the growing literature on the reality and therefore the possibility of non-state-centred mass collaboration, with Tapscott and Williams's (2006) survey as support, this sort of visceral opposition to the forms of decentralization being proposed has generated bizarre reactions to the very notion of governance (Paquet 2007b). This local reaction by the public administration tribe is nothing but a self-serving echo effect of a more dramatic fear of governance that is emerging. Fifty years of promises by the state about fictional social solidarity, however hollow yet hallowed, have left citizens psychosocially dependent on the state. When citizens feel unprotected by the state, and feel that they have no choice but the state or chaos, they lose faith in democracy as a state-producing machine. Unless citizens start seeing governance as a workable alternative to the state, they will be tempted to flush out democracy (Welzer 2008).

WHO'S AFRAID OF GOVERNANCE AND WHY?

The raising of shields against the notion of governance in significant segments of the intelligentsia, especially in the world of political science and public administration, is as impressive as it was predictable. The popularity of the notion in the population at large is great, but the anxiety is even greater in times of turmoil. At the same time, the omnipresence of the notion of governance in public usage is testimony that the citizens have come to realize that effective coordination in a world where power, resources and information are widely distributed, is the new frontier that needs to be probed. Yet unless one can flesh out this notion of governance, it is unlikely to tame the citizens' anxiety.

This is where the betrayal of the elites is most costly. Those who feel threatened are those who have invested political, organizational and intellectual capital in the old structures. For them this seemingly innocent linguistic shift from "Big G government" to "small g governance"

constitutes a major affront. What they have taken to be a
rock-solid basis for their operations is now being called
into question.

The first group is composed of the traditional lobbies
(private, public and social) that used to be able to use
the powers of the state to redistribute resources in their
direction. For them the decline of the power of the state
has meant that their task has become more difficult.

The second group is composed of the apparatchiks
who were able, until recently, to maintain the rules of
the game in the operations of organizations centralized in
the hands of a few stakeholders. In their case, the recent
erosion of the power bases of these happy few has meant
a significant loss of the margin of manoeuvrability.

The third group is composed of academics who have
seen their knowledge base in political science and public administration dramatically questioned and eroded.
While their stake in the old ways may well appear to be
trivial when compared to the real power shift at the other
two levels, it is at this third level that the resistance has
been the most vicious. Postmodernism has made everything a matter of opinion, evidence has no valence and
intellectual capital can be whimsically defended, even
though it has no market value, all just to save face.

The very reason that the resistance from the political science and public administration tribes has been
so phenomenal, is that the reduction in the importance
of the state raises questions about the very identity of
these practitioners. Therefore, the defence mechanisms
have been more robust there than anywhere else: a
bourgeois cannot really understand and use the notion
of "bourgeoisie" without being forced to question his
own self and being led thereby to cease to be a bourgeois.
Consequently, he is in stark denial of the very notion.

Such vehement rejection of the very notion of governance reminds me of an anecdote that my former
colleague, Scott Gordon, used to tell. It had to do with
the invention and widespread use of inside toilets to

replace chamber pots. Formerly, the contents of chamber pots had been merrily thrown out of the window in the morning, and a small group of people had developed the habit of collecting such waste for sale as fertilizer. Indoor plumbing deeply affected their livelihoods, and therefore they demonstrated forcefully against the new invention. Gordon concluded that this was proof that one can develop a vested interest in anything.

A vested interest in expertise that is becoming less pertinent can be explained, but it not easy to defend. Perhaps there was a time in the history of science when biologists who classified animals by number of legs agitated against the new abstruse biology that was on the way to using DNA. Or perhaps this is a phenomenon that is peculiar to the social sciences.

IN CLOSING

The difficulty of "unlearning" may be understandable, but when it leads to rearguard action that can only be regarded as obscurantist it clearly becomes reprehensible. It should be understood that a central blockage here is the natural if infantile reaction to the subversive suggestion of Harlan Cleveland (2002) that there is "nobody in charge". Mitchell Resnick (1994a; 1994b) has shown that there is a natural tendency to demand that someone be in charge. This is the foundation of the centralizing mindset. He uses the story of the reasoning of the daughter of a friend of his, Rachel, a bright young child who has a theory about everything. She explains that rain falls because the thunder tells the clouds to release water. There is a similar tendency in human beings to reassure themselves by presuming that somebody must be in charge, because otherwise all hell would break loose. This is still the dominant mindset.

This is probably the new frontier for sabotage and bricolage in the social sciences: debunking the myth of the necessity of someone being in charge, and magical thinking about leadership in general. There is some urgency in questioning the need for centralization, leadership and state-centricity, by showing that complex social phenomena may result from simple mechanisms. Resnick (1994b), Thomas Schelling (1978) and many others have begun to develop a whole literature on this subject, but their impact has been minimal.

This is a task that complexity theory and the theory of emergence have also begun to tackle, and that they may succeed in realizing. Such endeavours have done so in a negative way by showing the limits of the reductionism I complained about in the introduction to this volume, and by proposing a new scientific worldview that attempts to repair the injuries inflicted by reductionism, including the splits between the sciences and the humanities, facts and values, materiality and spirituality. Indeed, such an avenue even promises to reinvent the sacred (Kauffman 2008). While the harnessing of complexity and emergence is promising, this is only a hope for the longer term. In the short run, some bridging of the chasm generated by "methodism" and the old scientistic cosmology will be necessary through work in the trenches to prepare our minds for this new cosmology. The only way to legitimize the view that systems are emergent and self-organizing, will be to do much reconstructive work, to better explain the phenomenon of emergence, and to show how complex systems may self-steer and self-organize in particularly well-circumscribed milieus.

This has been the approach used by Resnick (1994b) and his colleagues, and it is the one governance specialists will have to use. Unless one can demonstrate in many concrete contexts that leaders are not necessary for systems to emerge, be creative, innovate and be reliable, it is unlikely that there is any hope of breaking the centralized mindset.

It is unclear just how long it might take for complexity and emergence theory, bolstered by demonstration projects, to generate a general debunking of the fixation on state-centricity, centralization and the leadership mystique as dogmas in public administration. It is easier to take a person out of Wonderland than to take Wonderland out of that person.

Acknowledgements

Most of the work that led to this book was carried out at the University of Ottawa, with the help of the Telfer School of Management and then under the auspices of the Centre on Governance. Substantial financial assistance has been provided by the Social Sciences and Humanities Research Council of Canada. I am most grateful for this support.

I have also received intellectual support and criticism from my younger colleagues Linda Cardinal, Robin Higham, Ruth Hubbard, Dan Lane, Paul Laurent, Christian Navarre, Jeffrey Roy and Chris Wilson. I have no alibi for the errors that have survived in this text: they must be ascribed to my inescapable learning disabilities.

Earlier versions of the chapters in this book have appeared elsewhere, as shown in the list below. I am especially grateful to Ruth Hubbard and John de la Mothe for their contributions to the papers that have become, respectively, Chapter 4 and Chapter 8.

Chapter 1: "Two Tramps in Mud Time: Social Sciences and Humanities in Modern Society," in *The Human Sciences: Contributions to Society and Future Research Needs*, ed. B. Abu-Laban and B. G. Rule. Edmonton: University of Alberta Press, 1988, 29–57.

Chapter 2: "*Savoirs, savoir-faire, savoir-être*: In Praise of Professional Wroughting and Wrighting," a report prepared for *Campus 2020: An Inquiry into the Future of British Columbia's Post-Secondary Education System*, July 31, 2006.

Chapter 3: "Corporate Culture and Governance: Canada in the Americas," in *Converging Disensus, Cultural Transformation and Corporate Culture: Canada and the Americas*, ed. P. Imbert. Ottawa: Research Chair on Social and Cultural Change in a Knowledge-Based Society, 2006, 79–115.

Chapter 4 (written with Ruth Hubbard): "Réinventer notre architecture institutionnelle." *Options politiques*, 27:7, 2006, 57–64.

Chapter 5: "Intelligent Accountability," at www.optimum online.ca, 37:3, 2007, 49–66.

Chapter 6: "Organization Design as Governance's Achilles' Heel," at www.governancia.com, 1:3, 2007, 1–11.

Chapter 7: "Nothing is More Rational than a Rationalization: Words of Caution about Public Policy Marksmanship," in *Public Sector Accounting: Shifting the Focus to Results*, ed. D. Zéghal. Ottawa: CGA Accounting Research Centre, 1997, 36–48.

Chapter 8 (written with John de la Mothe): "Circumstantial Evidence: A Note on Science Policy in Canada." *Science and Public Policy*, 21:4, 1994, 261–268.

Chapter 9: "The Many are Smarter than the Few," at www.optimumonline.ca, 36:4, 2006, 21–40.

Bibliography

Abrams, M. H. (1953). *The Mirror and the Lamp.* New York and Oxford: Oxford University Press.

Ackoff, R. L. (1994). *The Democratic Corporation.* New York and Oxford: Oxford University Press.

Akerlof, G. A., and R. E. Kranton. (2005). "Identity and the Economics of Organizations." *Journal of Economic Perspectives*, 19:1, 9–32.

Alexander, Christopher A. (1964). *Notes on the Synthesis of Form.* Cambridge, MA: Harvard University Press.

Anderson, Walter Truett. (2001). *All Connected Now: Life in the First Global Civilization.* Boulder and Oxford: Westview Press.

Andreski, Stanislav. (1974). *Social Sciences as Sorcery.* Harmondsworth, Middx: Penguin.

Angus, Ian. (2001). *Emergent Publics.* Winnipeg: Arbeiter Ring Publishing.

Archer, L. B. (1978). *Time for a Revolution in Arts and Design Education.* Royal College of Art Papers, no. 6.

Argyris, Chris, and Donald Schön. (1978). *Organizational Learning: A Theory of Action Perspective.* Reading, MA: Addison–Wesley.

Ashby, W. R. (1956). *Introduction to Cybernetics.* London: Chapman and Hall.

Authier, Michel, and Pierre Lévy. (1992). *Les arbres de la connaissance.* Paris: La Découverte.

Axworthy, T. S. (2005, Summer). "The Responsibility Crisis in Canada." *Canadian Parliamentary Review*, 7–12.

Bachelard, Gaston. (1972). *L'engagement rationaliste*. Paris: Presses Universitaires de France.

Bacon, Sir Francis. (1963). *Novum Organum* [1620] in *The Complete Essays*. Boston, MA: Washington Square Press.

Baumard, Philippe. (1996). *Organisations déconcertées*. Paris: Masson.

Becker, T. L. (1991). *Quantum Politics*. New York: Praeger.

Beinhocker, E. D. (2006). *The Origin of Wealth*. Boston, MA: Harvard Business School Press.

Bennis, Warren. (1976). *The Unconscious Conspiracy*. New York: AMACOM.

Ben-Porath, Yoram (1980). "The F-Connection: Families, Friends and Firms and the Organization of Exchange." *Population and Development Review*, 6:1, 1–30.

Blinder, A. S. (1997). "Is Government Too Political?" *Foreign Affairs*, 76:6, 115–126.

Boguslaw, Robert. (1965). *The New Utopians: A Study of System Design and Social Change*. Englewood Cliffs, NJ: Prentice–Hall.

Boisot, Max H. (1995). *Information Space: A Framework for Learning in Organizations, Institutions and Culture*. London: Routledge.

Boisvert, R. D. (1998). *John Dewey — Rethinking Our Time*. Albany: State University of New York Press.

Borges de Freitas, Alexandre. (1997). "Traços brasileiros para uma análise organizacional," in *Cultura organizacional e cultura brasileira*, ed. Fernando C. Prestes Motta and Miguel P. Caldas. São Paulo: Atlas, 38–54.

Braybrooke, David. (1987). *Meeting Needs*. Princeton, NJ: Princeton University Press.

Braybrooke, David, and Charles. E. Lindblom. (1963). *A Strategy of Decision*. New York: Free Press.

Burelle, André. (2007). "Deux lectures opposées de la Charte canadienne." *Options politiques*, 28:7, 106–108.

Business of Public Sector Procurement, Winter, 8–9.

Canadian Commission for UNESCO. (1977). *A Working Definition of Culture for the Canadian Commission for UNESCO*. Ottawa: UNESCO.

Carter, S. L. (1998). *The Dissent of the Governed*. Cambridge, MA: Harvard University Press.

Chait, R. P., W. P. Ryan, and B. E. Taylor. (2005). *Governance as Leadership*. Hoboken, NJ: Wiley.

Chandler, Alfred D., Jr. (1962). *Strategy and Structure: Chapters in the History of the American Industrial Enterprise*. Cambridge, MA: MIT Press.

Chesterton, G. K. (1908). *Orthodoxy*. London: Bodley Head.

CHL Global Associates. (2006). Website at www.chlglobalas sociates.com.

Chwe, M. S. Y. (2001). *Rational Ritual*. Princeton, NJ: Princeton University Press.

Cleveland, Harlan.(2002). *Nobody in Charge: Essays on the Future of Leadership*. San Francisco: Jossey–Bass.

Courchene, T. J. (1995). "Corporate Governance as Ideology." *Canadian Business Law Journal*, 26:1, 202–210.

Day, Patricia, and Rudolf Klein. (1987). *Accountabilities: Five Public Services*. London: Tavistock Publications.

de Bono, Edward. (1979). *Learning to Think*. Harmondsworth, Middx: Penguin.

DeLanda, Manuel. (2006). *A New Philosophy of Society*. London: Continuum.

de Rougemont, Denis. (1936). *Penser avec les mains*. Paris: Albin Michel.

Desautels, D. (1997). "Public Sector Accounting: Shifting the Focus to Results," in D. Zéghal (ed.), *Public Sector Accounting: Shifting the Focus to Results*. Ottawa: CGA Accounting Research Centre, University of Ottawa, 1–11.

Dewey, John. (1927). *The Public and Its Problems*. New York: Holt.

Donaldson, Thomas, and Thomas W. Dunfee. (1994). "Towards a Unified Conception of Business Ethics: Integrative Social Contracts Theory." *Academy of Management Review*, 19:2, 252–284.

Drath, W. H., and C. J. Palus. (1994). *Making Common Sense*. Greensboro, NC: Center for Creative Leadership.

Dror, Yehezkel. (2001). *The Capacity to Govern: A Report to the Club of Rome*. London: Frank Cass.

Dubnik, M. J. (1996). "Clarifying Accountability: An Ethical Theory Framework." Paper presented at the Fifth International Conference on Ethics in the Public Service, Brisbane, August 5–9.

Durkheim, Émile. (1895/1988). *Les règles de la méthode sociologique*. Paris: Flammarion.

Earle, T. C., and G. T. Cvetkovich. (1995). *Social Trust*. Westport, CT: Praeger.

Economist, The. (2006, April 1). "Battle of Britannica."

Elkins, D. J. (1995). *Beyond Sovereignty*. Toronto: University of Toronto Press.

Emery, F. E. (1981, Spring). "Educational Paradigms: An Epistemological Revolution." *Human Futures*, Spring, 1–17.

Emery, Merrelyn, and Ronald E. Purser. (1996). *The Search Conference: A Powerful Method for Planning Organizational Change and Community Action*. San Francisco: Jossey–Bass.

Energy, Mines and Resources Canada. (1988). *Energy and Canadians into the Twenty-first Century: A Report on the Energy Options Process*. Ottawa: Energy, Mines and Resources.

Evans, Philip, and Bob Wolf. (2005). "Collaboration Rules." *Harvard Business Review*, 83:7, 97–104.

Ferry, Jean-Marc. (1996). *L'éthique reconstructive*. Paris: Cerf.

Fish, Stanley. (1999). *The Trouble with Principles*. Cambridge, MA: Harvard University Press.

Fleiner, Thomas. (2001). *Models of Citizenship Rights*. Ottawa: Forum of Federations.

Flyvberg, Bent. (1998). *Rationality and Power*. Chicago: University of Chicago Press.

Flyvberg, Bent. (2001). *Making Social Sciences Matter*. Cambridge: Cambridge University Press.

Foa, U. G. (1971, January 29). "Interpersonal and Economic Resources." *Science*, 171:3969, 345–351.

Frankfurt, Harry G. (1988). *The Importance of What We Care About: Philosophical Essays*. Cambridge: Cambridge University Press.

Friedmann, John. (1978). "The Epistemology of Social Learning: A Critique of Objective Knowledge." *Theory and Society*, 6:1, 75–92.

Friedmann, John. (1979). *The Good Society.* Cambridge, MA: MIT Press.

Friedmann, John, and George Abonyi. (1976). "Social Learning: A Model for Policy Research." *Environment and Planning, A,* 8, 927–940.

Galbraith, John Kenneth. (1968). *The New Industrial State.* New York: Mentor.

Gallie, W. P. (1964). *Philosophy and the Historical Understanding.* London: Chatto & Windus.

Gattegno, C. (1972). *Ces enfants : nos maîtres ou la subordination de l'enseignement à l'apprentissage.* Neuchâtel: Delachaux et Niestlé.

Gibson, J. J. (1979). *The Ecological Approach to Visual Perception.* Boston, MA: Houghton Mifflin.

Gigerenzer, Gerd, and Reinhard Selten, eds. (2001). *Bounded Rationality: The Adaptive Toolbox.* Cambridge, MA: MIT Press.

Gilles, Willem, and Gilles Paquet. (1989). "On Delta Knowledge," in *Edging Toward the Year 2000,* ed. Gilles Paquet and Max von Zur-Muehlen. Ottawa: Canadian Federation of Deans of Management and Administrative Studies, 15–30.

Gintis, Herbert, et al., eds. (2005). *Moral Sentiments and Material Interest.* Cambridge, MA: MIT Press.

Gladwell, Malcolm. (2005). *Blink: The Power of Thinking Without Thinking.* New York: Little, Brown.

Goldsmith, Stephen, and William D. Eggers. (2004). *Governing by Network.* Washington, DC: Brookings Institution.

Gombrich, E. H. (1979). *Ideals and Idols.* New York: Phaidon.

Gordon, H. Scott. (1961). *The Economists versus the Bank of Canada.* Toronto: Ryerson Press.

Grafton, Anthony. (1996). "Descartes the Dreamer." *Wilson Quarterly,* 20:4, 36–46.

Grant, George. (1979). "Research in the Humanities," in *Humanities in the Present Day,* ed. John Woods and Harold G. Coward. Waterloo, ON: Wilfrid Laurier University Press, 47–50.

Gui, Benedetto. (2000). "Beyond Transactions: On the Interpersonal Dimension of Economic Reality." *Annals of Public and Cooperative Economics,* 71:2, 139–169.

Habermas, Jürgen. (1971). *Knowledge and Human Interests.* Boston, MA: Beacon Press.

Hampden-Turner, Charles, and Alfons Trompenaars. (1993). *Seven Cultures of Capitalism.* New York: Doubleday.

Handy, Charles. (1992). "Balancing Corporate Power: A New Federalist Paper." *Harvard Business Review*, 70:6, 59–72.

Hardin, Russell. (2002). "The Crippled Epistemology of Extremism," in *Political Extremism and Rationality*, ed. Albert Breton et al. Cambridge: Cambridge University Press, 3–22.

Harmon, M. M. (1995). *Responsibility as Paradox.* London: Sage.

Hayek, F. A. (1952). *Scientism and the Study of Society.* New York: Free Press.

Heath, Joseph. (2003). *The Myth of Shared Values in Canada.* Ottawa: Canadian Centre for Management Development.

Heider, Fritz. (1926). *On Perception and Event Structure and the Psychological Environment: Selected Papers.* New York: International Universities Press.

Heller, M. (2008). *The Gridlock Economy.* New York: Basic Books.

Hermet, Guy, et al., eds. (2005). *La gouvernance: un concept et ses applications.* Paris: Karthala.

Hinde, Robert A. (1995). "A Suggested Structure for a Science of Relationships." *Personal Relationships*, 2, 1–15.

Hirsch, E. D. (1988). *Cultural Literacy.* New York: Vintage.

Hirschman, Albert O. (1986). *Rival Views of Market Society.* Cambridge, MA: Harvard University Press.

Hirschman, Albert O. (1995). *A Propensity to Self-Subversion.* Cambridge, MA: Harvard University Press.

Hock, Dee Ward. (1995). "The Chaordic Organization: Out of Control and into Order." *World Business Academy Perspectives*, 9:1, 5–18.

Hock, Dee Ward. (1999). *Birth of the Chaordic Age.* San Francisco: Berrett–Koehler.

Hofstede, Geert H. (1967–2003). *Cultural Dimensions.* Materials accessible at www.geert-hofstede.com.

Hofstede, Geert H. (1991). *Cultures and Organizations: Software of the Mind.* New York: McGraw–Hill.

Holland, John H. (1995). *Hidden Order: How Adaptation Builds Complexity.* Reading, MA: Addison–Wesley.

Homer-Dixon, T. (1995). "The Ingenuity Gap: Can Poor Countries Adapt to Resource Scarcity?" *Population and Development Review,* 21:3, 1–26.

Hubbard, Ruth, and Gilles Paquet. (2002). "Ecologies of Governance and Institutional *Métissage." Optimum Online: The Journal of Public Sector Management,* 31:4, 25–34. Online at www.optimumonline.ca.

Hubbard, Ruth, and Gilles Paquet. (2005). "Betting on Mechanisms: The New Frontier for Federalism." *Optimum Online: The Journal of Public Sector Management,* 35:1, 2–25. Online at at www.optimumonline.ca.

Hubbard, Ruth, and Gilles Paquet. (2006). "Réinventer notre architecture institutionnelle." *Policy Options,* 27:7, 55–63.

Hubbard, Ruth, and Gilles Paquet. (2007a). *Gomery's Blinders and Canadian Federalism.* Ottawa: University of Ottawa Press.

Hubbard, Ruth, and Gilles Paquet. (2007b). "Cat's Cradling: APEX Forums on Wicked Problems." *Optimum Online: The Journal of Public Sector Management,* 37:2, 2–18. Online at www.optimumonline.ca.

Hubbard, Ruth, and Gilles Paquet. (2008). "Cat's Eyes: Intelligent Work versus Perverse Incentives." *Optimum Online: The Journal of Public Sector Management,* 38:3 (in press).

Innis, Harold A. (1952). *Changing Concepts of Time.* Toronto: University of Toronto Press.

Jentoft, Svein. (2006). "Beyond Fisheries Management: The Phronetic Dimension." *Marine Policy,* 30, 671–680.

Jessop, Bob. (2003). "Governance and Metagovernance: On Reflexivity, Requisite Variety, and Requisite Irony." Online at www.lancs.ac.uk/fass/sociology/papers/jessop-governance-and-metagovernance.pdf.

Johnson, Chalmers. (1964). *Revolution and the Social System.* Stanford, CA: Hoover Institution.

Jung Gi-woong. (2002). "How to Negotiate with North Korea: The Logic of Two-Face Games." *East Asian Review,* 14:4, 73–92.

Katouzian, Homa. (1980). *Ideology and Method in Economics.* New York: New York University Press.

Kauffman, Stuart A. (2008). *Reinventing the Sacred: A New View of Science, Reason, and Religion.* New York: Basic Books.

Kaufmann, Walter. (1977). *The Future of the Humanities.* New York: Reader's Digest Press.

Kekes, John. (1993). *The Morality of Pluralism.* Princeton, NJ: Princeton University Press.

Kets de Vries, Manfred F. R. (2001). *The Leadership Mystique: Leading Behavior in the Human Enterprise.* London: *Financial Times* and New York: Prentice Hall.

Kets de Vries, Manfred F. R., and Danny Miller. (1984). *The Neurotic Organization: Diagnosing and Changing Counterproductive Styles of Management.* San Francisco: Jossey–Bass.

Kindleberger, C. P. (1978). *The Aging Economy.* Kiel: Institut für Weltwirtschaft.

Kolm, S. C. (1985). *Le contrat social libéral.* Paris: Presses Universitaires de France.

Kreps, David M. (1990). "Corporate Culture and Economic Theory," in *Perspectives on Positive Political Economy,* ed. James E. Alt and Kenneth A. Shepsle. Cambridge: Cambridge University Press, 90–143.

Kroker, Arthur. (1984). *Technology and the Canadian Mind.* Montreal: New World Perspectives.

Ladeur, K. H. (2004). *Public Governance in the Age of Globalization.* Aldershot, Hants: Ashgate.

Laurent, Paul, and Gilles Paquet. (1998). *Epistémologie et économie de la relation: coordination et gouvernance distribuée.* Paris and Lyon: Vrin.

Law, John. (2004). *After Method.* New York: Routledge.

Le Goff, Jacques. (1957). *Les intellectuels au Moyen Age.* Paris: Éditions Seuil.

Leibenstein, Harvey. (1978). *General X-Efficiency Theory and Economic Development.* Oxford: Oxford University Press.

Leiss, William. (1990). *Under Technology's Thumb.* Montreal: McGill–Queen's University Press.

Lemoigne, Jean-Louis. (2007). "The Intelligence of Complexity." *Revista Sísifo/Educational Sciences Journal,* 4, 115–126.

Leontief, Wassily. "Academic Economics." *Science,* vol. 217, 9 July 1982, 104–105.

LeShan, Lawrence, and Henry Margenau. (1982). *Einstein's Space and Van Gogh's Sky*. New York: Collier.

Lester, R. K., and M. J. Piore. (2004). *Innovation — The Missing Dimension*. Cambridge, MA: Harvard University Press.

Lindblom, Charles E. (1992). *Inquiry and Change: The Troubled Attempt to Understand and Shape Society*. New Haven, CT: Yale University Press.

Lundvall, B. A. (1988). "Innovation as an Interactive Process: From User–Producer Interaction to the National System of Innovation," in *Technical Change and Economic Theory*, ed. Giovanni Dosi et al. London: Pinter, 349–369.

Machlup, Fritz. (1980–1983). *Knowledge: Its Creation, Distribution and Economic Significance*. 3 vols. Princeton, NJ: Princeton University Press.

Malcolm, Norman. (1984). *Ludwig Wittgenstein: A Memoir*. Oxford: Oxford University Press.

March, J. G. (1988). "The Technology of Foolishness," in *Decisions and Organizations*, ed. J. G. March. Oxford: Blackwell, 253–265.

March, J. G. (1991). "Exploration and Exploitation in Organizational Learning." *Organization Science*, 2, 71–87.

Marquand, David. (1988). *The Unprincipled Society: New Demands and Old Politics*. London: Cape.

Martin, Roger. (2004, Winter). "The Design of Business." *Rotman Magazine*, 7–11.

Martin, Roger. (2007, Fall). "Becoming an Integrative Thinker." *Rotman Magazine*, 5–9.

Merleau-Ponty, Maurice. (1964). *Signs*. Evanston, Ill.: Northwestern University Press.

Michael, D. N. (1993). "Governing by Learning: Boundaries, Myths and Metaphors." *Futures*, 25:1, 81–89.

Michael, D. N., et al. (1980). *The New Competence: The Organization as a Learning System*. San Francisco: Values and Lifestyles Program.

Mintzberg, Henry. (1996a). "Managing Government, Governing Management." *Harvard Business Review*, 74:3, 75–83.

Mintzberg, Henry. (1996b). "Musings on Management." *Harvard Business Review*, 74:4, 61–67.

Monnerot, Jules. (1946). *Les faits sociaux ne sont pas des choses*. Paris: Gallimard.

Moore, J. F. (1998). "The Rise of the New Corporate Form." *Washington Quarterly*, 21:1, 167–181.

Morgan, Gareth. (1988). *Riding the Waves of Change*. San Francisco: Jossey–Bass.

Nadler, David, and Michael Tushman. (1997). *Competing by Design*. Oxford: Oxford University Press.

Nathan, R. P. (1985, January–February). "The Missing Link in Applied Social Sciences." *Society*, 71–77.

Neill, Robin F. (1972). *A New Theory of Value: The Canadian Economics of H. A. Innis*. Toronto: University of Toronto Press.

Nelson, Richard. (1977). *The Moon and the Ghetto: An Essay on Public Policy Analysis*. New York: Norton.

Nisbet, Robert. (1976). *Sociology as Art Form*. Oxford: Oxford University Press.

Noë, Alva. (2006). *Action in Perception*. Cambridge, MA: MIT Press.

North, Douglass C. (2005). *Understanding the Process of Economic Change*. Princeton, NJ: Princeton University Press.

Nozick, Robert. (1981). *Philosophical Explanations*. Cambridge, MA: Harvard University Press.

OECD. (1998). *21st Century Technologies: Promises and Perils of a Dynamic Future*. Paris: OECD.

OECD. (1999). *The Future of the Global Economy: Toward a Long Boom?* Paris: OECD.

OECD. (2000). *The Creative Society of the 21st Century*. Paris: OECD.

OECD. (2001). *Governance in the 21st Century*. Paris: OECD.

OECD. (2003). *White Paper on Corporate Governance in Latin America*. Paris: OECD.

Office of the Auditor General. (1999, November). "Chapter 23—Involving Others in Governing—Accountability at Risk." *Report of the Auditor General of Canada*. Ottawa: Office of the Auditor General.

Olson, Mancur. (1982). *The Rise and Decline of Nations : Economic Growth, Stagflation, and Social Rigidities*. New Haven, CT: Yale University Press.

O'Neill, Onora. (2002). *A Question of Trust: The BBC Reith Lectures*. Cambridge: Cambridge University Press.

Ostrom, Elinor. (2005). *Understanding Institutional Diversity.* Princeton, NJ: Princeton University Press.

Ostry, Sylvia. (2001). "WTO: Institutional Design for Better Governance," in *Efficiency, Equity and Legitimacy: The Multilateral Trading System at the Millennium*, ed. Roger B. Porter et al. Washington, DC: Brookings Institution.

Pahl-Wostl, Claudia, et al. (2007). "Social Learning and Water Resources Management." *Ecology and Society*, 12:2:5, 1–19.

Paquet, Gilles. (1968). "The Economic Council as Phoenix," in *Agenda 1970 — Proposals for Creative Politics*, ed. T. Lloyd and J. McLeod. Toronto: University of Toronto Press, 135–158.

Paquet, Gilles. (1971). "Social Science Research as an Evaluative Instrument for Social Policy," in *Social Science and Social Policy*, ed. G. E. Nettler and K. Krotki. Edmonton: Human Resources Research Council, 49–66.

Paquet, Gilles. (1985). "The Optimal Amount of Coercion is Not Zero," in *Social Science Research in Canada: Stagnation or Regeneration?*, ed. J. P. Souque and John Trent. Ottawa: Science Council of Canada, 98–115.

Paquet, Gilles. (1987). "Le goût de l'improbable," in *Education Canada?*, ed. Gilles Paquet and Max von Zur-Muehlen. Ottawa: Canadian Higher Education Research Network, 61–92.

Paquet, Gilles. (1989a). "A Social Learning Framework for a Wicked Problem: The Case of Energy." *Energy Studies Review*, 1:1, 55–69.

Paquet, Gilles. (1989b). "Liberal Education as Synecdoche," in *Who's Afraid of Liberal Education?*, ed. Caroline Andrew and Steen B. Esbensen. Ottawa: University of Ottawa Press, 1–20.

Paquet, Gilles. (1991a). "The Best is Enemy of the Good." *Optimum*, 22:1, 7–15.

Paquet, Gilles. (1991b). "Policy as Process: Tackling Wicked Problems," in *Essays on Canadian Public Policy*, ed. T. J. Courchene and A. E. Stewart. Kingston, ON: Queen's University School of Policy Studies, 171–186.

Paquet, Gilles. (1992a). "Betting on Moral Contracts." *Optimum*, 22:3, 45–53.

Paquet, Gilles. (1992b). "The Strategic State," in *Finding Common Ground*, ed. J. Chrétien. Hull, QC: Voyageur, 85–101.

Paquet, Gilles. (1994). "Reinventing Governance." *Opinion Canada*, 2:2, 1–5.

Paquet, Gilles. (1996a). "Distributed Gouvernance and Transversal Leadership," in *Quebec–Canada After the Referendum: What is the Path Ahead?*, ed. Robert Young and John Trent. Ottawa: University of Ottawa Press, 317–332.

Paquet, Gilles. (1996b). "Contextualizing Alternative Service Delivery," in *Thinking Through the Alternative in Alternative Delivery*, ed. Robin Ford and David R. Zussman. Toronto: KPMG/IPAC.

Paquet, Gilles. (1997). "The Burden of Office, Ethics and Connoisseurship." *Canadian Public Administration/ Administration publique du Canada*, 40:1, 55–71.

Paquet, Gilles. (1999a). *Governance Through Social Learning.* Ottawa: University of Ottawa Press.

Paquet, Gilles. (1999b). "Auditing in a Learning Environment." *Optimum*, 29:1, 37–44.

Paquet, Gilles. (2000). "On Hemispheric Governance." *Transactions of the Royal Society of Canada*, Sixth Series, Vol. 10, 37–79.

Paquet, Gilles. (2004a). "There is More to Governance than Public Candelabras: E- Governance and Canada's Public Service," in *E-Government Reconsidered: Renewal of Governance for the Knowledge Age*, ed. E. Lynn Oliver and Larry Sanders. Regina: Saskatchewan Institute of Public Policy.

Paquet, Gilles. (2004b). *Pathologies de gouvernance.* Montreal: Liber.

Paquet, Gilles. (2005a). "Productivity and Innovation in Canada: A Case of Governance Failure." *Policy Options*, 26:3, 42–46.

Paquet, Gilles. (2005b). *The New Geo-Governance: A Baroque Approach.* Ottawa: University of Ottawa Press.

Paquet, Gilles. (2005c). *Gouvernance: une invitation à la subversion.* Montreal: Liber.

Paquet, Gilles. (2006a). "Une déprimante culture de l'adjudication." *Policy Options*, 27:5, 40–45.

Paquet, Gilles. (2006b). "APEX 2006 Symposium: A Curmudgeon's Commentary." *Optimum Online: The Journal of Public Sector Management*, 36:2, 54–62. Online at www.optimumonline.ca.

Paquet, Gilles. (2006c). "*Savoirs, savoir-faire, savoir-être*: In Praise of Professional Wroughting and Wrighting," a report prepared for *Campus 2020: An Inquiry into the Future of British Columbia's Post-Secondary Education System*. Online at www.campus2020.ca/EN/think_pieces.

Paquet, Gilles. (2006d). "Le palimseste de l'imputabilité." *Revue générale de droit*, 36:4, 561–578.

Paquet, Gilles. (2007a). "The Charter as Governance Story." *Canadian Diversity*, Fall, 80–83.

Paquet, Gilles. (2007b). "Letting the Cat Out of Gow's Bag." *Optimum Online: The Journal of Public Sector Management*, 37:4, 45–49. Online at www.optimumonline.ca.

Paquet, Gilles. (2008). *Gouvernance: mode d'emploi*. Montreal: Liber.

Paquet, Gilles. (2009). *Scheming Virtuously*. Ottawa: Invenire Press.

Paquin, S. (2005). "Quelle place pour les provinces canadiennes dans les organisations et négociations internationales du Canada à la lumière des pratiques au sein d'autres fédérations?" *Canadian Public Administration/Administration publique du Canada*, 48:4, 477–505.

Parker, Simon, and Niamh Gallagher. (2007). *The Collaborative State*. London: Demos.

Piore, Michael J. (1995). *Beyond Individualism*. Cambridge, MA: Harvard University Press.

Polanyi, Michael. (1966). *The Tacit Dimension*. New York: Doubleday.

Posner, Paul L. (2006). "Third-Party Governance: Accountability Challenges," in *Comparative Trends in Public Management*, ed. Colin Campbell et al. Ottawa: Canada School of Public Service, 48–70.

Power, Michael. (2007). *Organized Uncertainty: Designing a World of Risk Management*. Oxford: Oxford University Press.

Putnam, Robert D. (1988). "Diplomacy and Domestic Politics: The Logic of Two-Level Games." *International Organization*, 42:3, 427–60.

Quebec. (2006). *La politique internationale du Québec : la force de l'action concertée.* Quebec City: Ministère des affaires internationales.

Quinton, Anthony. (1980). *Francis Bacon.* Oxford: Oxford University Press.

Ramos, Alberto Guerreiro. (1981). *The New Science of Organizations.* Toronto: University of Toronto Press.

Raymond, Eric S. (1999). *The Cathedral and the Bazaar: Musings on Linux and Open Source by an Accidental Revolutionary.* Sebastopol, CA: O'Reilly & Associates.

Rescher, Nicholas. (1996). *Process Metaphysics: An Introduction to Process Philosophy.* Albany: State University of New York Press.

Rescher, Nicholas. (2000). *Process Philosophy: A Survey of Basic Issues.* Pittsburgh: University of Pittsburgh Press.

Resnick, Mitchel. (1994a). "Changing the Centralized Mindset." *Technology Review*, 97:5: 32–40.

Resnick, Mitchel. (1994b). *Turtles, Termites and Traffic Jams: Explorations in Massively Parallel Microworlds.* Cambridge, MA: MIT Press.

Rheingold, Howard. (2002). *Smart Mobs: The Next Social Revolution.* New York: Perseus.

Risner, Mary E. (2001). "Successful Fast-Food Franchising in Brazil and the Role of Culture: Four Cases." M.A. thesis, University of Florida.

Rittel, Horst W. J., and Melvin M. Webber. (1973, June). "Dilemmas in a General Theory of Planning." *Policy Sciences*, 4:2, 155–169.

Roberts, John. (2004). *The Modern Firm: Organizational Design for Performance and Growth.* Oxford: Oxford University Press.

Rocher, Guy. (1985). "Obstacles to the Creation and Use of Knowledge by the Social Sciences to Solve Social Problems," in *Social Science Research in Canada*, ed. J. P. Souque and John Trent. Ottawa: Science Council of Canada, 154–159.

Romme, A. G. L. (2003). "Making a Difference: Organization as Design." *Organization Science*, 14:5, 558–573.

Rosanvallon, Pierre. (2006). *La contre-démocratie.* Paris: Seuil.

Rosell, Steven A., ed. (1992). *Governing in an Information Society.* Montreal: IRPP.

Rosenau, James. (2003). *Distant Proximities.* Princeton, NJ: Princeton University Press.

Sabel, Charles F. (2001). "A Quiet Revolution of Democratic Governance: Towards Democratic Experimentalism," in *Governance in the 21st Century*, ed. OECD, Paris: OECD, 121–148.

Sabel, Charles F. (2004). "Beyond Principal–Agent Governance: Experimentalist Organizations, Learning and Accountability," in *De Staat van de Democratie. Democratie Voorbij de Staat*, ed. Ewald Engelen and Monika Sie Dhian Ho. WRR Verkenning 3. Amsterdam: Amsterdam University Press, 173–195.

Saint-Onge, Hubert, and Charles Armstrong. (2004). *The Conductive Organization: Building Beyond Sustainability.* Oxford and Burlington, MA: Butterworth–Heinemann.

Savoie, Donald J. (1995). "What is Wrong with the New Public Management?" *Canadian Public Administration/ Administration publique du Canada*, 38:1, 112–121.

Saxenian, AnnaLee. (1994). *Regional Advantage: Culture and Competition in Silicon Valley and Route 128.* Cambridge, MA: Harvard University Press.

Schein, Edgar H. (2001). *Organizational Culture and Leadership.* San Francisco: Jossey–Bass Publishers.

Schelling, Thomas C. (1978). *Micromotives and Macrobehavior.* New York: Norton.

Schön, Donald A. (1971). *Beyond the Stable State.* New York: Norton.

Schön, Donald A. (1983). *The Reflective Practitioner.* New York: Basic Books.

Schön, Donald A. (1988). *Educating the Reflective Practitioner.* San Francisco: Jossey–Bass.

Schön, Donald A. (1990). "The Design Process," in *Varieties of Thinking*, ed. V. A. Howard. New York: Routledge, 110–141.

Schön, Donald A., and Martin Rein. (1994). *Frame Reflection.* New York: Basic Books.

Schrag, Calvin O. (1980). *Radical Reflection and the Origin of the Human Sciences.* West Lafayette, IN: Purdue University Press.

Schrage, Michael. (2000). *Serious Play: How the World's Best Companies Simulate to Innovate.* Boston, MA: Harvard Business School Press.

Schumacher, E. F. (1977). *A Guide for the Perplexed.* London: Cape.

Searle, John. (1985). *Minds, Brains and Science.* Cambridge, MA: Harvard University Press.

Sen, Amartya. (1999a). *Development as Freedom.* New York: Knopf and Oxford: Oxford University Press.

Sen, Amartya. (1999b). "Galbraith and the Art of Description," in *Between Friends: Perspectives on John Kenneth Galbraith,* ed. Helen Sassoon. Boston, MA: Houghton Mifflin, 139–145.

Senate Special Committee on Science Policy. (1970). *A Science Policy for Canada: Report of the Senate Special Committee on Science Policy, Chairman: Maurice Lamontagne.* Vol. 1, *A Critical Review: Past and Present.* Ottawa: Queen's Printer for Canada.

Simon, Herbert A. ([1969] 1981). *The Sciences of the Artificial.* 2nd ed. Cambridge, MA: MIT Press.

Simon, Herbert A. (1983). *Reason in Human Affairs.* Palo Alto, CA: Stanford University Press.

Simons, Robert. (2005). *Levers of Organization Design: How Managers Use Accountability Systems for Greater Performance and Commitment.* Boston, MA: Harvard Business School Press.

Skyrms, Brian. (1996). *Evolution of the Social Contract.* Cambridge: Cambridge University Press.

Slater, D. W. (1967). "Economic Policy and Economic Research in Canada since 1950." *Queen's Quarterly,* 74, 1–20.

Slaughter, Anne-Marie. (2004). *A New World Order.* Princeton, NJ: Princeton University Press.

Smith, Janet R., and Carl A. Taylor, eds. (1996). *Strengthening Policy Capacity.* Ottawa: Canadian Centre for Management Development.

Snow, Charles C., Raymond E. Miles, and Henry J. Coleman, Jr. (1992). "Managing 21st-Century Network Organizations." *Organizational Dynamics,* 20:3, 5–21.

Souque, J. P., and J. Trent, ed. (1985). *Social Science Research in Canada: Stagnation or Regeneration?* Ottawa: Science Council of Canada.

Sparrow, Malcolm K. (2008). *The Character of Harms.* Cambridge: Cambridge University Press.

Spinosa, Charles, Fernando Flores, and Hubert L. Dreyfus. (1997). *Disclosing New Worlds: Entrepreneurship, Democratic Action, and the Cultivation of Solidarity.* Cambridge, MA: MIT Press.

Stercie, E. W. R. (1965). *Speeches of E. W. R. Stercie.* Ed. J. D. Babbitt. Toronto: University of Toronto Press.

Stiglitz, Joseph E. (1987). "Learning to Learn, Localized Learning and Technological Progress," in *Economic Policy and Technological Performance*, ed. Partha Dasgupta and Paul Stoneman. Cambridge: Cambridge University Press, 125–153.

Straus, Sharon E., and Finlay A. McAlister. 2000. "Evidence-Based Medicine: A Commentary on Common Criticisms." *Canadian Medical Association Journal*, 163:7, 837–841.

Sturrock, John, ed. (1979). *Structuralism and Since: From Lévi-Strauss to Derrida.* Oxford: Oxford University Press.

Surowiecki, James. (2004). *The Wisdom of Crowds.* New York: Doubleday.

Sutherland, Sharon L. (2006, December). "The Unaccountable Federal Accountability Act: Goodbye to Responsible Government?" *Revue Gouvernance*, 3:2, 30–42.

Symons, T. H. B. (1975). *To Know Ourselves: The Report of the Commission on Canadian Studies.* Ottawa: Association of Universities and Colleges of Canada.

Tapscott, Don, and David Agnew. (1999, December). "Governance in the Digital Economy." *Finance and Development*, 34–37.

Tapscott, Don, and Anthony D. Williams. (2006). *Wikinomics.* New York: Portfolio.

Tasar, Murat F. (2000, November/December). "A Long-Term Strategy for Latin America." *Journal of Management in Engineering*, 16:6, 23–28.

Tassé, Roger. (1996, July). *Ministerial Accountability and the Citizen-Centered Renewal Initiative.* Ottawa: Deputy Ministers' Task Force on Service Delivery Models.

Tassey, Gregory. (1992). *Technology Infrastructure and Competitive Position*, Norwell, MA: Kluwer Academic.

Tavistock Institute of Human Relations. (1964). *Social Research and a National Policy for Science*. London: Tavistock Publications.

Taylor, Carl. (1997). "The ACIDD Test: A Framework for Policy Planning and Decision-Making" *Optimum*, 27:4, 53–61.

Thacher, David, and Martin Rein. (2004). "Managing Value Conflict in Public Policy." *Governance*, 17:4, 454–486.

Thomas, P. G. (2007). "Public Service of the 21st Century: Trust, Leadership, and Accountability." *Optimum Online: The Journal of Public Sector Management*, 37:2, 19–24. Online at www.optimumonline.ca.

Tussman, Joseph. (1977). *Government and the Mind*. Oxford: Oxford University Press.

Tussman, Joseph. (1989). *The Burden of Office: Agamemnon and Other Losers*. Vancouver: Talonbooks.

Vickers, Sir Geoffrey. (1965). *The Art of Judgement: A Study of Policy-Making*. London: Methuen.

Vickers, Sir Geoffrey. (1972). *Freedom in a Rocking Boat: Changing Values in an Unstable Society*. Harmondsworth, Middx: Penguin.

Vickers, Sir Geoffrey. (1983). *Human Systems Are Different*. London: Harper & Row.

Vos, Cornelis M., and Cor L. Balfoort. (1989). "Strategic Conferencing: A New Approach in Science Policy." *Research Policy*, 18:1, 51–57.

Voss, Jan-Peter, et al., ed. (2006). *Reflexive Governance for Sustainable Development*. Cheltenham, Glos: Edward Elgar.

Wahl, Andrew. (2005, October 10–23). "Culture Shock: A Survey of Canadian Executives Reveals that Corporate Culture is in Need of Improvement." *Canadian Business Magazine*.

Webber, Alan M. (1993). "What's So New About the New Economy?" *Harvard Business Review*, 71:1, 24–42.

Weber, Max. (1978). *Economy and Society*. Los Angeles: University of California Press.

Weinberger, D. (2007). "The Folly of Accountabilism." *Harvard Business Review*, 85, 2, 54.

Welzer, Harald. (2008, August 14). "La démocratie occidentale, un avenir incertain." *Le Monde*.

Williams, T. A. (1979). "The Search Conference in Active
    Adaptive Planning." *Journal of Applied Behavioral
    Science*, 15:4, 470–483.
Winner, Langdon. (1977). *Autonomous Technology: Technics
    Out of Control as a Theme in Political Thought.*
    Cambridge, MA: MIT Press.
Woods, John, and Harold G. Coward, ed. (1979). *Humanities
    and the Present Day.* Waterloo, ON: Wilfrid Laurier
    University Press.
Wright, Robert. (2000). *Nonzero.* New York: Random House.
Wriston, Walter. B. (1992). *The Twilight of Sovereignty: How
    the Information Revolution Is Transforming Our World.*
    New York: Scribner's.
Zakaria, Fareed. (2003). *The Future of Freedom: Illiberal
    Democracy at Home and Abroad.* New York: Norton.

Index

10. Emmanuel Brunet-Jailly (ed.) 2007
   Borderlands – Comparing Border Security in North America and Europe

9. Christian Rouillard, E. Montpetit, I. Fortier, and A.G. Gagnon 2006
   Reengineering the State – Toward an Impoverishment of Quebec Governance

8. Jeffrey Roy 2006
   E-Government in Canada

7. Gilles Paquet 2005
   The New Geo-Governance – A Baroque Approach

6. C. Andrew, M. Gattinger, M.S. Jeannotte, W. Straw (eds.) 2005
   Accounting for Culture – Thinking Through Cultural Citizenship

5. P. Boyer, L. Cardinal, D. Headon (eds.) 2004
   From Subjects to Citizens – A Hundred Years of Citizenship in Australia and Canada

4. Linda Cardinal and D. Headon (eds.) 2002
   Shaping Nations – Constitutionalism and Society in Australia and Canada

3. Linda Cardinal et Caroline Andrew (dir.) 2001
   La démocratie à l'épreuve de la gouvernance

2. Gilles Paquet 1999
   Governance Through Social Learning

1. David McInnes 1999, 2005
   Taking It to the Hill – The Complete Guide to Appearing Before Parliamentary Committees

Composed in Sabon 10 on 12

The paper used in this publication is
Roland Opaque Natural 60lb

Printed and bound in Canada